Educating English Learners

Educating English Learners

What Every Classroom Teacher Needs to Know

Joyce W. Nutta

Carine Strebel

Kouider Mokhtari

Florin M. Mihai

Edwidge Crevecoeur-Bryant

Harvard Education Press

Cambridge, MA

Third printing, 2017

Library of Congress Control Number 2014935206

Paperback ISBN 978-1-61250-719-4
Library Edition ISBN 978-1-61250-720-0

Published by Harvard Education Press,
an imprint of the Harvard Education Publishing Group

Harvard Education Press
8 Story Street
Cambridge, MA 02138

Cover Design: Ciano Design
Cover Photo: iStock/GlobalStock
The typefaces used in this book are Aldine 401 and Univers Light.

Per Giorgio, per Amore.

—Joyce

For Ray, min beschte Fründ.

—Carine

For teachers of English learners everywhere.

—Kouider

✦

For my wife Cristina, with love.

—Florin

✦

For my wonderful dad and first English teacher,
Roland Crevecoeur.
You'll always be the best!

—Edwidge

Contents

Educating English Learners in Mainstream Classrooms

Many teachers we know feel overwhelmed and overworked. There are so many competing demands on their time—mounting paperwork and intensifying accountability measures. Rising standards and increasing student diversity. The list goes on. We know that teachers of all subjects and grade levels operate under challenging conditions. Yet, in spite of this, they continue working hard every day toward a single goal—to help *all* students reach their potential. Not just the privileged, not just those with every advantage. All students. And this, increasingly, means English learners (ELs).

Recent statistics released by the United States Department of Education identify approximately 4.7 million English learners in U.S. schools.[1] About three million of them are in at least one class taught by mainstream teachers.[2] While the growth in the number of English learners is unprecedented, these students bring extraordinarily rich linguistic and cultural backgrounds to the American education landscape, which stands to strengthen instruction for all students. Ironically, these cultural and linguistic assets also pose significant English language, literacy, and content learning challenges that often prevent English learners from doing well academically. Historically, native English speakers have consistently outperformed EL students on tests of academic achievement.[3] Federal legislation has recently begun holding public schools, state departments, and higher education institutions accountable for the education of EL students, requiring a close examination of their performance in comparison to their native-speaking peers.[4]

In addition to federal accountability measures, the Common Core State Standards present important new opportunities and challenges for EL students and their teachers. On one hand, the standards present EL students with an opportunity to gain equal access to rigorous instruction along with higher expectations for learning. On the other hand, teachers will need to make the challenging new standards accessible to English learners, regardless of their English proficiency. These opportunities and challenges will, in turn, require a change in how teachers view and implement instruction for English learners in the mainstream classroom. Educators in every state of our nation are confronting the challenges English learners face in accessing more rigorous instruction, a gap they need to address now more than ever. This book is about filling that gap.

BRIDGING THE CLASSROOM COMMUNICATION GAP

Unlike many other books that examine achievement gaps in aggregate, this book focuses on helping teachers meet the needs of individual English learners. In particular, we focus on analyzing and addressing the gap these students face in mainstream preK–12 settings between grade-level expectations for using listening, speaking, reading, and writing skills in English (also known as language demands) and each EL's proficiency in these skills. Let's call this the classroom communication gap. Understanding subject- and grade-specific language demands in relation to an individual's English proficiency—in other words, understanding the communication gap—is the first step for classroom teachers to make curriculum, instruction, and assessment accessible to English learners. And delivering that accessibility—in other words, narrowing the classroom communication gap—is an essential part of addressing the achievement gap.

With that goal in mind, three broad areas of focus permeate every chapter of this book. The first is communication and language in the mainstream classroom, predominant because it is directly under the control of classroom teachers. Of the many factors that impact English learners' achievement, what is said and done in the classroom is most likely to be affected by teachers' actions. The second area of focus is the process of second-language acquisition and how ELs progress from understanding and using little or no English to reaching parity with their native-speaking peers. No educator can make informed decisions about curriculum, instruction, or assessment for an English learner without a basic understanding of the second-language acquisition process, how it affects EL students' ability to comprehend and demonstrate mastery of new concepts presented in English, and what can be done to accelerate and promote attainment of the highest levels of proficiency in English listening, speaking, reading, and writing.

Examining the distance between these two areas of focus—mainstream classroom communication and ELs' developing English proficiency—brings us back to the classroom communication gap, and on to what teachers can do about it, the third area of focus. Throughout the book, through the stories of four English learners at different grades and proficiency levels and through descriptions of their lessons in different subjects, we show how the academic subject and the grade level impact ELs' performance. For each lesson example, we address the classroom communication gap for one of the four EL cases by applying protocols we have developed and used successfully in preK–12. One, the Academic Subjects Protocol, is intended for teaching academic subjects; the other, the Language Arts Protocol, is for teaching language arts/literacy. Both offer guidance on providing precisely what an English learner needs *in addition to* the general best practices teachers commonly use with all students. We developed the Academic Subjects Protocol and the Language Arts Protocol in collaboration with teachers of all subjects and grade levels who have one or more English learners at different levels of English proficiency in their classrooms. Unlike some other approaches to differentiating for English learners, which require that instruction be structured in a certain way, the protocols are flexible tools teachers can use with any type of lesson, enhancing and adapting it for the additional needs of their English learners.

Narrowing the classroom communication gap while fostering English learners' achievement of rigorous new standards may seem daunting. The great news is that no classroom teacher has to go it alone. Every educator has an essential role and responsibility in supporting English learners' academic achievement and language development. The role of each type of educator of English learners should complement the roles of others, forming an interconnected, unified system of support. Location and instructional delivery model notwithstanding, all English learners deserve educators who are informed, skilled, and capable of reaching them. That principle is the basis of this book and of our approach to teacher preparation and professional learning, the One Plus Model, which we described in depth in our previous book, *Preparing Every Teacher to Reach English Learners: A Practical Guide for Teacher Educators*.[5] In that book, we presented an EL infusion framework for preparing preservice teachers of all subjects and grade levels to reach and effectively teach English learners; we wrote *Educating English Learners* for current and future mainstream academic subject and language arts and literacy teachers with one or more English learners in their classrooms. Everything we share with you is based on our conviction that mainstream teachers, along with all other school-based professionals, can best serve English learners when they collaborate with specialists in bilingual education and in English language development (ELD), also referred to as English as a Second Language (ESL). Throughout the book we feature information about English learners that is essential for mainstream teachers, and we present examples of how they can work together with ELD and bilingual specialists and other professionals at their schools to support ELs' language development and academic achievement. We conclude the book with a summary of our One Plus Model of Professional Learning and Collaboration, suggesting knowledge and skills for teaching English learners that each type of educator should possess and ways in which they all can collaborate.

We, the authors, are teacher educators born in five different nations and raised speaking ten different languages (English being the one language we have in common). For the past twenty years we have been planning and leading professional learning for practicing and preservice teachers, concentrating on what is unique about reaching different types of English learners in the mainstream classroom. Our aim, in our work and in this book, is to provide practical guidance focused on what teachers of academic subjects as well as language arts/literacy can do to make curriculum, instruction, and assessment accessible for ELs at different levels of English proficiency, while addressing the same high standards required of all students. This book distills what we believe to be essential research, theory, and instructional practices that support this aim—to narrow the classroom communication gap—and presents them in a new way, one that is accessible to mainstream teachers and that is actionable in their classrooms. We begin this discussion by introducing English learners and how they learn in school.

WHO ARE ENGLISH LEARNERS AND HOW DO THEY LEARN?

There are many influences on English learners' second language acquisition. To present these influences in an individual context, throughout this book we share the stories of four English learners—Edith, Gero, Edgar, and Tasir—who represent common characteristics and issues of ELs that preK–12 educators need to understand and address. These student cases are based on real English learners we have worked with, but some details and names have been changed to protect their identities. Descriptions of the schools, classrooms, teachers, and other details of the stories will seem familiar, as they were drawn from schools that could be located anywhere. What may be unfamiliar is the complex array of factors that are specific to the home and school lives of these four English learners, who spend the majority of their day in mainstream classrooms.

Through the stories of Edith, Gero, Edgar, and Tasir, we portray common issues for English learners in primary and intermediate grades as well as middle and high school. Our four ELs represent typical characteristics of English learners at different levels of English proficiency, ranging from newcomers to those close to advancing out of the EL category. They also reflect differences in family circumstances, motivation, and engagement in school. In addition, many cultural, social, and affective factors form part of each student's portrait, offering complex considerations regarding the student's performance at school.

The stories take you to the scene, capturing a sliver of what we observed over the course of the academic year at actual school locations. Packed with details, the stories are subsequently explained in terms of research and theory. In other words, the stories are more than simply illustrative; they are also instructional. Through recounting these students' experiences in various lessons, we realistically depict the gaps they face in classroom communication and show how lessons can be adapted to better meet their needs, using the protocols we have developed.

Getting to Know English Learners: Edith, Gero, Edgar, and Tasir

So let's look a bit more closely at the protagonists of this book, Edith, Gero, Edgar, and Tasir, and the general issues that impact their English language development and academic achievement.

✦ Edith Rodriguez and Gero Jantiy at Pine Woods Elementary School, Harveston, Florida

"Why aren't you in class?" scolded an authoritative voice. "Do you have a hall pass?" Edith kept walking. It was her first day at Pine Woods Elementary, and she was fifty minutes late. The fourth-grade classroom was at the end of the long hallway, and Edith was walking as quickly as she could. "Excuse me!" Edith slowed and turned toward the assistant principal. "I'm talking to you."

"No . . . no inglés," Edith muttered. The assistant principal haltingly changed tone. "Oh . . . let me help you to your classroom, honey." "No entiendo," Edith whispered as they walked along.

"Ms. Oliver, this is your new student, Edith. She's an English learner," the assistant principal announced. "Are you sure she should be assigned to my class?" questioned Ms. Oliver. "I already have two English learners and three students with special needs. Wouldn't the other fourth-grade class have more room?" Edith glanced at the students seated at the table next to her. They fixed their eyes on her and giggled. Seeing that the assistant principal had no intention of reassigning the new student, Ms. Oliver motioned to Edith to join a small group at a table in the back. Drawing her shoulders inward and her head low, Edith moved hesitatingly to her spot. "Class, this is our new student, Edith Rodriguez. I hope you will all make her feel welcome."

Edith's family had moved from the Hidalgo region of Mexico a month earlier, settling in one of five trailers parked at the edge of a dirt road crossing fifty acres of strawberry fields. Her parents had decided to leave Mexico to join relatives with jobs, following the harvests northward during the season. Neither Edith's mother nor her father spoke English, so knowing someone from home who worked in the fields made it possible for them to join the crew. Edith had attended school in Mexico, but her town had been besieged by violent crime and insurgency, which caused her parents to relocate often for safety and for work. As a result, her schooling had been haphazard, and Edith's literacy skills in Spanish had suffered, along with her knowledge of math, science, and other subjects. In spite of these hardships, Edith loved school and enjoyed the attention of her teachers. She had been looking forward to finding out what school would be like in the United States.

Pine Woods Elementary had recently been rezoned to include the outskirts of town and its surrounding farmland. Before this year the school had seldom enrolled an English learner, but now every grade had at least a couple ELs, all at different levels of English proficiency. Six teachers had just returned from a national conference, energized with new tips and techniques for reaching the new students. Some of these teachers had begun professional learning to better understand how to teach English learners, participating in classes one night per week. Everyone knew that the school had to rise to the new challenge, but some teachers were more eager to get started than others.

That first morning, Edith attended an English language development class.[6] She immediately felt more comfortable among the other English learners and their patient, encouraging teacher. Most of her school day would be spent with English-speaking fourth graders whom she could barely understand, but in the ELD class Edith could communicate with her classmates and her teacher, using mostly Spanish interrupted by a few key words she knew in English. In no time, however, the bell rang and the other students began picking up their pencils and making their way out the door. Edith stayed put as a new group scampered in, planting themselves in the empty chairs. A lone boy inched his way into the room, moving toward Edith. "Edith, sweetie, you need to go back to your classroom," the ELD teacher told her. As she was leaving, Edith heard sniffles, growing louder and louder. "Come here, Gero," the teacher said sweetly. "Come here with me."

It was Gero's first day, too. Gero had come to Pine Woods Elementary after spending a few weeks of the new school year in another district. Gero's father, a civil engineer, had been transferred to a construction company in Harveston, so the whole family had to quickly adjust to their new neighborhood and schools. Gero's mother, a pediatrician, and his father spoke to him in French, as they insisted on doing with all of their children. However, Haitian Kreyòl, the native language of Gero's home country, Haiti, was also spoken in the home, mainly by Gero's brothers and sisters, and sometimes by his grandmother.

Gero was lucky to be placed with kindergarten teacher Ms. Levin, who had begun professional learning the summer before the school's zoning change. Ms. Levin had worked to create a welcoming environment for her English learners, labeling classroom objects in multiple languages and providing an enticing selection of bilingual picture books. "Welcome, byenveni, Gero!" Ms. Levin had greeted the doe-eyed boy at the door. At her side was a girl from Port-Au-Prince who had been in the United States two years, with English skills that had grown strong in a preschool program. Gero smiled and moved toward his class buddy. Kindergarten didn't look as scary as he had expected. Ms. Levin made sure of it. When it came time to go to lunch, Gero refused to leave Ms. Levin's side.

Within the different categories of ELs, Edith and Gero are considered to be beginning level. English learners entering school (either in preschool or kindergarten) at the beginning level of English proficiency may have been born in the United States, but live in homes and communities where their exposure to and use of English may not be extensive. This is not the case for Edith and Gero, however; they are both what are known as newcomers—ELs who have recently arrived in the United States, have limited English language skills, and likely have limited experience with American culture. As with all language learners, Edith and Gero will go through typical, predictable stages in their acquisition of English. EL students of all grade levels begin learning English by focusing mostly on comprehending their new language. They often show comprehension by nodding, pointing, and answering in their first language because they haven't yet acquired the wording and phrasing necessary to converse in English. Apart from language-related challenges, newcomers face issues linked to their adaptation to and integration into a new cultural environment. Schools need to recognize these difficulties and make an effort to include the family and the community in the cultural transition of ELs, as they play a critical role in the success of this process.[7]

Previous schooling experiences and first language literacy are both important factors in EL students' performance and progress. Edith likes school but her education has been irregular, a fact that can potentially affect her performance. Will her gaps in literacy be insurmountable? Do her teachers know that she might lack basic reading skills in Spanish, her first language? Unlike Edith, Gero is a bilingual French and Haitian Kreyòl speaker, but is more dominant in Haitian Kreyòl.[8] He is able to use a wider set of vocabulary words, sentence structure, and emotions when expressing himself in Kreyòl rather than French. He also has developed strong preliteracy skills in both home languages, thanks to time spent with his grandmother and mother, who read to him regularly. Do his teachers know that he is drawing from multiple home languages instead of just one? Do they know that his foundational literacy skills have been developed in his home languages? These are all important questions that we will look at more closely in subsequent chapters. Now that we have introduced our beginning English learners, Edith and Gero, it's time to meet our intermediate English learner, Edgar.

✦ Edgar Ponce at Highpoint High School, Chicago, Illinois

The apartment smelled moldy. Eliminating the dampness seemed impossible given the two narrow, 1970s-era column windows, neither facing south, and one of them broken. This city dwelling was far removed from the bright and airy home Edgar grew up in with his family in Puerto Rico. His "real" home wasn't big or fancy, but sea breezes blew across every sunlit room.

Edgar had become withdrawn and sullen after his father left the family one random Saturday evening fourteen months earlier. Edgar's mother said he'd be back, but that never happened. After six months she decided to move, along with her four children, to the U.S. mainland, to the big city where her sister lived. There was work, her sister told her, and starting anew near family gave her hope.

Every afternoon when Edgar came home to the dingy apartment, he remembered all they had left in Puerto Rico. His friends, the sunshine, even his school. Edgar had never liked school, but after eight months away from his "real" home, his memories of ninth grade and before became more pleasant. Even though he had struggled with reading and math, his teachers understood him.

Now school had become a nightmare. Edgar's eight months of English immersion gave him budding conversation skills, but that didn't equip him for the demands of tenth-grade subjects taught in English. On a good day, Edgar would simply tune out when he couldn't understand his social studies, math, or science teacher. For too many days, Edgar would impulsively act out, talking loudly to nearby Spanish-speaking classmates and even confronting the teacher as she explained a concept, incomprehensible to him.

But Edgar entered a different world for two hours each day at Highpoint High. There was one place where he felt at home again, where he felt understood. Ms. Myers, his English language development teacher, knew how to teach so he could comprehend. The other students, who spoke many different languages, had lived similar experiences, and felt homesick and tongue-tied like Edgar. When Ms. Myers introduced newcomers, Edgar approached each one eagerly, welcoming and helping them with maturity and empathy. During class, Ms. Myers often observed him leaning in to encourage a newly arrived group member, giving clues such as "Así se dice libro en inglés, boo-k." A childlike smile would spread from his eyes downward—he knew more English than someone else, and he could help. For now, though, this side of Edgar had to be suspended until the next day. The clanging bell interrupted end-of-class group work. "Remember to take your vocabulary practice sheets home," Ms. Meyers announced as she held up the empty form. Stepping out of the classroom oasis, Edgar folded his arms, tilted his head defiantly upward to the left, and mustered his toughest stance to survive in the mainstream.

While Edith and Gero are newcomers, Edgar is a U.S.-born EL. A great proportion of students classified as English learners were born in this country, entering preschool or kindergarten as beginners and continuing to receive ELD support as their levels of proficiency and grade levels rise. U.S.-born ELs bring a different set of challenges but they also share many common issues with newcomers, as is the case with Edgar, who moved from Puerto Rico, a U.S. territory with a distinct culture where Spanish is the primary language. As you saw in the story, it didn't take long before Edgar got into trouble at school. But this doesn't necessarily mean that Edgar is a bad kid. Edgar's discipline problems may simply be the result of a very difficult, yet common, period of cultural adjustment, known as the hostility or crisis phase of acculturation.[9] Edgar's displacement from his familiar environment has created feelings of frustration, irritability, and helplessness. It is likely that Edgar will need special assistance from various professionals to succeed in school. In addition to the support of his ELD and academic subject teachers, a guidance counselor who is familiar with cultural adjustment could talk with Edgar about why he may be feeling stressed, and a bilingual reading coach could offer the additional help Edgar needs to develop his academic and literacy skills in both languages.

If we compare Edgar's language performance to that of Edith and Gero, it's clear he is beyond a beginning EL. An intermediate EL, Edgar is able to communicate in English. He understands conversational English fairly well, but not in most academic contexts, such as his mainstream academic subject classes. Like many ELs at his level, Edgar's speech and writing at this stage have frequent errors as he tries to master the complexity of English grammar and sentence structure. This is a normal part of the process of second language acquisition. In many ways, Edgar is right where we would expect him to be. The big question facing Edgar is, where will he go next?

Now let's meet Tasir, our advanced English learner.

✦ Tasir Barad at Freedom Middle School, Summerfield, Arkansas

"Yes, I AM going to school dressed like this, Dad! This is how all the girls dress," Tasir insisted as she stormed out the door. Still smarting from the confrontation, Tasir replayed the scene in her mind as she hurried to the bus stop.

Why does he want me to dress, think, and act like someone thousands of miles away? *He* moved the family here, not me, so how can he expect us to live like we never left Egypt? As the bus to Freedom Middle wound through the tidy suburbs, Tasir glanced broodingly through the dusty windows at the driveways and ranch-style homes passing by.

More than anything, Tasir wanted to fit in, to look, think, and act like the popular girls in the seventh grade. She did all right imitating the cool kids, with her style, mannerisms, and even speech mimicking the latest tween fads. It had taken time to blend in, though. When she started school in the United States, back in the third grade, Tasir spoke not one word of English. Her reading skills in Arabic, her native language, were strong, but the shape and direction of the boxy letters in the English textbooks were all new to her. Four years later, she understands but rarely utters anything in the language she arrived speaking.

"I just don't see how Tasir is still categorized as an English learner. No one could tell she's not a native speaker. I have no time to make accommodations for her, and she doesn't need them anyway!"

"Ms. Parker," cautioned the ELD resource teacher, "Tasir may be able to talk about her favorite pop stars, but she can't keep up with your lectures. She tells me that just as she's starting to understand a new point, you move on to the next." Tasir had failed Ms. Parker's last test. Next to the 58 the teacher had written, "You can do better than this!" Tasir reached for the paper, felt the force of her limitations rush upward from her flushed neck, and flipped the test over quickly on her desk.

Tasir hated geography, math, and earth science. Home economics, where she could watch her teacher prepare meals and practice cutting vegetables, was the only class she liked. Most of Tasir's teachers thought she did poorly because of her "whatever" attitude. But even though she looked and sounded like a typical seventh grader, she read and wrote like a fourth grader. Catching up with the native speakers required learning a new alphabet at the same time she was absorbing the meaning of the most basic words and acquiring the unfamiliar structure of simple sentences and paragraphs. All this while she studied science and social studies and math in this backwards language that she had only just begun to understand. She'd had barely four years to catch up with the others, but now Ms. Parker only saw a seventh grader who could do well, if she just tried.

To understand Tasir's needs, Ms. Parker should become aware of how advanced English learners become fluent in social uses of language but are still developing proficiency in academic language. Social language is synonymous with what English learner expert Jim Cummins terms Basic Interpersonal Communication Skills (BICS). This is the type of language proficiency required to converse with others about daily life and basic needs. For example, when Tasir talks with her friends about what she is planning for the weekend, she is showing her command of social English. In contrast with social language, Cummins defines proficiency in academic English, which he has termed Cognitive Academic Language Proficiency (CALP), as that needed for learning school subjects.[10] Academic language is more complex and tends to refer to more abstract notions than social language. In addition, academic language use involves more reading and writing than social language, which is mostly conversational. Even advanced English learners like Tasir still need time and support to become proficient in academic English. Research has shown that if ELs have no prior schooling or have no support in their native language, it may take seven to ten years for them to catch up to their peers' proficiency in academic English.[11] Therefore, Tasir's teachers should not assume that advanced ELs like her, who show a high degree of fluency and accuracy in everyday spoken English, or social language, have an equally well-developed academic language proficiency in English.

We can see that Tasir needs more support and more time given the fact that her first language uses a script that is different from the English alphabet. She is fortunate that her literacy skills in Arabic were strong. Strong literacy in the first language helps tremendously with acquiring literacy in a second language. However, because she did not continue to receive literacy instruction in Arabic, her transition to English literacy has required more time and is not complete. Tasir is still classified as an English learner, but even ELs who have been exited from ELD programs are still in the process of catching up with their native English-speaking peers, and so they still need monitoring and support. Tasir has caught up with her peers when it comes to fitting in culturally. But this has cost Tasir the loss of her native culture and language, and a clash between her home and school lives.

Individual Characteristics of Our Four English Learners

Edith's, Gero's, Edgar's, and Tasir's stories show how complex EL-related issues are and the difficulty of a one-size-fits-all type of instructional approach. Differences in the first language, age, and social, cultural, and affective conditions of English learners have a powerful effect on the way they learn.

Although the majority of English learners in the United States speak Spanish, as do Edith and Edgar, English learners come from a multitude of home languages, and each one has particular influences on the way an EL learns English. Edith and Edgar can benefit from various similarities between Spanish and English, and their teachers should take advantage of every opportunity to make connections explicit. Similarly, French and Haitian Kreyòl, Gero's home languages, share many commonalities with English that can be built upon to his benefit. Unlike the other three ELs' home languages, Arabic, Tasir's home language, does not use the same alphabet as English, nor does it have many words that are based on the same roots (typically Latin and Greek words). However, the basic concepts of print and the notion of sound/symbol correspondence that Tasir brought with her from Egypt undoubtedly helped her develop an ability to understand and use their English counterparts.

As with the differences evident in the stories, some ELs have a positive attitude toward learning English, while others are more resistant if they view English as trying to displace their ethnic identity or if they see no clear or immediate benefits to developing strong skills in this "foreign" language. Like first language development, second language acquisition occurs in very rich contexts where social, cultural, and affective factors are an important part of the process. Second language acquisition scholars have studied social and affective influences on student learning, examining the relationship between two linguistically different groups of people who are in contact.[12] One group consists of people who have the same first language (such as Spanish) and are learning a second language (such as English), while the other group is made up of native speakers of the second language. The research suggests that a number of social factors can either promote or hinder contact between the two groups, which affects whether or not the second language learners from the same native language group adapt to the culture and consequently acquire the second language. The contact between the two groups can affect English learners' attitudes toward learning English. The type of contact between the community of speakers of the home languages of our four ELs and the larger community of English speakers varies greatly, and the more our ELs' teachers know about the languages used in their homes, the better the teachers will understand how their native language impacts their learning.

As with learning anything, motivation, like attitude, affects learners' second language acquisition process and outcomes. Two types of motivation, integrative and instrumental, have been identified as influencing individuals' second language development in particular.[13] *Integrative motivation* alludes to the learner's interest in learning the language and his attitudes toward the teacher, the school, and the second language and its speakers. *Instrumental motivation* entails the learner's perceived benefits of learning the second language. Both types of motivation have been found to influence second language acquisition, with integrative motivation seeming slightly more influential than instrumental motivation. We can see with Edith, Gero, Edgar, and Tasir that teachers and other educators at their schools have a profound influence on their interest in developing English proficiency. Similarly, we will see in upcoming chapters how their teachers will clue them in to the direct benefits of developing proficiency in English listening, speaking, reading, writing, vocabulary, and grammar and to their progress toward reaching grade-level expectations.

Age also plays an important role in language development, since older ELs have to acquire highly complex academic content at the same time they learn English. As we have seen with our four English learners, the age ELs begin learning English has a major effect on their language development. This is true for both internal factors—for example, cognitive development and maturation—and external factors, such as different instructional approaches.

Several studies have compared the development of older and younger learners in similar situations, finding that at the early stages of language development, adult learners are, contrary to what many assume, actually more efficient than younger learners.[14] In formal second language learning settings, older learners are successful because they have several skills younger learners do not yet possess: metalinguistic knowledge (they can compare the new language with their home language), memory strategies, and problem-solving skills. This means that they can benefit from more formal instruction about their new language, which calls upon those more complex skills to learn new grammatical structures. So Tasir and Edgar, adolescent English learners in middle and high school, can benefit more from the formal study of English grammar, as we will see in more detail in part II. This doesn't mean, however, that older students are better at learning second languages. Younger students like Gero and Edith have many advantages, including more time to catch up, a learning environment that is generally more conducive to language acquisition, and internal developmental factors that promote the eventual attainment of native-like pronunciation and grammar use. All of these issues play key roles in the progress of our four English learners.

Their stories illustrate the many differences in classifications and terms used (newcomer, native-born, etc.) to describe the students we focus on in this book, preK–12 students who are not fully proficient in English, their second (or third, etc.) language.[15] English learners' education in their native languages and home countries may have been interrupted and ineffective, or it may have been continuous and rigorous. They may come from financially stable families or live in abject poverty. The diversity among English learners can be as vast as that of any other group of students.

Classroom Communication and Language Learning for Our Four English Learners

As we have seen, how one learns a second language can vary greatly, with individual factors such as native language, prior education, family background, motivation, and age affecting the process and the outcome. Along with these key issues, the school context in which ELs learn has a major impact as well. In fact, the school and classroom context is so important to English learners' success that it is the focus of the rest of the book. Considering the quality of communication for English learners in mainstream classrooms is a crucial first step for teachers to understand how to help ELs learn academic subjects and develop proficiency in English.

Just from our brief snapshot of the elementary, middle, and high school classrooms of our EL subjects, we see that the goal of successful communication with these students can vary greatly. Gero's teacher, Ms. Levin, is working hard to narrow the communication gap between classroom language use and Gero's English proficiency. Being in a kindergarten environment certainly helps, but Ms. Levin supports communication with Gero with what she has learned about ELs. In contrast, Edgar's tenth-grade academic subject teachers mostly teach their classes as if he weren't there, with no special attention to improving communication with Edgar. If they knew even a little bit about narrowing the classroom communication gap, they could help him master their subjects and even contribute to his language development. Teachers who know how to support English learners in this way can make all the difference for students like Gero, Edith, Edgar, and Tasir.

In the upcoming chapters, your understanding of the school context, class-room communication, language instruction, and other issues affecting English learner achievement will deepen as you come to know Edith, Gero, Edgar, and Tasir. Their unfolding stories and the discussions that follow them present the experiences of these students and their teachers realistically, showing how, despite the challenging circumstances that face so many schools and classrooms around the nation, educators *can* reach English learners.

OVERVIEW OF UPCOMING CHAPTERS

This introduction presents our four English learners and the contexts in which these students live and learn. The rest of the book is divided into two major parts—teaching academic subjects and teaching language arts and literacy—followed by a concluding chapter that brings the book full circle, explaining how the information from the previous chapters can be implemented in a school-based, collaborative model of instruction for English learners, our One Plus Model of Professional Learning and Collaboration.

Part I—Teaching Academic Subjects to English Learners

Part I begins with an orientation to the research and theory that underlie our approach to teaching academic subjects to English learners. Placing communication at the center of this discussion, chapter 1 shows how the primary goal of teaching academic subjects differs from the primary goal of teaching language arts and literacy. To illustrate how the level of English proficiency affects mastery of academic subjects, stories of our four English learners include dialogue from actual interview transcripts and illustrate other important factors, such as their first language literacy and prior knowledge of the academic subjects. After the preliminary discussion of classroom communication of academic subjects and English learner levels of proficiency, we discuss the gap between them and how it is affected by grade level. Last, we introduce our Academic Subjects Protocol, which is an articulated series of analyses and decisions that narrow the gap between communication in curriculum, instruction, and assessment of academic subjects and English learners at beginning, intermediate, and advanced levels of proficiency.

This protocol is then applied in chapters 2 through 5, which provide research-based practical guidance for teaching academic subjects to English learners. Each chapter focuses on teaching a specific subject to one of our four English learners, Gero, Edith, Tasir, or Edgar. Unlike this introduction, which presented our four ELs in order from beginning to advanced levels of English proficiency to introduce that concept, the chapters in part I are sequenced by grade level, progressing from kindergarten to fourth, seventh, and tenth grade.

Chapter 2 presents general considerations in teaching social studies to English learners, followed by a classroom application of these principles to a kindergarten social studies lesson and then use of the Academic Subjects Protocol to analyze where and decide how Gero will be provided necessary support. In addition to this detailed description of how we used this protocol to narrow the gap for Gero, we provide briefer adaptation examples for English learners at higher or lower levels of English proficiency. The remaining chapters of part I follow the same structure, with chapter 3 focusing on Edith and science instruction, chapter 4 on Tasir and interdisciplinary, thematic instruction, and chapter 5 on Edgar and mathematics instruction. The lessons presented are standards-based, and each uses a different pedagogical approach, which illustrates how various common instructional practices present particular challenges and opportunities for English learners.

Part II—Teaching Language Arts and Literacy to English Learners

As with part I, part II begins with an orientation to the research and theory that underlie our approach to teaching English learners, but focuses on teaching language arts and literacy. Maintaining the centrality of communication to all types of learning, in chapter 6 we isolate the primary means of communication—language—and analyze how it develops through instruction, or what is known as instructed second language acquisition. In noting the difference between teaching through language, teaching about language, and teaching language, we argue that teaching language/teaching about language to English learners requires a greater degree of linguistic precision than teaching academic subjects to ELs.[16] We subsequently deepen our discussion of English proficiency, describing five levels and how to target language arts and literacy instruction to these more precise proficiency levels. After discussing how implementation of instructed second language acquisition (what we term "targeted language instruction" for English learners) might range from nearly complete overlap with grade-level language arts instruction to nearly complete separation from it, we move on to how this language gap can be addressed in the mainstream and English language development classrooms. We then show how our Language Arts Protocol, an articulated series of analyses and decisions that target language arts and literacy instruction to specific levels of English proficiency, helps guide mainstream language arts and literacy teachers to ensure that curriculum, instruction, and assessment in their classrooms and, where appropriate, in ELD classes, meet English learners at their precise level of English proficiency.

The Language Arts Protocol is then applied in chapters 7 through 10, which provide research-based practical guidance for teaching listening, speaking, reading, and writing to English learners. Each chapter focuses on one of our four English learners, integrating the teaching of listening and speaking with reading or writing instruction. Based on the grade levels of the English learners, we begin each chapter by discussing grade-level expectations for language arts and literacy. We then highlight major research and theory on language arts and literacy instruction for English learners within the grade bands of focus and present actual reading and writing samples for the English learners in the context of their stories. This all leads to an analysis of the gap between grade-level instruction and the English learners' proficiency, followed by a classroom application of the Language Arts Protocol to standards-based English language arts lessons.

Maintaining the pattern described above, chapter 7 begins with a summary of the English language arts Common Core State Standards for kindergarten, followed by a presentation of general research and theory on language and literacy development for English learners in primary grades. Gero's oral proficiency in English and the influence of his first language on his English language development are discussed, followed by a classroom application. This practical section begins with samples of Gero's reading and writing, and then describes his language arts teacher's writing lesson and how she applied the Language Arts Protocol to make sure it was targeted to Gero's specific level of English proficiency. Chapters 8 and 9 use this same pattern. Chapter 8 focuses on teaching language arts and literacy to English learners in the intermediate grades, looking specifically at teaching Edith in the mainstream classroom at her level of English proficiency. Chapter 9 presents teaching language arts and literacy to English learners at the middle school level, discussing teaching Tasir in the mainstream classroom at her English proficiency level. Chapter 10 focuses on teaching language arts and literacy to English learners at the high school level, but it diverges from the previous pattern of chapters 7 through 9 by showing how Edgar's language instruction needs are best met in the English language development rather than mainstream language arts classroom.

Conclusion

After experiencing key research, theory, and practical issues in teaching English learners through the cases of Gero, Edith, Tasir, Edgar, and their teachers, you will be prepared to take action in your own classroom and school. The conclusion shows how educators who have developed essential knowledge and skills in teaching English learners can collaborate to serve their best interests. We describe how teachers and other school professionals can work together, spanning simple coordinated efforts to more cooperative approaches, and finally to collaboration, the most integrated and connected way of working together. We then present an overview of the major topics and concepts in each category of our One Plus Model of Professional Learning, with references to online and other resources for free and easily accessible content for professional learning. We close by revisiting our four English learners, now at the end of the school year in which we have come to know them.

Features Common to the Entire Book

As the overarching theme of this book is the communication gap, envisioned as the space in which every teacher works to address the specific needs of an English learner, the content of every chapter is organized by a common sequence: first, a general description of the language demands of the subject or skill of focus, followed by a discussion of the challenges in studying that subject or skill for ELs at specific levels of English proficiency. In other words, each chapter sizes up the gap, then offers practical suggestions for narrowing it. This book provides an overarching theoretical framework, a big picture, so to speak, for the specific practices that illustrate what teachers can do to reach English learners, and we believe that big-picture books need big (and lots of) pictures. Therefore, in the theory-to-practice chapters 1 and 6, we have placed diagrams and infographics that illustrate and summarize major points. We included these visuals also to walk our talk about the importance of using both verbal (language) and nonverbal (visual) communication in teaching English learners.

Each chapter ends with "Stop and Reflect Questions" and "Go and Practice Activities," which offer preK–12 teachers and other education professionals myriad opportunities to apply the book's content to their own instructional contexts. We collaborated to keep the book comprehensive, yet concise, so we excluded far more than we included. Our Web site, http://www.englishlearnerachievement.com, provides suggestions and resources for further study. We believe these will be most useful after reading the book and developing a sense of the full landscape of teaching English learners in mainstream classrooms.

This book wasn't written for a perfect world. It doesn't lay out a gold standard of practice that can only be implemented in ideal conditions with bountiful resources. It was written for you and all the other educators who are doing the best they can to help all their students reach their potential. We believe what you read here will be actionable in your classroom, and we hope it helps you to foster excellent communication and provide effective support for closing your English learners' language gaps.

STOP AND REFLECT QUESTIONS

1. How are you preparing to assist your ELs to meet the rigorous requirements of the Common Core Standards?
2. You know the professionals at your school. In your opinion, is there a sense of collaboration among all? If not, what can you do to foster greater collaboration among your colleagues to meet the needs of English learners?
3. Do you perceive students as being effective communicators? Do you encourage communication in your classroom?
4. Why is it necessary to accelerate the English language development of English learners?
5. Compare Edith's overall demeanor upon entering the mainstream class and when entering the ELD class. Why did her attitude change? What were the contributing factors that allowed her to feel more comfortable in the ELD class?
6. Think about the English learners in your class(es). Do any of your students share characteristics with Gero, Edith, Edgar, and Tasir? If so, how are they similar?

GO AND PRACTICE ACTIVITIES

1. Review the Common Core Standards. Identify the standards that may be challenging for the ELs in your class, depending on their levels of English proficiency. Start to develop a plan for how you will help your ELs meet those challenges.

2. During the course of a week, analyze your communication patterns in the classroom. Reflect on the exchanges that you think occur. Then, have a colleague videotape one of your class sessions during an unannounced visit. View the video with your colleague and discuss your verbal interactions with your English learners. How often do you call on them? Do you elaborate on their answers? Do you share your opinion on a given answer to model dialogues?

3. Once you have analyzed the video recording of your session, write down any behaviors that need improvement in order to enhance communication between you and your English learners.

PART I

Teaching Academic Subjects to English Learners

CHAPTER 1

Narrowing the Classroom Communication Gap for Academic Subjects

Teachers need to know a lot to reach English learners. There are entire academic degrees in that subject. In this book, we distill what our research and experience tell us is essential. To get to our core goal, closing English learners' language gap, we have divided the book into two areas of focus: instruction in academic subjects and instruction in English language arts for English learners. In teaching academic subjects to ELs, we define the goal as *narrowing the classroom communication gap* between grade-level communication and ELs' English proficiency. That is the subject of this chapter and the rest of part I. In part II, we address English language arts instruction for English learners, which we define as *targeted language instruction*, identifying students' precise level of English proficiency and targeting communication and instruction around it. Because we believe communication is the foundation of learning all subjects and skills, we begin part I by considering its essence.

COMMUNICATION—THE CURRENCY OF EDUCATION

Most would agree that communication is paramount in teaching. Teachers communicate information about topics, concepts, and skills that students are expected to master. Likewise, communication by and among students is central to learning. Students communicate their understanding of a new concept or their questions about a skill they are developing. Communication is, in a sense, the currency of education. A great deal hinges on successful communicative interchanges between teacher and students as well as those among classmates. All teachers need to attend to the quality of communication in the classroom, reflecting on their own and their students' use of language and other means of expressing and comprehending meaning. Without communication, little is taught or learned.

Communication scholar James Carey once stated that prominent twentieth-century educator John Dewey positioned communication at the center of humanity, asserting that society exists both *through* and *in* communication.[1] Drawing on Dewey's work, Carey expanded a prevailing definition of communication from the conveyance of information from one person to another, to a communal process of constructing a symbolic reality. Carey pointed to the common root of the word *communication*, the term *community*, going as far as viewing communication as culture itself.[2] In this perspective, communication is much more than the simple transmission of a message from sender to receiver—it acts as a binding force of interpersonal connection, an exchange of meaning affected by and affecting the communicators.

Similar to Carey's culture-building model of communication is the assertion by language scholar M. A. K. Halliday that culture forms the context for making meaning through language, which he defined as a "social semiotic system" (that is, language as a sign or symbol referring to real objects, concepts, etc.).[3] Halliday's view of language, the most significant form of human communication, is similar to that of learning theorist Lev Vygotsky, who defines language as a cultural tool that serves social interaction. Language can be described in multiple ways, but there is no denying its principal function of creating shared meaning.

In the preK–12 school environment, with its many different uses of language, communication both forms and is shaped by the culture of the classroom. Each individual in the class brings cultural and linguistic assets from life outside of school, creating the potential for a rich collective expression and exploration of meaning. In addition to this collective classroom culture, the socially constructed content of schooling—the knowledge and skills communicated through curriculum and instruction—exists in and through communication as well. If a child's own language and culture closely align with the larger society's language and culture as experienced at school, the gap between the child's abilities and the performance expectations is small. If the gap is large, such as that between the rigorous language demands of the Common Core State Standards and the English proficiency of a beginning English learner like Edith, a substantial degree of support is necessary.[4]

COMMUNICATING ABOUT ACADEMIC SUBJECTS THROUGH LANGUAGE

According to Halliday, there are three aspects of language use in schooling. The first is *learning through language*, such as when studying a subject like history. Information regarding the topic is presented through spoken and written language, and students develop understandings through discussion or other instances of listening, speaking, reading, or writing about the topic. Learning through language is the main mode of communication in teaching and learning academic subjects. Another aspect of language use in school is *learning the language*. This is typically done in language arts classes, where students develop competence in the four skills or modalities of language use—listening and speaking (oral language) and reading and writing (literacy). Lesson objectives and activities provide opportunities to practice these skills, often stressing strategies for improving outcomes. An example of learning the language is a lesson on composing a persuasive essay. Halliday's last element of language use is *learning about the language*, which involves analysis of the form, structure, and rules of language, such as learning grammar, punctuation, or spelling. This type of learning would typically take place in language arts classes, and could easily be part of the persuasive essay lesson just mentioned.

Halliday's distinctions of classroom language functions help illustrate the difference between teaching academic subjects and teaching language arts to English learners. While both types of instruction are clearly interdependent, the overall goals of each differ in emphasis. With academic subject instruction for ELs, the primary goal is to master the subject matter, and if communication of the subject matter is at an appropriate level for the English learner, the EL is able to also develop related English language proficiency. Academic subject teachers play a critical role in ELs' language development through focusing on successful communication. English learners can use newly acquired language related to the academic subject to better learn new content and skills, and therefore a cycle of success in learning the subject and the language of the subject continues.

As English learners develop greater English language proficiency, they are able to comprehend more complex subject matter through language, discuss the content in more complex terms, and demonstrate mastery through higher-level language-based assessments. This process is a mutually beneficial, upwardly mobile system, leading concurrently to increased English proficiency and subject matter knowledge. This cycle is illustrated in figure 1.1.

Conversely, with language arts instruction for English learners, the primary goal is to develop proficiency in English listening, speaking, reading, and writing, which involves learning language and learning about language. Yet by acquiring English language skills and, more specifically, academic language skills, ELs are able to master more

FIGURE 1.1

Purpose of Teaching Academic Subjects to ELs

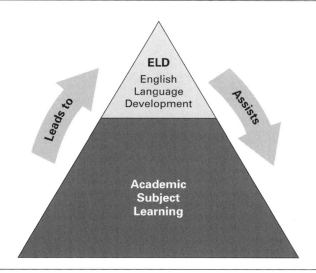

FIGURE 1.2

Purpose of Teaching Language Arts to ELs

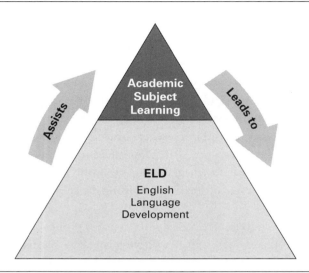

complex academic subject content in English.[5] In part II we will explore the dimensions of language arts/literacy instruction for English learners in more detail. As shown in figure 1.2, just as with academic subject instruction, the process is mutually beneficial.

Given that all teachers need to be mindful of effective communication, teachers of English learners bear additional responsibilities. English learners are acquiring the language of instruction, so communicating with them and helping them to communicate what they are learning takes extra knowledge, skills, and effort. In essence, the primary goal of all teachers of ELs is to communicate successfully with and support the successful communication of these students, whose academic achievement and English language development depend on it. We believe that if culture can be defined as communication, so can teaching.

COMMUNICATION *FOR, BETWEEN,* AND *OF* ENGLISH LEARNERS

Extending Carey's and Halliday's play on prepositions, we can consider mainstream teachers' role in academic subject instruction for English learners in terms of communication *for, between,* and *of* students. Teachers attend to their communication *for* all their students. Lessons of every type involve some sort of teacher communication that is *for,* or directed to, the learners. Similarly, teachers plan and orchestrate communication *between* students, making sure the back and forth sharing of meaning between teacher and student, and between student and student, goes smoothly and purposefully. Teachers also enable communication *of* their students, providing support to help them say or write what they know about the subject being learned, such as with assigned homework or in-class quizzes. No one can deny that these communication relationships are important to teachers. This is especially true for teachers of English learners. Let's take a look at Edith's class to get an idea of how communication in a mainstream classroom can help her learn mathematics and develop English proficiency.

Edith's fourth-grade teacher, Ms. Oliver, often presents new information or skills through the gradual release of instruction, or what is sometimes known as the *I do, we do, you all do, you do* approach.[6] When Ms. Oliver taught her class how to add fractions, she began by writing ¼ + ¼ = on the interactive whiteboard, naming the number and describing what she was doing with each number and symbol she wrote. She continued the same process of writing and describing, adding the top numbers and writing 2 above a line she drew, and then 4 beneath it, and so on until she had solved the problem (the *I do* part of the lesson). After she had walked the class through a couple more examples, she let them know that they would now do a few problems together. By questioning the class at each step, she had them direct her calculations on the whiteboard, coming to the correct answer by consensus (*we do*). She then projected a poem on the whiteboard to help them remember the process: "If adding or subtracting is your aim, the bottom numbers must be the same!" At this point, it was time for students to work together at their tables, solving more problems first in pairs, then sharing their answers, back and forth, with the other pairs (*you all do*). Finally, she turned off the projector and gave each student a handout with four problems to solve individually (*you do*), asking them to write out each step of solving the problem as well as the answer. For extra credit, she challenged them to write the rhyme from memory.

Ms. Oliver's gradual release lesson format involved the three communication relationships we discussed. For each stage of the lesson, she set up communication *for*, *between*, and *of* her students. Let's rename these three prepositions that represent the direction of classroom communication with their recognized terms in the field of second language acquisition—input (communication for students), interaction (communication between students and between teacher and student), and output (communication of students). In the first part of the lesson, Ms. Oliver presented and demonstrated new information, which provided *input* to the learners. Then the teacher led the give-and-take instructional process, which is a form of *interaction* between the teacher and individual students. After that, students had an opportunity for *interaction* with each other, first in pairs, and then with their small groups. Finally, individual students showed what they learned through their written *output* on the handout.

Second language acquisition research and theory have shown that language input, interaction, and output are necessary for anyone to develop proficiency in a new language, but just providing the three aspects of communication is not enough to ensure language learning. They must also be accessible.[7] What does this mean? Essentially, English learners like Gero, Edith, Edgar, and Tasir must be exposed to unknown language forms and structures that they can comprehend; they must engage in meaningful communication, using these new forms and structures with other speakers of the language; and they must express themselves understandably using the newly acquired forms and structures. Comprehensible language in the preK–12 classroom means that when unknown forms and structures are directed at English learners (communication *for* ELs), they are able to comprehend them through reference to real objects or actions (and, in some instances, through background knowledge learned in the native language) or through inferring their meaning from closely related language they already know. In other words, the language English learners are exposed to becomes comprehensible through being at the level of, or a slight step beyond, the language the learner already knows, and also by being closely linked to nonverbal items and experiences the learner can understand.[8] For example, if Edith hears "Write your name, Edith" when her teacher holds a pencil as she points to the top of a blank page, Edith knows to put her name on the paper. This association is described by the term that second language acquisition theorist Stephen Krashen coined, *comprehensible input.*[9] We can contrast this with hearing a radio broadcast in an unknown language—there is input (the sound of the spoken information), but it is not comprehensible. In any learning environment, the more comprehensible input available for the learner, the better.

The counterpart to comprehensible input is comprehensible output, which means that the learner expresses meaning in the second language (communication *of* ELs) that another speaker (native or otherwise) of the language can understand.[10] Because this is an important requirement for developing proficiency, English learners who are moving beyond the earliest stages of second language acquisition, when they mostly listen, must have opportunities to express their thoughts in English, through either speaking or writing. In addition, there needs to be an audience for the English learner's output. The audience can be someone evaluating the output at a later point (as in a testing situation), or someone who is speaking or writing extemporaneously with the English learner (communication *between* ELs and *between* ELs and others—or *interaction*).[11]

Interaction, as the word implies, signifies an exchange between two people, in this case two communicators. The beauty of communicative interaction is that it includes both input and output, and they are connected in a meaningful way. For example, if Edgar asks his English-speaking friend, "Can I use your kay?" and the friend doesn't know what he means, Edgar might say, "for open door" or he can repeat "kay" and hold out his fist, grasping an invisible key and twisting it left and right. His friend would then say, "Oh, you mean my key!" and would hand it to him. This exchange enables Edgar to use the language for a real purpose and builds his vocabulary through his attempt at using an unfamiliar word and his friend's confirmation of the correct term and object. This attempt at communication is like a little lesson, one that uses negotiation of meaning between Edgar and a more advanced or native speaker of English as a route to language growth.[12]

In preK–12 classrooms of all subjects, teachers should do everything possible to provide the most accessible input, interaction, and output for English learners.[13] This means making instruction comprehensible, setting up and supporting interaction with English learners and between English learners and other students, and enabling English learners to express what they know and can do in the subject through multiple means, appropriate to their level of English proficiency. As we saw with Ms. Oliver's gradual release lesson, and with most types of lessons, instruction or presentation of new information is a major form of input (with some teacher-student interaction when the teacher calls on individuals to answer questions), pair and group activities offer opportunities for interaction, and classroom-based assessment requires varying degrees of output.[14] When the classroom teacher is keenly aware of the importance of accessibility for all three elements, she can make adjustments that not only improve the EL's understanding of the subject being learned but will also naturally increase the EL's English language development.[15]

No matter the subject or grade level of instruction, accessible input, interaction, and output is the essence of successful communication *for*, *between*, and *of* English learners. Successful communication promotes learning of the academic content and fosters English language development. We know that accessible input, interaction, and output are necessary for English language development, but as we'll see in the next section, their feasibility differs by grade level.

COMMUNICATING ABOUT ACADEMIC SUBJECTS ACROSS GRADE LEVELS

To get a more complete sense of the nature of communication in instruction at different grade levels, start with a look at the curriculum in the early grades—it would show concepts and topics that are concrete and can be presented by using real objects, role playing, making crafts, and engaging in hands-on activities rather than solely by offering spoken and written explanations. This is what second language acquisition expert Jim Cummins calls "context-embedded instruction."[16] A simple comparison of the physical arrangement of Gero's kindergarten and Edgar's tenth-grade classrooms illustrates this point. Gero's classroom has centers where he and other children play-act different kinds of jobs and handle toys representing the tools or equipment used. His classroom is highly visual and colorful, with labeled objects and word walls that show the alphabet, accompanied by words and pictures. There are bins and crates overflowing with sorting objects, models, flashcards with pictures and words, and sentence strip holders. Parts of walls are dedicated to vocabulary-building resources. There is abundant correspondence between objects and the printed word. By contrast, most of Edgar's high school classrooms contain fewer objects and other resources that make vocabulary and concepts more concrete. Many of the posters on the wall address good study habits and attitudes, but they don't display objects and images depicting topics and concepts that relate to the curriculum.

Because young learners like Gero have not fully mastered literacy in the language of instruction, much of the academic subject instruction in the early grades is communicated through oral language, accompanied by copious amounts of hands-on objects and experiences, pictures and visual communication, and labels and other forms of accompanying text, among other resources. Once children have learned to read, however, much more of the information they have to acquire is conveyed through text, and their comprehension of the content is often assessed through writing. Measures of text complexity generally show an increasing level of difficulty in materials spanning preK–12. For example, the following texts show an increasing amount of information and complexity, including discipline-specific vocabulary by grade levels, which Gero, Edith, Edgar, and Tasir could be expected to read and learn in their respective grades.

> *Kindergarten Water Cycle Text:* The sun evaporates water from oceans, and it turns into water vapor.
>
> *Grade 4 Water Cycle Text:* The constant recycling of water on Earth is called the water cycle. Heat from the sun causes the water particles to move faster and faster. In time, the water particles have enough energy to release into the air as water vapor. This phase of the water cycle is evaporation, the process by which a liquid changes to a gas.
>
> *Grade 7 Water Cycle Text:* The water cycle, also known as the hydrologic cycle, is the continuous movement of water between the surface of Earth and the troposphere. The water cycle happens because of three repeating processes: evaporation, condensation, and precipitation. Evaporation is the process by which liquid water changes into invisible water vapor (water in the form of a gas). Heat from the sunlight causes evaporation.
>
> *Grade 10 Water Cycle Text:* Water vapor rearranges energy from the sun through atmospheric circulation. This happens because water absorbs a large amount of energy when it transforms its state from liquid to gas. When it evaporates from liquid water, the resulting vapor contains more energy, which is referred to as latent heat. Solar radiation drives evaporation by heating water so that it changes to water vapor at a faster rate.

From these examples we see that the language demands of these grade-level texts become more complex, and the amount of language used to convey information about topics and concepts and to develop skills in academic subjects increases with each grade. But what about *oral* language complexity?

We know that academic language demands include listening, speaking, reading, and writing, but most research on their increased difficulty across the grade levels focuses on text and reading. A good deal of research has been conducted on the degree of text complexity from prekindergarten to the twelfth grade, with formulas for calculating readability and grade-level passages as well as specific types of linguistic analyses, but scant attention has been paid to listening and speaking (oral language) complexity in the classroom.[17] Educators assume discussions focusing on complex texts require higher levels of language proficiency to comprehend and participate in lesson activities. Unfortunately, there is limited research on the demands of listening and speaking skills at any grade level. We anticipate that there will be more research on this topic as the Common Core State Standards for listening and speaking skills are implemented. Until that time, we can look to various linguistic factors of oral language, such as the rate and complexity of speech, including word choices, phrasing, and discourse types, to understand the communication challenges in comprehending instruction.

One way to see how grade level may affect oral language demands is to consider how adults speak with young children. Research on adults' speech to babies and toddlers shows that they focus on the here and now, slow their speech, use short, simple sentences, and repeat words frequently. When adults talk to kindergarten-age children, they speak more slowly than with adults, adding pauses between each word. They naturally use what are called "sentence frames," which are set phrase patterns that allow simple substitutions, such as, "Where's____? Look at_____."[18] When adults speak with older children or other adults, they tend not to use these natural adaptations made to help younger children develop first language competence. This means that English learners in mainstream classrooms at the middle and high school levels, such as Tasir and Edgar, don't normally receive the same quality of oral language development, or accessible input and interaction, that Gero and Edith receive in their mainstream elementary school classrooms.

To illustrate the differences in expectations for listening, speaking, reading, and writing as well as the amount of contextualized instruction in early grades versus upper grades, in figure 1.3 we show the ratio of context-embedded instruction (nonverbal classroom communication) to the language demands (verbal classroom communication). The graph highlights the decrease in nonverbal types of communication and increase in verbal ones as we move from prekindergarten to the twelfth grade.[19] In Gero's kindergarten class the portion of academic subject instruction communicated solely by language—for example, listening to the teacher and reading books—is smaller than that communicated by other means, such as hands-on experiences. However, for Edgar, in grade 10, language bears a greater proportion of classroom communication. In Gero's classroom, in addition to the higher proportion of nonverbal communication, the correspondence between nonverbal and verbal classroom communication is very close, with Ms. Levin referring pointedly to real objects and pictures to contextualize their verbal descriptions. Moreover, the integration of oral and print communication is explicit and consistent, providing a bridge between them for young children. This is less true for Edgar in tenth grade.[20]

FIGURE 1.3

Proportion of Verbal and Nonverbal Communication Across Grades

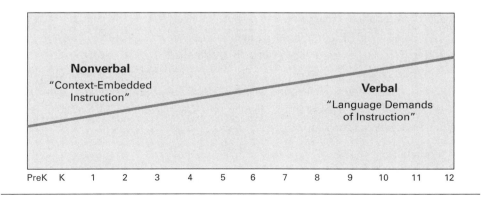

We now have a sense of the different academic subject and language learning environments for Gero, Edith, Edgar, and Tasir. To better understand the gap between communication in their classrooms and their level of English proficiency, we share the following stories about their experiences and communication at school.

INDIVIDUAL FACTORS IN ENGLISH LEARNERS' ACADEMIC SUBJECT ACHIEVEMENT

Gero, Edith, Edgar, and Tasir represent common oral language behaviors for English learners at different levels of English proficiency. Although they are in different grades, their listening and speaking skills are less representational of their grade than their English proficiency level. In other words, a sixth-grade beginning EL has many of the same listening and speaking behaviors in English as a ninth-grade beginning EL, and a ninth-grade advanced EL has many of the same listening and speaking behaviors in English as a twelfth-grade advanced EL. The following stories include transcripts of their speech, which gives a sense of what a learner at each level of proficiency can say and understand in English and how he or she says it.

✦ Edith and Gero

"How long have you been in the United States?" "Uhhh . . . " Edith wanted to respond. She longed to please her teacher with the correct answer. She just couldn't understand the question. "Umm, one month . . . in Florida?" Ms. Oliver held up her index finger as her rising pitch signaled a question. "One . . . one month," Edith confirmed as she bobbed her head and smiled.

Even though an English language development specialist had tested Edith and placed English proficiency scores in the file according to district guidelines, these scores were practically meaningless to Ms. Oliver, who had no prior familiarity with English language development assessment data. "Why don't you just sit down with Edith and have a conversation?" suggested the other fourth-grade teacher. "Whenever I get a newcomer, I make sure to have a lot of pictures and props when we talk."

Ms. Oliver had followed that advice, and after asking Edith about her background, she opened a magazine and pointed to a cartoon. "Who is this?" "Uh . . . eh-Stitch?" Edith offered. "Stitch, that's right, that's Stitch! Do you like Stitch?" Edith nodded with a flutter of affirmation, a wave of relief rising toward her piercing black eyes. "Uh-huh!" "Yeah, me too!" agreed Ms. Oliver. "He makes me laugh." Sitting side by side, the magazine between them, Ms. Oliver and Edith were communicating. Ms. Oliver went on. "What color is Stitch?" (Transcript follows.)

> **EDITH:** Uhh . . .
> **MS. OLIVER:** Is he green, is he black, is he yellow? What color?
> **EDITH:** Eh, blue.

MS. OLIVER: Blue, very good, he's blue! And, can you point to the bed? [no response] Do you see a bed in the picture? [no response] Is there a bed there?

EDITH: Uhh . . . [asks to use a little Spanish—poquito español]

MS. OLIVER: Poquito español? OK.

EDITH: Uhh . . . Poquito español? [pleads for clarification in Spanish]

MS. OLIVER: La cama (Spanish for bed). Can you point to it? The bed.

EDITH: La cama?

MS. OLIVER: Uh-huh. In the picture, show me where it is in the picture.

EDITH: La cama. Eso? (Translation: The bed? This?) [points to the bed]

MS. OLIVER: Yeah, that's the bed. And what color is the bed? Is it the same color as Stitch?

EDITH: Uhh.

Their conversation was strenuous, with both of them grasping for words that made sense to the other. Despite the strain to communicate, Edith's and Ms. Oliver's give-and-take began to form a strong basis for tailoring instruction to Edith's needs. From these interactions, Ms. Oliver gained an understanding of what a beginning English learner can say and do in a second language. She knew, though, that she needed to learn more.

✦ ✦ ✦

Ms. Levin was not surprised that Gero hadn't yet spoken in English. He had, however, begun to nod and point, and follow simple commands. Even when his Kreyòl-speaking classmate, Merline, wasn't nearby, Gero would express himself in Kreyòl, but when an adult pressed him to speak up in English, his response was consistently, "Je ne comprends pas." With a classmate, it was always, "Mwen pa konprann."

Edith's listening comprehension and speech in English represent the beginning level of oral language proficiency. Kindergartner Gero is nearly identical to fourth-grader Edith in both listening and speaking. Common characteristics of the beginning level, which can last up to a year, often include an initial "silent period" when ELs are not yet speaking in English.[21] They might not talk, but they can show comprehension by pointing, performing, gesturing, and nodding. As they progress through the beginning level, English learners develop a vocabulary of five hundred to a thousand words they can understand, some of which they might not use yet. They become more capable of speaking, albeit limited to one- or two-word phrases or short answers to simple questions. For example, once beyond the silent period, English learners can answer simple questions such as yes/no (Is this a flag?), or who (Who has the flag?), either/or (Is this a flag or a globe?), what (What is this?), and where (Where is the flag?). In addition, they are able to understand and say memorized frequent, formulaic language, such as "Whatcha doin'?" even though they aren't yet able to build a sentence that complex word by word, as in "What are you doing?" We saw in Edith's story that she frequently used her first language, Spanish, to clarify a question or supply an answer. It is common for beginning ELs to spontaneously use the language they know well when they are put in situations where they don't know enough English to express their thoughts, even if the person they are addressing doesn't know the EL's first language.

✦ Edgar

Losing patience after her previous warnings to Edgar, the dean of students spoke sternly. "Here we are again, Edgar. Your fourth referral this month. You've got to straighten up soon, or we'll be looking at more serious measures."

"Like . . . like what?" Edgar questioned.

"We can talk about that when the time comes," the dean replied. "I mean, if the time comes. Hopefully, that won't happen."

Edgar stared at the freshly painted wall behind the dean's desk. Grooves the width of his index finger marked each horizontal row of cinderblocks. The semi-gloss sheen of the gray paint highlighted underlying peeled splotches of various pastel colors from the past, their cheerful hues painted over to muffle potential distraction. Gray, and only gray, loomed everywhere. (Transcript follows.)

> **DEAN:** "Edgar, are you listening to anything I'm saying? I just told you the behaviors we expect of you in every class. Ms. Myers describes a well-behaved young man in her ELD class. If you can follow the rules in her class, why are you so disruptive in history class?"
>
> **EDGAR:** 'Cause the other class is boring. I don't like it.
>
> **DEAN:** Why is it boring?
>
> **EDGAR:** 'Cause, sometime I don't understand the work what I have to do. You know.
>
> **DEAN:** Do you understand everything in ELD class?
>
> **EDGAR:** Yeah, and I talk with everybody.
>
> **DEAN:** So what kinds of things do you learn in ELD class?
>
> **EDGAR:** We read, write, and talk, we need to talk, and the teacher, umm . . . , they help, umm . . . , everyone do the other for the other class. In the other class, yeah when, when someone got some problems in some class, yeah, they help with.

This was the longest the dean had spoken with Edgar in the eight months since he had been placed in tenth grade. Maybe knowing a bit more about him could help improve his behavior. Forging ahead, the dean inquired about Edgar's home life.

> **DEAN:** Can you tell me anything interesting about your family?
>
> **EDGAR:** My brother he come from this school, my sister she go to Kennedy, um, my little sister she go to King Highway, something like that. Yeah, and my little brother he don't go to school because she's four year old but he's in the chilled [sic] care.

The second-period bell interrupted the getting-to-know-you interview that the dean had been improvising in simple English. If Edgar stayed out of trouble, there might be no further reason to continue the conversation. The dean hoped this was all she ever needed to know about Edgar.

Common characteristics of students, like Edgar, at the intermediate level, which may last up to two years, are a vocabulary of around three thousand words and the ability to use short phrases and simple sentences to communicate. Intermediate-level English learners are able to ask and answer questions that use and require a bit more language than the simple questions that are appropriate for beginners. In the interview, Edgar could understand, "Do you understand everything in ELD class?" and even elaborated beyond a *yeah* to make it known that he talks with everybody in that class. However, when trying to produce longer sentences, his language, typical of intermediate ELs, contained grammatical errors that obscure meaning. For example, when Edgar referred to his little brother, he alternated between *he* and *she* because he had not yet acquired the correct form in English. Another error that is typical of English learners at this level is not adding the -*s* to the end of verbs, as in, "he come" and "she go." He also uses *don't* instead of *doesn't* in "he don't go," an error that may be due to his developing learner language or to language modeled by his native-speaker peers.

✦ Tasir

Suite 115A . . . 115B . . . 115C. 115J had to be coming up. "Have you heard her with her friends? She sounds like any seventh grader. You may think you're helping her in ELD class, but you're actually holding her back." The voices got louder as Tasir approached the end of the hall. "The problem with Tasir," Ms. Parker continued, "is she's basically lazy. She won't push herself, so we have to." Tasir paused outside the doorway. "Uh, Tasir, how long have you been there?" "Just got here," she chirped. "Come in. We've been waiting for you." Tasir's ELD teacher, Ms. Marlin, pulled a chair out from the conference table's edge. "We'd like to ask you a few questions about your classes." Tasir shrugged her right shoulder as she replied with an abrupt "sure."

> **MS. MARLIN:** Tell me about your favorite class.
> **TASIR:** Um, home ec, 'cause it's fun and it's not—it's not hard.
> **MS. MARLIN:** What kind of things do you do in there?
> **TASIR:** Um, we were gonna cook, but we didn't like cook yet, and, um, uh, we, we learn about like what kind of food we eat and stuff.
> **MS. MARLIN:** Oh, so do you like to cook?
> **TASIR:** Oh, no, not really, not really.

Tasir chattered freely as Ms. Parker and Ms. Marlin recorded her responses in their notepads. Manila folders labeled with Tasir's full legal name were stacked, unopened, at the table's edge. The school counselor and testing coordinator sat at the end of the table, listening while typing on their laptops.

Avoiding looking at Ms. Parker, whose gaze was fixed on her notepad, Tasir volunteered unexpected details, sounding more and more like a seventh grader who was raised speaking English.

> **MS. MARLIN:** What is your hardest class?
>
> **TASIR:** Geography.
>
> **MS. MARLIN:** Geography. And what's hard about geography?
>
> **TASIR:** Um, Ms. Parker don't give us like time to do stuff, when she says do something, she just like gives us a second and she goes OK, next person.
>
> **MS. MARLIN:** So, it goes too fast, huh?
>
> **TASIR:** Yeah.
>
> **MS. MARLIN:** Do you have to do a lot of reading in geography?
>
> **TASIR:** Uh-huh.

Ms. Parker glanced at the other educators around the table for a split second. With Tasir seated in front of her, and surrounded by her coworkers, especially the sympathetic Ms. Marlin, Ms. Parker for once kept her opinions to herself. Ms. Marlin stopped her questions and reached for one of the cumulative folders. "Tasir, let's look at your progress in reading." Tasir didn't respond. Her mind had drifted to Ms. Parker's earlier outburst, to those condemning pronouncements that carried down the hallway. Tasir is a problem. Tasir is lazy. Was that the real reason for her failures at school?

Students at the advanced level, which might last two to three years, typically have a vocabulary of close to six thousand words. Advanced-level English learners like Tasir are able to construct complex statements, state their opinions, and speak at length. However, they are still in the process of learning academic English and they still need language support when they experience difficulty with academic tasks at grade level. Depending on the age of initial exposure and the amount of exposure to English as well as other individual factors, it can take from four to seven years (or even longer) for an English learner to reach grade-level academic language proficiency.[22] From the interview we can see that Tasir has clearly mastered social language, but she is struggling with academic language. Her reading and writing in English are well below grade level (we will see samples of her work in those areas in part II), but that isn't her only difficulty. She has trouble understanding her teachers' explanations and discussions during academic subject instruction, which perplexes her teachers who don't know about the process of developing English proficiency.

The stories thus far have illustrated that a number of factors may explain individual differences among English learners in academic subject achievement. These factors include English learners' level of English proficiency, and oral proficiency in particular; their literacy in the first and second language; and the extent of their prior knowledge of the academic subject.[23] We look at these factors more closely in the next section.

English Language Proficiency Level

Learning a second language is a process that progresses from knowing and understanding nothing about the language to becoming fully proficient. The intervals, or stages, can be categorized in various ways. Traditional foreign or second language instruction often divides levels of proficiency into five or more segments, until full proficiency is achieved. In part II, we will show how teaching language arts and literacy to ELs requires fine-tuning instruction in listening, speaking, reading, and writing to individuals' levels of English proficiency, and we will describe the WIDA Consortium six stages of proficiency (see chapter 6 for specifics).[24]

For narrowing the classroom communication gap in academic subject instruction, however, we believe that a basic categorization of three levels of proficiency—beginning, intermediate, and advanced—is most useful.[25] With three levels, there are very clear distinctions for what each student can understand and do in English. Similarly, for teachers, there are very clear distinctions for what they can do to enable successful communication for, between, and of these students. Table 1.1 describes common characteristics of English learners at each of the three levels, categorizing Gero and Edith at the beginning, Edgar at the intermediate, and Tasir at the advanced level. This categorization is an important basic tool for reaching each English learner at her or his level, and will be referred to again throughout part I.

Prior Knowledge of Subject Matter and First Language Literacy

Gero's, Edith's, Edgar's, and Tasir's teachers face similar, yet unique, challenges. They all strive to help their English learners learn academic subjects, but this can only occur if the content is made accessible. Because curriculum, instruction, and assessment are

TABLE 1.1

English Learner Communication—Levels of Proficiency

BEGINNING Gero and Edith	INTERMEDIATE Edgar	ADVANCED Tasir
• Points to items • Follows commands • Listens initially—receptive skill development • One- to two-word responses • Labels and matches items • Lists items • Memorizes common phrases	• Uses novel phrases and simple sentences • Describes items in simple terms • Frequent grammatical errors in word form (he go) • Frequent sentence structure errors (Why you don't like it?) • Pronunciation errors (in spontaneous speech and read-aloud) • Vocabulary gaps and circumlocution	• Beginning academic language use • Dialogue and discourse with some grammatical and rhetorical errors • Can read/write decontextualized passages with support • Grammatical errors in writing

largely afforded through language, English learners' developing second language proficiency influences their developing knowledge and skills in academic subjects.

English learners may already know the academic content or focus in their first language, which would mean that they are learning the English phrasing and terms of a topic they already understand. Let's take a look at Edgar to see how this works. Fortunately, Edgar had learned about plate tectonics in Puerto Rico, so when his earth and space science class at Highpoint High studied continental drift and the earth's lithosphere and asthenosphere, he was able to catch on to the content more readily since the concepts were not new to him. This freed up information-processing capacity for him to concentrate on the English terms used. Considering what Jim Cummins refers to as cognitive demand of instruction for English learners, we can see that the cognitive demand placed on Edgar in learning a topic he already knows is low, but he still has much to learn about the language used to teach and assess the topic. If the curriculum in Puerto Rico had not included plate tectonics prior to his arrival in Chicago, he would most likely have felt overwhelmed, trying to understand the content and its related English explanations at the same time. In this case, he would have a high cognitive demand because he would have twice the content to learn, the science concept and its related language in English.

First language literacy has a positive effect on second language literacy. Years of research have shown this to be true. English learners who are literate in their first language have an advantage over peers with few or no literacy skills in their first language.[26] So Edith, who missed a lot of school while her family moved from town to town in Mexico, has deficits in academic subject knowledge as well as literacy in her native language, Spanish.[27] This will present additional challenges because in fourth grade, Edith is expected to learn academic subjects through reading and writing about them. Students who read widely and frequently in any language, not just English, are higher achievers than students who read rarely and narrowly.[28] Fortunately, important aspects of language and literacy knowledge and skills are transferable, even across languages that differ markedly in the type of letters, spelling conventions, word formation, sentence structure, and direction of print (e.g., Arabic, English, and French).[29] If English learners are competent readers in their first language, they will never need to learn to read again. They may need to learn new symbols, and they will need to learn new language, but much of what they know about reading in their first language will help them read in their second one.[30] And, of course, there is reading involved in learning academic subjects, so their first language reading competence can ultimately help them to learn academic subjects in English.

In spite of clear individual differences, we have seen that our four English learners share several characteristics. They all go through predictable stages in their acquisition of English, from primarily listening in the classroom to developing advanced fluency in speaking, listening, reading, and writing. Their social English develops more quickly than their academic English, which needs more time and more direct support from classroom teachers.

In addition to common characteristics of English learners that affect the process of developing proficiency in English, we have seen that classroom environments can vary in the degree that they narrow the gap between classroom communication and ELs' English proficiency levels. Classrooms with accessible input, interaction, and output narrow this communication gap and thus foster both academic subject learning and language growth. When English learners are doubly tasked with learning the academic content and its associated academic language, accessible curriculum, instruction, and assessment depend primarily, or perhaps even exclusively, on successful communication.

ANALYZING THE GAP BETWEEN ELs' ENGLISH PROFICIENCY AND GRADE-LEVEL LANGUAGE DEMANDS OF ACADEMIC SUBJECT INSTRUCTION

The stories of Gero, Edith, Edgar, and Tasir illustrate the challenges in making curriculum, instruction, and assessment accessible for English learners studying academic subjects. From their examples, we can see how grade level affects verbal and nonverbal classroom communication. But what happens when the verbal communication in whole-class instruction is too far above an English learner's proficiency level and the topic or concept is new as well? This is the situation facing many secondary teachers, such as those who teach Edgar. For example, if Edgar is expected in social studies class to listen to, read about, and discuss complex aspects of the relationships among science, technology, and society, learning this new content through language that is appropriate for tenth-grade native speakers will likely cause him to struggle to comprehend every detail and nuance presented. On the other hand, Gero, who may not know the grade-level concepts of voting and majority rule, will more easily grasp them if his kindergarten class learns about them through voting for a class treat. So, the gap between grade-level classroom communication and the English learner's proficiency level is the space in which the teacher adapts curriculum, instruction, and assessment.

To get a clearer understanding of this space for adaptation, let's look at a visual representation of the gap between the English proficiency of each of our four English learners and the language demands, or verbal classroom communication, of each EL's grade, presented in figure 1.4. Gero, a beginning English learner in kindergarten, has a smaller gap between his proficiency level and the language demands in his class than Edith, who is also a beginner but is in the fourth grade. Tasir, an advanced English learner in the seventh grade, has a smaller gap than the three other ELs. If Tasir had come to the United States as a toddler, attended a good-quality preschool, and consequently entered kindergarten at an advanced level of proficiency, her gap would be very small, almost negligible. Enrolled in the uppermost grade of our four English learners, Edgar has a large spread between his intermediate English proficiency and the language demands of tenth grade. This classroom communication gap diagram depicts students who are literate (to varying degrees) in their native language. If they lacked basic literacy skills (or in Gero's case, preliteracy skills) in their native language, then the shaded 'gap' bar would begin below the beginner level, creating an even greater classroom communication gap.

FIGURE 1.4

Classroom Communication Gaps for the Four ELs

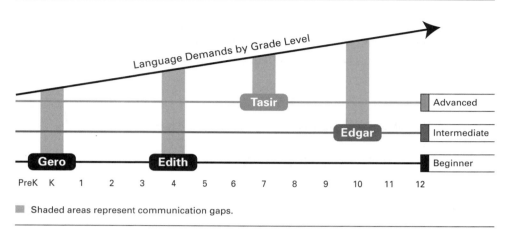

Shaded areas represent communication gaps.

The gap is real. Its size differs by grade level, English proficiency, and other individual factors, but we can't ignore small gaps because they seem inconsequential, nor should we throw up our hands at large gaps that seem too big to take on in mainstream classes. We owe every student the best we can give. We must do all we can to narrow every gap.

ACADEMIC SUBJECTS PROTOCOL

Now that you've read about our four English learners and the communication gaps they and their teachers face, it's time to look at how you can approach the gap in your classroom. After working with mainstream teachers of all academic subjects and grade levels, we found that teachers weren't looking for a specific instructional format for English learners. They had tried that approach but ran into two major problems, equally detrimental. Teachers told us that if they had only one or maybe a handful of English learners in their classrooms, it wasn't feasible or reasonable to revise all their lessons specifically for them. There wasn't time to develop double plans for every lesson objective, and even if there were, how could they put the one for ELs into practice when they had to teach a whole class of primarily native speakers? If they taught everyone the lesson designed especially for their ELs, then the native speakers would not be adequately challenged verbally. On the other hand, if they taught the lesson designed for native speakers to everyone, then the curriculum, instruction, and assessment would not be accessible to their ELs.

To avoid these competing lesson approaches, many of the teachers had turned to "differentiation strategies"—using multiple ways to present and test information—to reach their English learners. That seemed like a feasible and reasonable way, especially since they were already differentiating for their students with special needs. The problem with extending those strategies to English learners, we came to learn, was that for many teachers all this differentiation became one big blur. For them differentiation was a set of practices they saw as "just good teaching" for all students, and they lost sight of the unique needs of English learners. And who could blame them? At face value, differentiation strategies do look strikingly similar. But something deeper is going on for English learners. The process of acquiring English, of moving through levels of English proficiency, leaves a gap between ELs' current understanding and use of English, and what goes on in the English-speaking (and listening, reading, and writing) classroom. That gap—the classroom communication gap—is what is unique about English learners, and it is the teacher's workspace for differentiating instruction for ELs. No one lesson can close the language gap for ELs; that occurs over time. But if each lesson makes curriculum, instruction, and assessment accessible for English learners, they will learn more content and develop more English proficiency as a result. And, as we discussed earlier, these are two mutually supportive objectives that propel English learners' eventual achievement of grade-level expectations.

So, when you think about making classroom communication accessible for your ELs, picture the gap as presented in figure 1.4. This is the space that you will need to narrow in your academic subject lessons. How do you go about doing this? To foster this process, we have developed a protocol that walks teachers step by step through specific decision points for determining the appropriate support for English learners in any academic subject lesson, at any level of proficiency. We call it the Academic Subjects Protocol. Rather than asking mainstream content teachers to design special lessons for the English learners in their classes, the protocol targets how teachers can adjust their standard lessons to make the curriculum, instruction, and assessment accessible to their ELs as well.

To narrow the gap for each English learner participating in a mainstream lesson, you need the right tools, materials, and people. The Academic Subjects Protocol helps you develop a work habit for every lesson—to size up the gap and identify the resources needed. And everything you do in putting this protocol into practice serves the research-informed goal of successful communication *for*, *between*, and *of* English learners in mainstream classes. Through doing this day by day, you'll help raise your ELs' English proficiency in subtle, yet essential, ways.

After reading this chapter and the rest of part I, which applies the Academic Subjects Protocol to lessons for different academic subjects and grade levels, pick a lesson or activity description you or someone else developed, and give the protocol a try. There are many free tools and materials at our Web site (http://www.englishlearnerachievement .com) for putting the protocol into practice. We encourage you to try them and to refer to the protocol description the first few times you use it; then the process of making classroom communication accessible for any English learner will become a habit.

So now we'll take a closer look at the steps of the Academic Subjects Protocol. Summarized visually at the end of the chapter (and in appendix A), the protocol is divided into two phases. Following instructional design principles, phase I starts with an analysis of the task, the student, and the gap between them; phase II involves instructional decision making. The box provides an outline of the upcoming section, which describes each part of the protocol.

ACADEMIC SUBJECTS PROTOCOL

PHASE I: Understanding the Task and the Student

STEP 1: Understanding the Task
- How is nonverbal communication used in the lesson? ("SLIDE" analysis)
- How is verbal communication used in the lesson? ("TREAD" analysis)

STEP 2: Understanding the Student
- Is the student a beginning, intermediate, or advanced EL?

PHASE II: Narrowing the Gap Between the Task and the Student

STEP 1: Supporting Instruction
- What types of nonverbal supports are needed?
- What types of verbal supports are needed?
  - Moderating language demands
  - Elevating learner language

STEP 2: Use of Nonverbal and Verbal Supports
- Can nonverbal and verbal supports be used for the whole class? (universal)
- Can verbal and nonverbal supports be provided alongside instruction? (supplemental)
- Is a different instructional approach needed for this student? (alternative)

STEP 3: Time and Scaffolding Provider
- At what time should supports be provided?
  - Pre-teach
  - Teach or co-teach
  - Post-teach (follow-up)
- Who should lead the supported instruction?
  - Classroom teacher
  - Bilingual paraprofessional
  - ELD/bilingual specialist
  - Volunteer
  - Technology-based resource

PHASE I: Understanding the Task and the Student

Phase I consists of two considerations, namely what language demands each task (of the lesson, activity, or assessment) places on all students, and the proficiency level of each English learner.

STEP 1: UNDERSTANDING THE TASK

Before thinking about making curriculum, instruction, or assessment accessible for English learners, it's important to figure out how much of the lesson is conveyed primarily through written and spoken language (verbal communication) versus how much is conveyed primarily through hands-on experiences, manipulatives, pictures, and visual models (nonverbal forms of communication). This applies to communication *for*, *between*, and *of* English learners, or to put it more technically, it applies to the input, interaction, and output elements of curriculum, instruction, and assessment.

Some lessons include lots of nonverbal forms of communication, which helps make instruction (encompassing curriculum, instruction, and assessment, unless noted otherwise) accessible for English learners. Other lessons are exclusively or primarily verbal (language-dependent). And, of course, there are many lessons somewhere in between. When tasks are primarily verbal, English learners need extra support.

Over the years, when we asked teachers to review lesson and activity descriptions in various academic subject areas to determine where English learners would need support, we were struck that they were often blind to the language used by teachers and students. If a description indicated that the teacher should explain a concept, such as how the seasons occur, teachers often would miss that the term *explaining* most likely involves speaking. If a lesson plan required students to discuss an issue in small groups, teachers didn't always notice that this requires verbal skills in English that many ELs might not yet possess. To help teachers develop habits of practice that analyze the degree of nonverbal and verbal communication of academic subject lessons, we developed a two-part mnemonic device: "SLIDE" and "TREAD." SLIDE and TREAD are acronyms for verbs conveying common student and teacher actions that point toward aspects of lessons or activities where information is conveyed largely through nonverbal or verbal means, respectively. Table 1.2 lists some of the most common verbs and their synonyms.[31]

To review an activity or lesson description for its degree of verbal communication (language demands) and nonverbal communication (context-embedded instruction), begin by underlining verbs indicating what the teacher or students are doing. Then analyze whether those verbs signify a heavy dependence on language, marking each task

TABLE 1.2
SLIDE and TREAD Verbs

Less language-intensive (not primarily language-conveyed) lesson aspects tend to be described by verbs like these:	**More language-intensive** (primarily language-conveyed) lesson aspects tend to be described by verbs like these:
• **S**how (also watch, pantomime, model, display, project [a picture/graphic]) • **L**ook (also smell, taste, feel, and other nonverbal senses) • **I**nvestigate (also measure, weigh, categorize, classify, connect) • **D**emonstrate (also draw, design, act out) • **E**xperience (also act, move, do, make, create)	• **T**ell (also present information, lecture, narrate, recount, go over, report out, share) • **R**ead (also skim, scan, review) • **E**xplain (also listen) • **A**sk/Answer (also solicit, write, respond, predict) • **D**iscuss (also describe, define, brainstorm)

that requires support for English learners, which will be added in phase II of the Academic Subjects Protocol. The point here is not to analyze grammar, but rather to use the verb as a key to the type of teacher and student communication—verbal or nonverbal, or both.

Let's take a look at the following second-grade activity description to see how this works. We have underlined the verbs that indicate what the teacher or student does in the lesson (we don't underline the verbs that tell what other people or objects do).

> Tell students that each table group will design a boat using one sheet of paper and a roll of tape. Explain that they will test their boat, so it must fit inside the testing container and must hold as many pennies as possible.
>
> Each group makes its boat and displays it to the class, giving the name of the boat and explaining its design.
>
> Each group puts its boat in the testing container and places pennies into the boat until it begins to sink.
>
> Each group weighs the number of pennies its boat held before sinking.
>
> Each group discusses the strengths and weaknesses of their designs and students write the information in their science journals.

We can see that this lesson description uses both SLIDE and TREAD verbs. The first verb is *tell*, which is how the teacher will give directions about the activity to the students. As shown in table 1.2, *tell* is the T in TREAD, so it is a major clue that there is verbal communication (the teacher tells the students what to do) for which an English learner may need support. The next verb says what the students do, *design*, and this is a SLIDE verb because it involves hands-on, experiential (nonverbal) actions rather than primarily verbal ones. Then we go back to the teacher action, with the heavy TREAD word *explain*. This word is a red flag when considering the challenges of any task for English learners. One underlined verb, *giving the name*, is another way to say *tell* or *state the name*, so it is a TREAD verb. However, it asks for only one or two words, so that is less difficult than a similar term like *give a rationale*, which involves more complex language. Many of the verbs that describe what the students do involve working with concrete objects, so the tasks they describe are accessible to English learners. Some of them, especially at the end of the activity, involve verbal tasks, such as *discuss* and *write*, so we know that we will have to provide support to enable ELs to participate. And you can probably guess that beginning and advanced ELs need different types of support.

So now, let's relabel figure 1.3 with our acronyms, showing that in general we would expect that academic subject instruction uses less nonverbal communication, "SLIDE" words, and more verbal communication, "TREAD" terms, as we progress up the grade levels. Figure 1.5 depicts this sliding scale. To use the terms discussed earlier (and shown in figure 1.3), the language demands increase while the context-embedded

FIGURE 1.5

Proportion of SLIDE and TREAD Words Used Across Grades

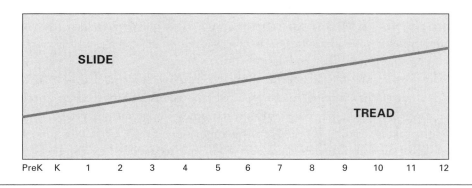

instruction decreases. We believe this general principle of increasing language demands/decreasing context applies across all academic subjects, although the degree of SLIDE to TREAD varies somewhat by the nature of the subject, as we will see in chapters 2 through 5. This has implications for the amount of nonverbal and verbal support needed by English learners at different grades and English proficiency levels.

Both verbal and nonverbal communication are important, but as we'll see in phase II of the Academic Subjects Protocol, ELs need balance between the two and special support for TREAD-heavy activities since they are language-dependent.

STEP 2: UNDERSTANDING THE STUDENT

Equally important in this analysis phase is understanding each English learner in your classroom. In addition to the student's English proficiency level, the individual's cultural background, native language and degree of native-language literacy, and knowledge of the academic subject matter are essential in planning instruction.

After you have analyzed the TREAD and SLIDE words for a task, consider whether your English learners at any of the three English proficiency levels can participate fully. For example, if a task requires small groups of students to debate an issue in social studies, is it likely that an intermediate EL could do that successfully without extra support? After determining the gap between the task and each English learner's level of proficiency, you can plan support to meet their individual needs while ensuring that instruction for non-ELs remains appropriately challenging. Of course, you must first know your English learners' general levels of proficiency (beginning, intermediate, or advanced). After examining what they generally can understand and do in English (refer again to table 1.1 for an overview), you then compare their skills to what the lesson's tasks demand. We also provide a more detailed description of learner characteristics and behaviors for each level on our Web site, http://www.englishlearnerachievement.com.

PHASE II: Narrowing the Gap Between the Task and the Student

After you have analyzed the extent of the communication gap, the next step is to narrow it—to decide how to make curriculum, instruction, and assessment accessible. But what exactly does *accessible for English learners* mean? As we noted previously, classroom communication in academic subjects can take place through language (verbal communication) or other (nonverbal) means.

Nonverbal communication occurs through perceiving or using objects, images, graphics, multisensory activities, gestures, facial expressions, and movement, among other means.[32] Language-based, or verbal, communication, on the other hand, involves listening, speaking, reading, writing, or any combination of the four. If we add nonverbal and verbal support to any lesson, we are attempting to support ELs' comprehension and expression of subject matter content while developing language proficiency in the process. Phase II of the Academic Subjects Protocol thus begins with a determination of what instructional support teachers can implement to make their lessons more accessible for English learners.

STEP 1: SUPPORTING INSTRUCTION

We see nonverbal support as universal, because it really benefits all students. However, nonverbal support is especially important for those ELs who are at the beginning and intermediate levels of English proficiency because it naturally reduces the language load by adding other ways of perceiving information. The second type of communication support you need to consider is verbal. Because it is language-specific, verbal support is not only intended to facilitate communication with English learners rather than all students, but it also needs to be targeted to the English learners' level of proficiency.

Nonverbal Support

We define nonverbal support as either nonverbal additions to primarily verbal instruction, such as pointing to objects, gesturing, and showing pictures, or as primarily nonverbal information that includes verbal elements, such as concept maps with graphics and titles. Nonverbal support is generally helpful for all students. Any academic subject can incorporate nonverbal support, from manipulatives in mathematics to dramatization in social studies. If you only increased nonverbal support, this would go a long way to improve accessibility for English learners. These suggestions for nonverbal communication support indicate its variety:

- Gestures/acting out/pantomiming
- Visuals—photos, pictures, video clips, animations
- Pointing to real objects, demonstrating a process, and modeling tasks
- Hands-on activities and experiences
- Referring to picture dictionaries
- Using props and dramatizations
- Experiential learning

- Simple graphic organizers and infographics[33] using pictures and words
- Using mobile devices, tablets, and other visual communication technologies

Although nonverbal support benefits all students, we recommend adding it wherever possible for the explicit benefit of English learners to enhance their comprehension and their ability to demonstrate knowledge. Even though the second-grade science activity we analyzed previously includes many forms of nonverbal communication, it could be improved by having the teacher model the directions while stating them. This could be an ideal opportunity to not only make the directions accessible to English learners but also help their English development by associating any new words with known objects and actions.

Verbal Support

While nonverbal support is vital, it's not enough to fully support ELs' subject matter achievement and English language development. You will also need to adjust verbal communication to enable English learners at different levels of English proficiency to comprehend and participate in lessons and show what they have learned to the fullest extent.

The type and amount of this verbal support varies by the EL's proficiency level, so if you had a beginning English learner, you would incorporate a different type and greater amount of verbal support than for an advanced EL. When the communication gap between any EL's proficiency level and the language demands of the task is vast, using both nonverbal and verbal support throughout all parts of a lesson, activity, or assessment can help narrow the gap and improve comprehension and language growth.

We categorize verbal support into two types: support that (1) moderates the language demands of the lesson (bringing the demands down) and (2) temporarily elevates English learners' spoken and written language above what they could produce on their own at their current proficiency level (bringing the learner up). Figure 1.6 incorporates these two types of support, displaying their directionality and how they help

FIGURE 1.6

Two Directions of Verbal Support

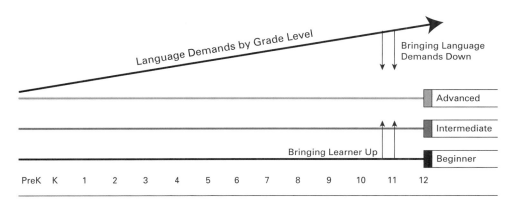

to reduce the gap for the English learner. Our experience working with mainstream teachers has taught us that the consistent implementation of both types of verbal support, geared to the English learners' unique needs and based on their proficiency levels, yields strong results.

Moderation of Language Demands

Moderating language demands means reducing the complexity and amount of language an academic subject lesson requires to a level slightly above the English proficiency of the EL. While this may seem like watering down the curriculum, it needn't be so. There is a relationship between topical and linguistic complexity. That's indisputable—a beginning English learner placed in a mainstream eleventh-grade American history class will probably not be able to access the content solely through grade-level reading and discussion activities, even when the teacher adds ample nonverbal support, such as diagrams, graphic organizers, and interactive media that show complex relationships.[34] Simplified and elaborated (through additional paraphrasing) texts are necessary when there is such a substantial gap between grade-level language use and the EL's English proficiency. In such cases, native language resources can also be used to help fill in any details that are lost so that the academic subject is represented in grade-level complexity. Another way to moderate language demands is to provide leveled questions and tasks. These types of verbal support can provide accessible input, output, and interaction through using language that is a step above what the English learner has already acquired, which will increase language development over time. We look more closely now at these two go-to tools to moderate language demands.[35]

TEXT SIMPLIFICATION AND ELABORATION. Text simplification and elaboration facilitate comprehension and language development if the language structure is not too far beyond the learner's current level of proficiency. Second language learners' comprehension of vocabulary and structures in receptive language (listening and reading) is typically more varied and complex than their competence in productive language (speaking and writing). In other words, ELs are capable of understanding more than they can express accurately (without developmental grammatical errors). However, if the reading or speech they are attempting to understand uses very complex grammatical structures and lots of unfamiliar vocabulary, comprehension is impeded.

Let's look at an original and a simplified/expanded text in Italian to experience the benefit firsthand. The following is an original social studies text at the fifth-grade level:

> *Si dice che Mastro Giorgio non svelasse mai a nessuno la sua maniera, ma da lui i ceramisti di Gubbio qualche cosa devono aver imparato, se ormai da cinque secoli producono terraglia di squisita fattura; e in particolare (con una tecnica scoperta mezzo secolo fa) quei vasi neri e lucidi chiamati búccheri, che ripetono le forme e i fregi degli antichissimi modelli originali etruschi.*

Did you get all that? Were you able to use your strong reading skills to learn the content? Check yourself with the following translation:

> It is said that Master Giorgio never revealed to anyone his method, but from him the ceramicists of Gubbio must have learned something, if by now for five centuries they produce earthenware of exquisite nature; and in particular (with a technique discovered a half century ago) those black, shiny vases called búccheri, which repeat the forms and friezes of the original Etruscan models from antiquity.

In contrast, let's look at a simplified/elaborated version. The sentences are shorter. There are fewer complex clauses and unusual or embedded phrasings.

> *Il ceramista famoso di Gubbio, Mastro Giorgio, non ha mostrato il suo metodo. Però, i cera-misti di Gubbio hanno imparato il suo modo di fare ceramiche. Dal 1513 i ceramisti di Gub-bio fanno ceramiche squisite. Dal 1963 i ceramisti di Gubbio fanno búccheri, vasi neri e lucidi. Questi búccheri sembrano i vasi antichi etruschi.*

Here's what it looks like simplified in English:

> The famous ceramicist from Gubbio, Master Giorgio, did not demonstrate his method. But, the ceramicists of Gubbio learned his manner of making ceramics. Since 1513 the ceramicists of Gubbio have made exquisite ceramics. Since 1963 the ceramicists of Gubbio have made *búccheri*—black, shiny vases. These *búccheri* resemble ancient Etruscan vases.

We can see in this example that some information is lost in the simplification, but most of the main topics and points are maintained. The simpler language allows the second language learner to break down and build back up the structure and meaning of the text, so that both the content and the language can be comprehended and acquired. Many commercial materials have been developed for teaching academic subjects to English learners at different levels of proficiency, so these can be a convenient means of providing leveled texts.[36] Many commercial materials also provide elaborated texts, which unpack notions that are expressed tersely, offering added description and other details. For example, the original wording above might need this elaboration:

> . . . if by now for five centuries, in other words since 1513, ceramic artists produce what is called earthenware, or terra cotta pottery . . .

This expands embedded sentences and paraphrases unusual words or wording. When simplified or elaborated texts are not available, reducing the amount of text through outlines, graphic organizers, and infographics can help the English learner master the lesson objectives and meet the standards. These resources can be presented together with the original class texts so the English learners are exposed to grade-level text even if it is largely inaccessible and overwhelming without supplemental support.[37]

LEVELED QUESTIONS. Another very useful strategy to moderate language demands is leveled questions. Teachers who are knowledgeable about the comprehension and expression of English learners at different levels of proficiency can attune their questions about academic subject matter for each EL. For example, Edith, who can understand and answer simple yes/no, either/or, and one-word-answer questions, could be asked, "Does Master Giorgio make ceramics or glass?" Edgar, who can understand and answer more grammatically complex questions, could be asked, "For how many years have people made ceramics in Gubbio?" Tasir, who can understand and answer grammatically complex and abstract questions, could be asked, "If Master Giorgio didn't share his method with the ceramicists, how do you think they were able to develop specialized techniques?" Table 1.3 provides a sample of how to write leveled questions for any academic subject area.

In addition to phrasing instructional questions at each student's level of English proficiency, adjusting the language of existing test questions can help make them accessible to English learners. Several language features make academic subject test questions difficult for English learners to comprehend. These include unfamiliar vocabulary, complex grammatical structures, language abstractions, and passive voice.[38] Questions and tasks need to be carefully worded to make assessments more reliable, more valid, and more accessible to ELs. Table 1.4 shows examples of these linguistically complex structures, which are typically acquired at the advanced levels of English proficiency, in comparison to those with less complex grammatical structures.

Elevation of Learner Language

Conditions that provide ELs with accessible input, interaction, and output in the new language lead to their improvement of English language proficiency over time. While raising their level of English proficiency is intended to narrow the communication gap, these conditions can also accelerate language development because the ELs are given opportunities to produce spoken and written academic language. Following are two of our go-to verbal support tools.

SENTENCE FRAMES. One strategy to support ELs to speak or write beyond their level of proficiency is to use sentence frames as conversation prompts in pair activities. To help facilitate peer assessment among classmates, Margaret Heritage offers the following conversation prompts for all students:[39]

I'd like to suggest . . .

Have you thought about . . .

A strength I see in your work is . . .

You could improve this by . . .

TABLE 1.3

Leveled Questions for Each Proficiency Level

Beginning Proficiency	Simple yes/no questions—Is this a book?
	Questions that allow pointing, selecting, showing—Show me the book.
	Either/or questions—Is this a book or a pencil?
	Simple who, what, and where questions—Who has the book? What is this (point to book)? Where is the book?
	Questions that require only one-word answers—What is this?
	Questions that require simple or common two- or three-word phrase responses—Where is the book? On the table.
	Frequent vocabulary questions/answers (questions that use and elicit high-frequency vocabulary, such as the word *book* rather than *manuscript*)
	Formation of simple identification questions
Intermediate Proficiency	Restricted-tense questions
	• Simple present—What do you do every day?
	• Present progressive—What are you doing?
	• Simple past—What did you do yesterday?
	• Past progressive—What were you doing yesterday morning?
	• Simple future—What will you do tomorrow?
	• Present perfect—Have you read *Harry Potter*?
	Simple description (what) questions
	Simple explanation (how and why) questions
	Formation of simple questions and negative statements
Advanced Proficiency	Questions using complex tenses and moods
	• Past perfect—Had Harry seen Voldemort before he began following him?
	• Future perfect—Will he have finished his homework when he comes to class tomorrow?
	• Hypothetical, conditional—If Dumbledore asked you to move to Hogwarts, would you do it? Why or why not?
	Questions using complex passive and negative sentence structure
	• Passive construction—Could Harry have been hurt by Snape's magic? Why or why not?
	• Formation of complex negative statements—Should Harry not have gone to Hogwarts? Why or why not?
	Formation of complex analysis, justification, and evaluation questions and statements

Depending on the EL's level of proficiency, the conversation prompts could be further prescribed by providing word banks, as shown in table 1.5, which gives two scenarios for a beginner in a high school graphic arts class.

Deciding whether to provide a word bank in addition to sentence frames for complex sentences depends on the English learners' proficiency level, with more support being necessary for beginners than for intermediate or advanced students.

TABLE 1.4

Complex Versus Simple Phrasing in Assessment Questions

Complex Phrasing of a Test Item	Simple Phrasing of a Test Item
Unfamiliar Words *Jim expects that each orange tree will bear 50 oranges.*	Familiar Words *Jim expects that each orange tree will have 50 oranges.*
Passive Verbs *A game is bought for $12.95. If the sales tax on this item is 7.5 percent, what is the total amount that must be paid for the item, including tax?*	Active Verbs *Sue buys a game for $12.95. Sue pays 7.5% sales tax on the game. What is the total cost of the game, including tax?*
Conditional Clauses *If John is driving at 70 miles per hour, what is his approximate speed in kilometers per hour?*	Separate Sentences *John is driving at 70 miles per hour. What is his speed in kilometers per hour?*
Long and Complex Phrases *Which of the following numerical expressions gives the area of the square below?*	Simple Words *Which expression describes the area of the square?*
Relative Clauses *The first heart transplant that was a success took place in South Africa.*	Removed or Separated *(removed) The first successful heart transplant took place in South Africa.* *(separated) Heart transplants become successful. The first one was in South Africa.*

Source: Edynn Sato, Stanley Rabinowitz, Carole Gallagher, and Chun-Wei Huang, *Accommodations for English Language Learner Students: The Effect of Linguistic Modification of Math Test Item Sets* (NCEE 2009-4079), Institute of Education Sciences, National Center for Education Evaluation and Regional Assistance (Washington, DC: United States Government Printing Office, 2010).

TABLE 1.5

Sentence Frames

	Example 1	Example 2
Sentence Frame	I'd like to suggest that you _____.	Have you thought about _____?
Verb Word Bank	lighten, raise, erase, shade	making, elongating, darkening, translating, featuring
Object Word Bank	the heading, the background, the template, the shape	the fonts, the template, the title, the graph
Completed Sentences	"I'd like to suggest that you erase the heading." "I'd like to suggest that you shade the background."	"Have you thought about making a graph?" "Have you thought about translating the title?"

Either way, sentence frames enable English learners to produce higher-level structures than they could utter by constructing them word by word. The dependence on sentence frames lessens over the course of the academic year as ELs hear and produce similar sentences.

WORD BANKS AND GLOSSARIES. Word banks enable all students, but especially English learners, to use the academic vocabulary as it relates to the lesson when they would otherwise have struggled to think of the words needed. Not only do they reduce ELs' frustration levels by enabling them to express themselves successfully, they also save precious instructional time in that students don't need to refer to a dictionary each time they want to use the new vocabulary in the target language. As the lesson topics change and new content is introduced, the teacher changes the word bank. One point to keep in mind is that ELs at the beginning and intermediate levels of English proficiency may need more word lists or banks than their native-English-speaking peers, who only have to become familiar with content-specific vocabulary. For example, English learners have to acquire everyday nouns, verbs, and adjectives like *pencil*, *book*, *question*, *think*, *return*, *large*, and *round* at the same time that they learn the academic vocabulary and phrases.

When using text for instruction, there are different means of drawing the students' attention to important academic words, phrases, or concepts. While many textbooks assist teachers in this task by providing glossaries in the margins, English learners likely need more than what is provided by the publisher. Instead you could read through the text prior to assigning it to determine, possibly with the assistance of an ELD specialist (see phase II, steps 3–5), which additional explanations are necessary for your ELs to comprehend the text.

In summary, when the communication gap between the EL's proficiency level and the language demands of the task is vast, using nonverbal support coupled with both types of verbal support is necessary to help reduce the gap's effect on comprehension and language growth. We have presented four "go-to" verbal support tools that you can use with your English learners every day.

There are many other tools for verbal support that can narrow the communication gap, either by moderating the language demands or by temporarily elevating the English learner's proficiency. Our Web site, http://www.englishlearnerachievement.com, provides a classification of these verbal as well as nonverbal support tools by proficiency level. We suggest that you begin by trying out one or two of these tools, getting comfortable with how they work for your English learners, and then adding one or two tools every so often to your repertoire. We believe it's better to use a few choice communication support tools regularly, purposely, and skillfully with your English learners than to try to use every type of tool that comes your way.

STEP 2: USE OF NONVERBAL AND VERBAL SUPPORTS

Once you have identified the most advantageous types of nonverbal and verbal support for the English learner's level of proficiency, you need to examine the feasibility of their use. We divide levels of use into three categories: universal, supplemental, and alternative, as shown in the graphic at the end of the chapter (and in appendix A).

Universal

As previously stated, nonverbal support can almost always be used for all students, which is why we term this application *universal*. In cases where the language demands are only slightly above an EL's English proficiency, such as with an advanced EL in kindergarten, the verbal support used to reach the EL would be universal as well. ELs with beginning and intermediate proficiency, however, need targeted verbal support that isn't appropriate for the whole class. Universal support tools for English learners may lead educators to assume that general best practices are all that English learners need. In the case of nonverbal universal support, this is true. Verbal support, however, depends on the grade level and the EL's level of English proficiency.

Supplemental

If the gap for an EL allows participation in instruction and interaction with additional support, the support may be *supplemental* to instruction, such as a handout with support in the EL's first language for a complex concept or a fill-in-the-blank form with sentence frames to supplement group discussion.

Alternative

When the gap is enormous, as with beginning ELs who lack prior schooling in their home countries in addition to being admitted to secondary schools in the United States, support that is alternative to what the native speakers are engaged in may be necessary. For example, if eleventh graders in a mainstream class are rehearsing debates on the U.S. Civil War, a beginning EL could be given an alternative task of viewing a computer-based, graphic-enhanced timeline of events of the war to develop background knowledge and vocabulary.

Closely related to the decisions about the use of communication support for each EL is determining when the support would have the greatest impact. This is the next step of the Academic Subjects Protocol.

STEP 3: TIME AND SUPPORT PROVIDER

Would supplemental or alternative background information in the EL's first language help the most if it were provided in advance of the lesson? Or should the English learner be immersed in the activity and receive support on an as-needed basis? Can misconceptions that emerged be addressed after instruction? These are but three circumstances that show the time-sensitive nature of communication gap support. Sometimes the time of implementation is dictated more by logistics and available providers than by what would be optimal for the English learner. This balance between optimal and actual practices is the reality for most English learners and their teachers.

While you may be able to find time to implement the support strategies through creative lesson configurations, as a mainstream classroom teacher you may not always be the ideal educator to deliver them. This fact leads us to the final decision point in planning communication support that meets the needs of your English learners—who is best suited to provide the support, given the type and time of support needed?

The person best suited and available to implement the support strategies chosen by the lesson designer is to a large extent dictated by the resources at the school and the EL program model used. Can the classroom teacher work one-on-one with the English learner or with a group of ELs before, during, or after class? Does the school have a bilingual aide who can help with interpretation or translation? If there is an English language development or bilingual teacher, can that person support the EL while the teacher works with the rest of the class? At schools with small numbers of ELs, parent or community volunteers can help provide communication gap support. These volunteers may or may not know the first language of the English learner, which would affect the type of support used. We have seen that, increasingly, instructional technology can offer individualized, targeted support, using both the home language and English, or may be the basis for pair or small-group interaction with the selected support tool (for example, texts with glossaries or definitions that are linked to some or all of the words).

VISUALIZING THE ACADEMIC SUBJECTS PROTOCOL

You've read a description of the elements of the Academic Subjects Protocol and have seen examples of recommended communication support tools for teaching academic subjects to English learners. The infographic on the next page summarizes the steps of the protocol (for easy reference, it also appears as appendix A). We suggest that you duplicate this graphic and keep in your planner.

In chapters 2 through 5 we apply the Academic Subjects Protocol to lessons developed for different academic subjects and grade levels. You will get more ideas about how it works from those examples. We suggest that you get started by flipping through teacher resource books and surfing the Web to find lesson descriptions to try out with the protocol. Once you get the hang of it, it will change the way you teach. We hope your English learners will thank you for your extra effort, but even if they don't, we do. Thank you for taking the time to make your curriculum, instruction, and assessment accessible for your English learners. It will make a difference.

ACADEMIC SUBJECTS PROTOCOL

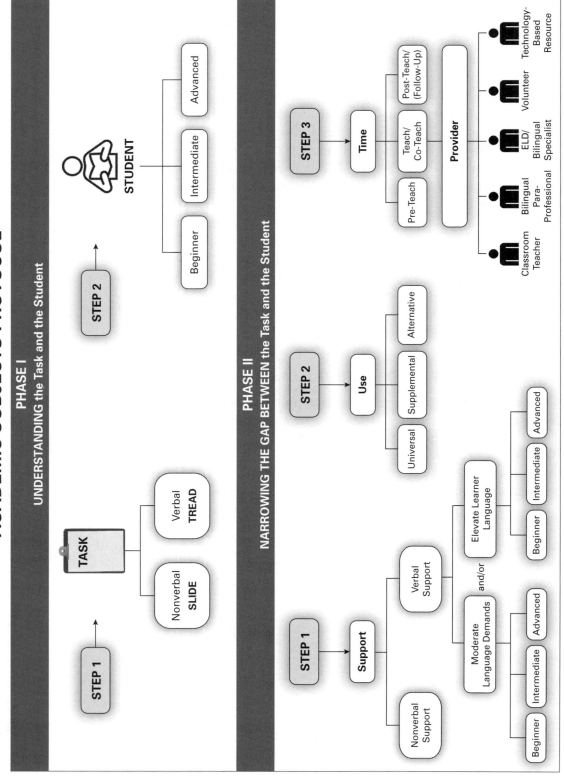

PHASE I
UNDERSTANDING the Task and the Student

STEP 1

TASK
- Nonverbal **SLIDE**
- Verbal **TREAD**

STEP 2

STUDENT
- Beginner
- Intermediate
- Advanced

PHASE II
NARROWING THE GAP BETWEEN the Task and the Student

STEP 1

Support
- Nonverbal Support
- Verbal Support
  - Moderate Language Demands
    - Beginner
    - Intermediate
    - Advanced
  - and/or
  - Elevate Learner Language
    - Beginner
    - Intermediate
    - Advanced

STEP 2

Use
- Universal
- Supplemental
- Alternative

STEP 3

Time
- Pre-Teach
- Teach/Co-Teach
- Post-Teach/(Follow-Up)

Provider
- Classroom Teacher
- Bilingual Para-Professional
- ELD/Bilingual Specialist
- Volunteer
- Technology-Based Resource

STOP AND REFLECT QUESTIONS

1. As a teacher, do you consider yourself to be an effective communicator? If so, describe the characteristics of an effective communicator. If not, what skills do you need to learn in order to communicate with your students more effectively?

2. Do you agree with the notion that the basic function of language is to create shared meaning? How is shared meaning created in the classroom?

3. Where do you think the greatest emphasis on shared meaning occurs? In the home? With friends? Or in the classroom?

4. In this chapter, you read that the conversation between Ms. Oliver and Edith was a bit strenuous, but how do you think Edith felt about the interaction? How did she feel about Ms. Oliver? In a classroom context, why should Edith's feelings matter?

5. Scenario: Two English learners are at the beginning level of English proficiency. One is in the eighth grade and the other in the ninth. Do you think they exhibit the same receptive (listening/reading) and productive (speaking/writing) skill levels in English? If so, how would you describe the similarities in skill levels given that one is in a higher grade than the other. How does research support your answer?

6. Go to http://www.iteachilearn.org/cummins/index.htm. Be sure to listen to "Aspects of English Language Proficiency," discussed by Jim Cummins, and read his many articles on BICS and CALP.

GO AND PRACTICE ACTIVITIES

1. In this chapter, you read about English learners at the beginning level who developed a 500- to 1,000-word vocabulary yet could not produce all of the words. Why was that so? Do receptive skills develop at a faster rate than productive skills? What evidence can you provide to support your answer? If you don't have a beginning-level English learner in your class, ask if you could observe and interview one in a colleague's class or at another school. You can also listen to the interview with Edith, Edgar, and Tasir at http://www.englishlearnerachievement.com to get a better sense of their oral proficiency.

2. Analyze the communication gap between the classroom language demands and the level of proficiency of an English learner with few or no literacy skills in his native language who has been placed in the eleventh grade. How wide would this student's gap be? What kinds of verbal and nonverbal support would such a second language learner need? Would this student need to first become literate in his native language prior to doing beginning-level work? How would native language literacy development help ELs in general to acquire literacy skills in English?

CHAPTER 2

Teaching Gero About American Symbols

Academic Vocabulary in Social Studies

That smile. Tepid at first, but growing expansive as he sat alongside Ms. Levin, Gero's smile gauged his sense of belonging. Before the lesson on community helpers, while his classmates worked in groups, Gero pronounced the new words with Ms. Levin in a heavy Kreyòl accent. "Ahm—boo—láhns, oe—spee—táhl, fie—air—tróek," he half whispered. "Gero, show me the police officer." His hand glided falteringly over the tabletop to the picture book. He paused, looked right at Ms. Levin, and thumped the illustration with his fingertip. "Yes, that's the police officer. She helps keep us safe. You learned so much today, Gero! Let's review our new words quickly before I read the class a story. Class!" Ms. Levin called out, "Let's get ready for story time!"

Ms. Levin gathered her class on the rug in front of her rocking chair. Her left hand gripping the opened, oversized book, her right hand suspended like a magic wand turned inward, she smiled at the students and began to read.

COMMUNICATION IN TEACHING AND LEARNING SOCIAL STUDIES

Academic content areas have their own language, discourse, and communication demands that vary across the preK–12 curriculum. The National Council for the Social Studies defines social studies as the integrated study of the social sciences and humanities with the purpose of promoting civic competence.[1] As they bridge the content from one discipline to the ideas of another, social studies teachers and their students encounter various forms of academic language in their readings, discussions, and critical thinking exercises.[2]

Social studies teachers may wonder whether abstract concepts can even be made comprehensible for English learners like Gero, Edith, and Edgar, who are at beginning and intermediate proficiency levels. Our response to this question is an emphatic "yes!" Social studies, much like science and mathematics, lends itself to an inquiry-based lesson format where second language learners can be involved in meaningful interactions with their peers and the content, which assist them with language development. We focus in this chapter on discipline-specific challenges English learners face in social studies, and show how teachers can provide the necessary communication support to foster their acquisition of both subject matter content and academic language.

Social Studies Texts

Of all content areas, social studies has traditionally required the most reading of informational text. Scholars note that history texts are information dense and may not make connections clear.[3] They describe history texts as having short sections with a wide variety of discourse patterns, including retelling events, describing, explaining, and debating. Let's take a look at some of these assertions and other important challenges of social studies textbooks in more detail by examining a brief selection from *TimeLinks: Third Grade*, a K–12 social studies textbook that builds geographic mastery:[4]

> Jill Staton Bullard started the Inter-Faith Food Shuttle in 1989. She saw a restaurant cashier throwing away leftover food and decided to do something about it. She serves seven counties in North Carolina and feeds more than 5,000 hungry people a day with donations.

The first apparent difficulty an English learner may face in approaching this paragraph is possible *lack of background knowledge or personal experiences*, as we noted in chapter 1. Contrary to their native-English-speaking peers, concepts such as "throwing away leftover food" might be unfamiliar to ELs who come from deeply impoverished countries where hunger is common and having leftover food never occurs. This lack of background knowledge is further reflected in ELs' lack of familiarity with vocabulary.

Another language-related challenge is *text density with fact, details, and language complexity*. In social studies texts, facts and details are often condensed and textbooks often contain a high concentration of new vocabulary or sophisticated sentence structure. Social studies texts contain complex sentences, an occurrence perfectly illustrated in the last two sentences in the text example. First of all, these sentences are complex because they consist of two clauses linked by the coordinating conjunction *and*. Second, the use of the pronoun *she* forces the English learner to figure out to whom the pronoun refers (the antecedent). A third language complexity factor in social studies texts, although not present in the sample above, is the common use of passive voice constructions. For example, instead of "I observed no significant increase in economic development," which is already loaded with academic language to decipher, textbooks will typically state, "No significant increase in economic development was observed." The passive voice, in both spoken and written language, is difficult for English learners to comprehend because its formation is learned relatively late in the process of acquiring English.[5] As we showed in chapter 1, teachers can make texts more accessible to English learners at the beginning and intermediate proficiency levels by simplifying or elaborating text.

Social Studies Vocabulary

Social studies language contains multiple examples of problematic words that have one meaning in social English and another meaning in academic English (polysemous words). For example, the word *party* is defined as a social gathering in social everyday English, but is defined as a group of persons with common political interests in the academic language common to social studies. Likewise, the word *house* has a general meaning, such as "I saw your cousin in front of your *house*." It also has a specific meaning in social studies, as with the sentence "The *House* is in session." The word *front*, as in "Meet me in *front* of the cafeteria," has a very different meaning in the sentence "Unlike previous wars, this war was waged on one *front*."

In chapter 1 we discussed Cummins's important distinction between the language ELs need for social conversation and the language they need for academic purposes.[6] Social English or Basic Interpersonal Communication Skills (BICS) are developed through informal settings such as the school playground or cafeteria. However, BICS are not enough. To perform successfully in school, ELs must also acquire the ability to use language for academic purposes. This type of language expertise is called Cognitive Academic Language Proficiency (CALP) and is developed in the classroom. In our vocabulary examples, ELs might know what a house is in a social context, but that will not help them in a social studies class where the same word has a completely different meaning.

TEACHING ENGLISH LEARNERS SOCIAL STUDIES

One of the main challenges ELs deal with in social studies classrooms, more so than in other content areas, is the lack of the background knowledge needed to understand key concepts. It is obvious that the cultural and societal norms in the home countries of immigrant ELs can differ considerably from the values and norms represented in our schools. This is the case not only for children whose ethnic and cultural backgrounds are substantially different from what most would describe as, even among the vast diversity encountered here, "typically American." Recent immigrants from Western countries, too, may have different understandings of concepts like values, personal rights and responsibilities, and the role of community.[7] The good news is that children who received some schooling in their home countries may be able to transfer some of their experiential knowledge to English. Social studies teachers who are aware of the main cultural and societal norms in the students' home countries can gauge what concepts are similar and can be transferred without much adjustment, and what concepts may need to be built into the lesson plan by pre-teaching. That same cultural awareness needs to be present when working with U.S.-born EL students. These students may have culture-specific background knowledge that may or may not be valued at school. The more familiarity teachers have with their students' cultures, the easier it is to integrate them into the curriculum.

There are several ways in which social studies teachers can build background knowledge useful in the academic context through students' previous knowledge and new experiences. For instance, when teaching about migration patterns, teachers can ask ELs to bring objects, photographs, or drawings related to their own family stories regarding immigration. More than one in five children in the United States has at least one immigrant parent. ELs' or their families' previous experiences with migration will help them understand the upcoming lessons about immigration and settlement patterns of American people.

In the case of migration patterns, the background experiences of many ELs make new learning possible. However, many social studies concepts are not easily bridged. When this is the case, social studies teachers at the elementary level may consider using role play as a means of constructing the background knowledge necessary for understanding new information.[8] Following models provided by teachers (videos, dialogues, illustrations), ELs can play the roles of colonists, the king of England, and the king's representative to dramatize the concept of taxation without representation. Making difficult concepts more concrete by acting them out can make classroom communication more accessible, stimulate interest in the topic, and engage ELs in language practice.[9]

Developing English Learners' Academic Vocabulary Skills

A well-developed vocabulary helps ELs build background knowledge and comprehend text and lectures in social studies classrooms. Starting with No Child Left Behind (NCLB), there has been a distinct emphasis on academic vocabulary development for ELs. A result of this effort is the creation of vocabulary lists that are content-area specific. One example is the Tennessee Vocabulary Project.[10] Based on the research conducted by Robert Marzano, this project focuses on the academic vocabulary in mathematics, science, language arts, and social studies and it is a valuable tool for all teachers.[11]

Teachers who have a student like Gero can use this list to establish an instructional plan that includes deliberate vocabulary development activities. It is important to note that this list and others like it contain general terms that all preK–12 students, not only English learners, have to master. Therefore, mainstream classroom teachers who have English learners should consider which of the words are in essence generic, or collective, terms. It is highly likely that native English-speaking students already know many of the specific words that are grouped under collective terms, so they only have to learn to use the new term. To illustrate this point, let's look at an example from the kindergarten list: basic needs (food, clothing, shelter). Beginning English learners like Gero not only have to learn the generic term *food*, but they also have to learn a handful of words for individual food items such as *apple*, *carrot*, or *tomato*.[12]

Fortunately, in kindergarten these words can be taught through visual cues, such as pictures or drawings. When going up in grade levels, however, the vocabulary gets more abstract, and teachers will need to find additional means to illustrate the concepts. For example, the essential social studies vocabulary that needs to be addressed in kindergarten consists of words such as *neighborhood* and *transportation*. These are generic terms that are typically covered in a picture dictionary. Moving on to first and second grade, the list contains concepts such *rights* and *responsibilities*, *rural* and *urban*, or *distribution* and *economy*. Teaching such terms to English learners is trickier because they require the teacher to use descriptions while offering examples. Descriptions require verbal comprehension skills that beginning and intermediate ELs don't yet possess. Therefore, teachers need to find places in the curriculum for explicit vocabulary instruction for English learners before they commence a new unit. If the school has a push-in, pull-out, or content-based ELD instruction program, collaboration between the ELD specialist and the mainstream teacher, especially at the secondary level, is necessary.[13]

To promote vocabulary learning and development with students like Gero, social studies teachers can use word walls, an instructional strategy that has been used quite successfully in teaching first language literacy in English, especially in the lower grades. We recommend that secondary teachers adopt and adapt the practice. Content-specific words strategically placed in the classroom allow English learners to refer to them during verbal exchanges and/or when writing. In addition to asking ELs to use a dictionary to look up the meaning of new words, teachers can add to the word wall while providing written and oral explanations and examples, or after drawing a concept to help convey meaning. The words remain on the wall throughout the unit, and teachers can refer back to them whenever those words occur. Frequent repetition and active learning are key to vocabulary expansion, which in turn leads to content comprehension and acquisition via language development.

✦ CLASSROOM APPLICATION ✦

"Class, come back together on the floor." As the groups of students moved to the front of the classroom, Ms. Levin collected the work sheets. "All right," she said as she pointed to the sample sentence displayed on the chart next to her rocking chair, "repeat after me: 'A heart stands for love.' Yes, that's right. Let's try it again. 'A heart. . . .'"

Speaking in a low voice in the safety of the entire group, Gero did not know that the teacher focused on listening to his speech during the second repetition. Ms. Levin, on the other hand, was encouraged by what she heard Gero say, even though he didn't accurately pronounce the word *heart*. After all, words with the initial *h*-sound are seldom found in the Haitian Kreyòl language.

After a few rounds of asking individual students what symbol she was holding up, and asking the entire class what the symbol stands for, Ms. Levin was confident that her students, including Gero, knew enough about the topic and language to participate in the upcoming unit on American symbols on Monday. As was her routine, Ms. Levin shook every single student's hand at the door on the way out. When Gero left the classroom, Ms. Levin said, "Sweetie, I'm so proud of how you said our sentences this afternoon. You're doing great!" Was it her imagination or did Gero grow a half inch?

AMERICAN SYMBOLS LESSON DESCRIPTION

Ms. Levin had had great success with the unit on American symbols in the past few years when she did not have any English learners in her class. Because of the professional learning work she had engaged in during the past summer, as well as Gero's progress during the preceding weeks, she knew that she would not have to go back to the drawing board to meaningfully engage him. Instead, she decided to simply tweak a few tasks in the learning centers with Gero's unique cultural and linguistic needs in mind. After reviewing the lesson plan modifications, she smiled, thinking, "I can't wait to see Gero learn alongside his peers in this unit."[14]

Content Standards

GA-SSKH2: The student will identify important American symbols and explain their meaning.[15]

Literacy Standards:

CCSS.ELA-LITERACY-L.K.1: Demonstrate command of the conventions of Standard English grammar and usage when writing or speaking.

> **CCSS.ELA-LITERACY-L.K.1.F:** Produce and expand complete sentences in shared language activities.

OBJECTIVES

- The student will be able to identify and name four symbols of American democracy.
- The student will be able to identify similarities and differences between American symbols and equivalent symbols from other countries.
- The student will be able to draw two American symbols and verbally explain why the symbols are important to American democracy.
- The student will ask questions to get information, seek help, or clarify something that is not understood.
- The student will produce and expand complete sentences in shared writing about a given topic (e.g., symbols in America).

INTRODUCTION

Call the students to the floor by the rocking chair.[16] Display a collage of American symbols on the whiteboard, and ask what they are. Tell the students that for the whole week they are going to explore the meaning of these symbols just like they did with the previous symbols (heart, stop sign, etc.), but that they will also learn about the history of these symbols. Point to one of the symbols on the collage and state that it represents what the children will learn about today.[17]

DIRECTIONS

1. Walk the students through each of the four centers, explaining what they will do there. Tell them that they will spend twenty minutes at each center to complete the task.

   Listening Center: Each student is given a work sheet that contains a word bank on top.[18] Together they view a narrated, teacher-created presentation that provides facts about the symbol.[19] They copy the words into the appropriate spaces on the work sheet.

   Drawing Center: Each student draws the symbol of the day on a work sheet that has a large empty space for the illustration on the left-hand side and three to four boxes for writing on the right-hand side.[20]

   Writing Center: Looking at a picture of the symbol of the day and an equivalent symbol from another country, the students compare the two symbols as a group and each student completes his or her own Venn diagram.[21]

   Reading Center: The teacher conducts a read-aloud on the symbol, working on conceptual understanding of the symbolism and vocabulary development.

2. Divide students into equal groups and tell them to go to the centers; rotate the groups every twenty minutes.

3. After all groups have completed the four centers, they discuss what they learned back on the floor.

4. Students write three facts about what they learned on their work sheet from the drawing center.

EVALUATION

Discussion, group participation, and daily journaling/writing.

APPLICATION OF THE ACADEMIC SUBJECTS PROTOCOL
to the American Symbols Lesson

To meet Gero's academic content and language needs, Ms. Levin first has to examine the lesson and then consider appropriate modifications.

PHASE I: Understanding the Task and Gero

In phase I we describe the nonverbal and verbal elements of the lesson, which are based on the underlined verbs and verb phrases in the lesson description, and we compare them to Gero's level of proficiency.

STEP 1: UNDERSTANDING THE TASK

TASK

To size up the gap between the language demands of each task in the lesson and Gero's English proficiency, we first examine the degree of nonverbal communication (SLIDE), then analyze the ways Gero is required to listen, speak, read, and write (TREAD). See table 1.2 for details of SLIDE and TREAD.

SLIDE ANALYSIS. From the underlined verbs we see a number of nonverbal elements, including *display, point,* and *draw.* In the introduction to the lesson there are only two nonverbal elements, the display of the American symbols and Ms. Levin pointing to one of the symbols as she starts out the lesson. Therefore, she will have to modify her introduction in order for Gero to understand the connection to the previous symbols lesson and what he will be learning in this unit.

The identified nonverbal elements relate mostly to the physical movement of the students (e.g., walk the students through, create groups, rotate the group, etc.). This is consistent with what often occurs in a kindergarten classroom where directions are modeled rather than spoken. Only two nonverbal tasks can be described as instructionally related: draw the symbol of the day (drawing center) and look at a picture of the two symbols (writing center).

TREAD ANALYSIS. As with the SLIDE analysis, the underlined verbs that describe what the teacher and students are doing are the key to analyzing the lesson's verbal demands. In the lesson we see numerous verbal tasks, such as *ask, tell,* and *explain.*

With the exception of the drawing center, the students will be performing more verbal than nonverbal tasks to learn about the American symbols' history and meaning. The verbal elements are strongly linked to instructional tasks (i.e., tell, complete, compare, discuss, copy, etc.). If Gero cannot understand these verbs and is not given opportunities to interact with his peers and the content at his beginning English proficiency level, he will not be able to meet two of the lesson objectives. This means that Ms. Levin needs to focus her modifications on finding scaffolds for him in three out of the four centers, as well as during the lesson closing, where the students write about what they learned about the symbol of the day.

STEP 2: UNDERSTANDING THE STUDENT

For a description of Gero's proficiency, Ms. Levin consulted table 1.1, which shows that English learners at the beginning level, like Gero, can point to items, follow commands, give one- or two-word responses, memorize common phrases, and label, match, and list items.

PHASE II: Narrowing the Gap Between the Task and Gero

Based on the analysis of the task and Gero's English proficiency, Ms. Levin is now ready to pinpoint areas within the lesson where Gero may need additional support as well as how, when, and by whom it will be provided.

STEP 1: SUPPORTING INSTRUCTION

First Ms. Levin needs to determine the types of nonverbal and verbal support that Gero needs for comprehensible input, interaction, and output, as well as what support can be provided for this lesson.

WHAT TYPES OF NONVERBAL SUPPORTS ARE NEEDED? The introduction to any lesson sets the stage for what the students are going to learn. It provides background information on the topic and activates prior knowledge. Making not only lesson introductions but also directions and routines comprehensible in kindergarten is especially important because all the students have to learn about movement and behavior in a classroom. When called together, they are learning that the teacher is going to say or do something important and that they must pay attention and listen. English learners like Gero often use these floor announcement/discussion opportunities to pay particular attention to what the teacher is saying in an attempt to catch on to what is expected of them. Because of the professional development sessions she attended, Ms. Levin is aware of this fact and always makes sure to place Gero directly in front of her and not in the back so he can watch her lips as she forms the words and hear the pronunciation of each word as she enunciates every syllable.

To assist Gero in understanding the verbal elements of the lesson, Ms. Levin also decides to make a habit of using gestures while using the words to describe the activities and actions. For example, when calling the students to the floor by the rocking chair, she purposely looks at him while waving her hands, palms face up, to demonstrate to him that he should move forward with the other children. In the Haitian culture such a gesture is considered to be acceptable.[22]

WHAT TYPES OF VERBAL SUPPORTS ARE NEEDED? While each center requires specific linguistic adaptations for Gero, one constant modification that Ms. Levin can implement is to have her other Haitian student, Merline, sit near him at all times. This way, she can quickly redirect him when he is lost or translate a word or two when he is really unable to comprehend what Ms. Levin or others say.

Since Ms. Levin uses her own narrated PowerPoint slides in the Listening Center, she should listen carefully to her presentation and decide whether the pace is appropriate or whether it would be wise to rerecord the voice-over a bit more slowly to increase Gero's chances to understand more words. She could also use a different font color for important information in the slides. She definitely should increase the wait time between slides so that the students have a chance to copy the words from the word bank into the cloze sentences on the work sheet.

The read-aloud activity in the Reading Center gives Ms. Levin maximum opportunity to monitor Gero's conceptual understanding and to work on vocabulary development.[23] Not only does she show the class each picture from the text she is reading, but she can engage Gero and his classmates by changing her voice, using different intonation patterns, and including lots of gestures. At times, she stops, poses questions to the students, and pretends to be thinking about the answer, with one finger on her chin and eyes turned upward, her head slightly tilted to the side. This way Gero recognizes easily that she is trying to find an answer and may even dare to offer her an answer. She can facilitate the exchange by asking leveled questions that require Gero to respond with one word only, or she can ask him to point to the object in the picture that contains the response. Similarly, by developing the habit of placing emphasis on the word she intends for Gero to know or concentrate on, Ms. Levin can formulate such a leveled question by asking, "Can you point to one of the *red* stripes in the American flag?" After he does so, she can then say, "Yes, this is one of the *red* stripes in the American flag," thus providing Gero not only with confirmation that he responded correctly, but giving him another opportunity to hear the sentence.

STEPS 2 AND 3: USE, TIME, AND PROVIDER OF SUPPORTED INSTRUCTION

All suggested supports for Gero could be added for the whole class (universal) or provided alongside instruction (supplemental), so no alternative would be necessary for Gero during class time. The Writing Center is one of the occasions where assigning Merline to work alongside Gero is highly beneficial. To reduce his dependence on others, though, Ms. Levin may want to give Gero a modified work sheet that lists the colors, shapes, and other details in both English and Kreyòl; then he can copy the words once the group decides on what to write.

Given the language-intensive nature of discussing similarities and differences of the symbols with his group during the Writing Center, Gero will need extensive support to be able to participate and learn social and academic language while interacting with his group members. Although students in Haiti engage in comparing and contrasting activities, this is most often done through verbal interaction and not through the use of a graphic organizer. He will therefore need to be explicitly taught how to complete the diagram prior to the unit.[24] The task of explaining Venn diagrams could be assumed by a bilingual aide, the ELD teacher, or even a classroom volunteer who can work with Gero while the other children do silent reading a few days before the start of the unit.

INSTRUCTIONAL MODIFICATIONS FOR OTHER ENGLISH LEARNERS

Table 2.1 shows suggested strategies for assisting learners at an intermediate or advanced level of oral proficiency for this lesson, based on the preceding SLIDE and TREAD analysis.

TABLE 2.1

Support for Intermediate and Advanced Students

	Nonverbal Support	**Verbal Support**
Intermediate	• Use gestures; point to items or pictures when talking	• Listening Center: Same as for beginning-level student • Writing Center: Sentence strips that the student can place in the correct position in the Venn diagram • Reading Center: Leveled questions, such as "What is this symbol?" or "What does this symbol stand for?" • Debriefing: Leveled questions • Fact writing at end of lesson: Sentence starters provided
Advanced	• No extra nonverbal support necessary	• Pair student with a native-speaking partner to write and proof sentences

STOP AND REFLECT QUESTIONS

1. Many students have stated that they were unaware of the polysemous words used in social studies. Prior to reading this chapter, were you aware of such terms? If so, when were you first made aware of them? If not, and more importantly, why do you think native English speakers are not made aware of polysemous words? What are the underlying assumptions educators make about polysemous word use among native English speakers? How are those same assumptions about knowledge of polysemous words transferred to teaching ELs?

2. When teaching social studies, have you used the following strategies specifically with your ELs: pre-reading, vocabulary overview, prediction guides, section reading, graphic organizers, and note taking? How effective were the strategies? Did they bring about the desired results?

GO AND PRACTICE ACTIVITIES

1. Review the textbook you are currently using and identify the polysemous words. Highlight them and create a list of the general meanings and social studies meanings and review them with your English learners. Plan time to discuss the words with your ELs as they may initially be confusing. Have a bilingual aide assist your ELs in identifying other polysemous words throughout the remainder of the chapters and create a list with their meanings for reference.

2. Create a word wall from the social studies unit you are currently using. Then be sure to document the effectiveness of using word walls. For example, have you noticed greater participation among your ELs as a result of using this word wall? If possible, jot down how often and in what ways your ELs use the word walls. Provide specific examples.

CHAPTER 3

Teaching Edith
About the Earth's Rotation

Inquiry-Based Science and Language Development

"Sit next to *me*, Edith!" Edith's classmate swatted the air, motioning to the empty chair nearby. The children rushed to their team tables for directions. "On each table, there is a piece of paper, a roll of tape, and a pile of pennies," Ms. Oliver explained. "Every team will design a boat, using only the paper and tape. Your team's goal is to create a boat that holds the most pennies without sinking. We will test your designs by placing the boats in a basin filled with water." Ms. Oliver flicked her number spinner. "Teammm . . . memberrr . . . *three*! will lead the discussion of the design plan for each group. Let's get started!"

"Hey, Edith!" shouted the boy sitting across from her. "You're number three!"

COMMUNICATION IN TEACHING AND LEARNING SCIENCE

Science instruction can provide many opportunities for English learners to comprehend concepts and topics through observing, measuring, weighing, and using just about every sense to take in and make sense of new information. By fourth grade, students should have experienced instruction that shows and explains, for example, properties of objects and materials, position and motion of objects, properties and changes of properties in matter, and motions and forces, among other concepts. All of these topics lend themselves to a hands-on approach to learning, linking objects and actions with language that describes them. However, like any other academic subject, science has language demands that challenge English learners in listening, speaking, reading, and writing.

Language Features of Science Discourse and Text

Students learning academic subjects such as science in a new language face various challenges as they negotiate the language, literacy, and content needs of the disciplines. A major challenge for teachers is to structure instruction so that they can reduce the language demands for participation while maintaining the rigor of science content and process. The academic language used in science classrooms is built around expressing specific functions. Science students, ELs included, are expected to formulate hypotheses, propose alternative solutions, describe and classify phenomena, use time and spatial relations, infer, interpret data, predict, generalize, and communicate findings.[1]

Language scholars Fang and Schleppegrell note that science is replete with technical vocabulary.[2] In addition, science texts, in particular, use abstract language, such as abstract nouns that are formed from verbs, as in *discover/discovery*. Another challenging aspect of the communication of science is the density of scientific texts. A great deal of information is packed into a clause, as in this example of an embedded clause:[3]

> A pattern of evolution in which distantly related organisms evolve similar traits is called convergent evolution.

The last feature of scientific texts that Fang and Schleppegrell identify is its tightly knit rhetorical nature. Referencing the "zig-zagging" pattern of thematic progression described by Eggins, they show how science follows a chain of reference from a new topic in one sentence to its further explanation and discussion in one or more following sentences, often using pronouns or other referents to link the second mention of the topic with the first.[4]

All four of these qualities of scientific texts pose challenges for English learners; the text complexity, the EL's level of English proficiency, and, depending on the EL's age, the first language reading ability of the student also affect the extent of the challenge and the support needed.

Components of Science Learning

In teaching science to English learners, it is helpful to consider what defines the constructs of science learning. Science and language experts Okhee Lee and Sandra Fradd have categorized the constructs as summarized in table 3.1; characteristics of scientific inquiry are shown in table 3.2, "Science Habits of Mind."[5] For each of these components, we further explain EL-specific issues—those teachers need to consider regarding the unique position in which English learners may find themselves when "doing science."[6]

If English learners are experiencing any of the issues described in the tables, it may affect their ability to fully engage in the science lesson. Addressing these linguistic differences or cultural viewpoints prior to teaching science will enable your English learner to focus on the lesson rather than on those linguistic or cultural differences.

TABLE 3.1
Components of Science Knowledge

Component	Characteristics	EL-Specific Issues
Knowing science (science understanding)	• Building on prior knowledge • Using appropriate science vocabulary • Understanding concepts and relationships	• Terms and concepts do not always translate accurately across languages. • ELs may lack specific language or communication patterns to express precise meanings.
Doing science (science inquiry)	• Engaging in inquiry • Solving real-world problems	• ELs with little or no formal schooling or those from oral language traditions may have difficulties with scientific inquiry in school if their cultural background does not encourage asking questions or devising plans for investigation.
Talking science (science discourses)	• Participating in social and academic discourse • Using multiple representational formats • Appropriating the discourse of science	• ELs may have difficulty following discussions and sharing their points of view, especially at the lower levels of English proficiency. • ELs may have different interpretations of nonverbal expressions (body language) exhibited during discussions. • ELs with limited literacy experience may have problems interpreting data and expressing themselves in written, graphic, or electronic formats.

TABLE 3.2
Science Habits of Mind

Component	Characteristics	EL-Specific Issues
Science values and attitudes	• Manifesting generic values and attitudes • Appropriating culturally mediated values and attitudes	• ELs from cultures that value group harmony above all may have difficulty critiquing their peers and arguing their perspectives.
Science world view	• Recognizing scientific ways of knowing	• ELs may interpret natural phenomena as the interaction among social, personal, and supranatural forces; this view might be rejected as personally useful and socially relevant, but not scientific.

TEACHING ENGLISH LEARNERS SCIENCE

Science lessons provide a very meaningful context for learning language and acquiring literacy. For example, when doing science inquiry, ELs use language associated with objects, visual representations and pictures, hands-on activities, and experiences with the local environment.[7] Moreover, ELs have the opportunity to develop their literacy through science discourse when they express their understanding in writing or by creating tables and graphs. When English learners discuss science in science class, they describe, hypothesize, explain, justify, argue, and summarize, all of which support the understanding of science concepts and the development of language skills.

Therefore, the relationship between science learning and language learning is reciprocal. The use of verbal and nonverbal communication in science classes allows ELs to develop and practice complex language forms and functions. Conversely, the use of language functions such as description, explanation, and discussion allows ELs to develop their understanding of science content.

Focus on Vocabulary

A well-developed vocabulary helps ELs build background knowledge and facilitates content comprehension of text and lectures in science classrooms. As with teaching and learning social studies, the Tennessee Vocabulary Project is a resource for science teachers. It lists the essential vocabulary items Edith's science teachers will need to teach. Teaching words is an important part of teaching concepts, so the integration between the content and language domains is quite clear in vocabulary development. For example, third-grade words such as *solar system* and *stratus*, fourth-grade words like *climate* and *condensation*, and fifth-grade words like *states of matter* and *symbiosis* should be identified and defined in tandem with teaching conceptual knowledge and skills.

A useful vocabulary-building strategy for science suggested by Nutta, Bautista, and Butler is to address cognates explicitly.[8] Cognates are words that sound or look similar. More important, however, they mean the same thing in different languages. Science uses many terms derived from Latin, the origin of Romance languages such as Spanish, Italian, French, Romanian, and Portuguese. Consequently, Spanish and English share many cognates.[9] Cognates such as *agricultura* and *agriculture*, *analice* and *analyze*, *actividad* and *activity*, and *aire* and *air* can be compared and prefix, root, and suffix patterns can be contrasted, as with *-dad* in Spanish and *-ity* in English. Explicit instruction in these similar words and their prefixes, suffixes, and roots can be an effective way of building vocabulary for Spanish-speaking English learners.

An interesting fact about cognates is that some cognate words are highly frequent in Spanish but less frequent in English. As a result, Spanish-speaking ELs like Edith possess a first language vocabulary bank that includes many words that are common in Spanish (e.g., *sol, luna*) but are used only in scientific and academic language in English (e.g., *solar, lunar*). Such words might help Spanish-speaking ELs understand science texts. To activate this resource, Edith's science teachers can begin by pointing out examples of cognates and then challenging her to find as many as possible in her science textbook unit. Then, cognates can constitute the basis for a student-generated glossary Edith can use when she needs help remembering the meaning of previously covered science content, or when connecting new content to her existing science knowledge.

Promoting Language Interaction

In chapter 1 we discussed the importance of interaction for acquiring a new language. Discussions are part of science instruction, and they often follow a communication pattern of Initiation/Response/Evaluation (IRE). The IRE communication pattern starts with the teacher asking a student a question. The student's answer is then evaluated by the teacher, who makes a brief statement such as "Good" or "No, that's not correct," after which the interaction ends. However, to integrate science with academic language development, science classrooms should include many opportunities for students to engage in classroom discussions in which they practice talking about science, challenge each other's ideas, and influence the direction of the discourse.

A better approach for English learners might be the Initiation/Response/Follow-Up (IRF) communication pattern, in which either the teacher or the student asks a question or introduces a topic. After a response is given, the initiator uses the response to move the conversation forward, which can continue for as long as the participants wish to talk about the subject. In contrast to the IRE pattern, IRF may include contributions from other students in the class. For example, a science teacher could engage ELs in discussing the evaporation and condensation of water. If the first answer the teacher gets is "Condenses," it would be easy to assume that the ELs lack the necessary language to express their ideas clearly. However, if the teacher uses the first response as a starting point and continues to ask questions such as "What is *condenses*?" and "How does it condense?" the students' responses become more comprehensive, moving from "Condenses" and "It condenses" to "The water vapor condenses" and then "The water vapor condenses as it cools." After more discussion, one student states, "The hot water in the bottom cup evaporated to the top cup, and the water vapor cooled with the ice and condensed in little drops." These changes represent the integration of science learning with language development using the IRF pattern. Initially, students learning English may use present tense verbs only ("condenses"), without specified nouns and pronouns. As their discourse becomes more complete, it also grows in complexity to include adverbs, adjectives, dependent clauses, and tense changes.[10] By describing and explaining their observations in science activities, ELs acquire the language of science as well as science content.[11]

In spite of decades of education reform that has aimed to make science accessible for all students, there still are important achievement gaps between native English speakers and English learners.[12] Moreover, English learners are less likely to see science as relevant to their lives outside of school or to pursue advanced degrees in science.[13] We believe that more accessible communication in science teaching and learning can lead to greater involvement of English learners in science-related activities.

✦ CLASSROOM APPLICATION ✦

As Ms. Oliver leaned over group two's table, she overheard laughter from the left. She turned quickly toward group four and saw Edith staring at the linoleum. "So . . . Edith . . . what do we do *now*?" the boy asked, intoning his question with sarcasm. "Let's have Sophia lead this discussion today because I need to borrow Edith for a second," said Ms. Oliver as she hurriedly placed her hand on Edith's shoulder. Edith followed Ms. Oliver to her desk, where they both did their best to communicate about the activity. Ms. Oliver had swooped in for the save, but she knew she could have set up the lesson better. She just didn't know how yet.

Preparing for the workshop she was scheduled to attend, Ms. Oliver searched teacher Web sites for just the right activity. With the upcoming schoolwide professional learning initiative, she had the opportunity to co-plan a lesson with the English language development specialist. "I want to do all I can for Edith," Ms. Oliver told her principal as the activity pages stacked up in the printer tray, "but I can't turn my class upside down to reach one student."

"I know what you mean, Ms. Oliver," the principal replied. "I want you to be the best teacher for all students, and I think you'll find that if you continue to concentrate on that goal, the professional learning will show you how to tweak the way you go about achieving it for Edith."

The Earth's Rotation Lesson Description

Edith and her fourth-grade classmates are learning that the earth revolves around the sun in a year and rotates on its axis in a day, or twenty-four hours. Inquiry-based lessons offer ample opportunities for English learners to interact with the topic, thus assisting with the development of conceptual understanding through hands-on exploration. They also invite verbal interaction with academic language in a low-risk environment when working in small groups. Despite the many elements that make inquiry-based lessons like the one we highlight here comprehensible for Edith, she will need extra support for some tasks, including small-group interactions. The activity modified with the Academic Subjects Protocol is the beginning of a lesson on the earth's rotation[14] that is built on the 5E Learning Cycle Model.[15]

Content Standard:
SC.4.E.5.4: Relate that the rotation of Earth (day and night) and apparent movements of the sun, moon, and stars are connected.[16]

Literacy Standards:
CCSS.ELA-LITERACY.SL.4.1.C: Pose and respond to specific questions to clarify or follow up on information, and make comments that contribute to the discussion and link to the remarks of others.
CCSS.ELA-LITERACY.SL.4.1.D: Review the key ideas expressed and explain their own ideas and understanding in light of the discussion.

OBJECTIVE

By demonstrating the earth's movement around the sun, students will explain how day and night occur as a result of rotation.

INTRODUCTION

Show a picture of you and a friend, and tell the class a story about wanting to call your friend who lives in New Delhi, India.[17] Ask the class what time would be the best to call her, since she will be on the other side of the world. Ask the class how the rotation of the earth affects day and night.

DIRECTIONS

1. Create groups of four and give a materials bag to each group.
2. Tell students to number off in fours.
3. Explain each group member's task. Tell them that student 2 selects a sphere from the materials bag and holds it up. Tell them that student 1 makes a chart and writes the size of the sphere on the chart. Then tell them that student 3 turns on the flashlight and shines it on the sphere, holding it about eight inches from the sphere.
4. The group observes the sphere to determine about how much of the sphere is lighted.
5. Then the group estimates the amount and student 1 records the estimation on the chart.
6. Student 4 holds up the second sphere and the group repeats the activity.
7. Group members then discuss why they think that much of the sphere was lighted by the flashlight.
8. Bring the groups back together and discuss their findings, asking:
   a. What did you find?
   b. Why do you think this occurred?
9. Guide the class discussion toward the correct answer: light spreads only to the widest part of the object; it can't bend around the sides. So, one half ends up being dark.
10. Ask the class what shape the earth is, and show pictures of the actual sun and earth with the back side of the earth dark.
11. Using one lamp for the class and globes for each group, guide the class discussion toward how the earth's rotation takes twenty-four hours and causes dawn, day, dusk, and night.
12. Allow students to explore different times around the globe.

EVALUATION

Answer the following questions:

1. What is the shape of the earth? Provide an example of this shape.
2. What causes day and night? Explain completely.

3. How long is the earth's day?

4. When it is daytime in the United States, what time of day is it in India? Why?

APPLICATION OF THE ACADEMIC SUBJECTS PROTOCOL
to the Earth's Rotation Lesson

To meet Edith's academic content and language needs, Ms. Oliver first examines the lesson and then considers appropriate modifications.

PHASE I: Understanding the Task and Edith

In phase I we describe the nonverbal and the verbal elements of the lesson, which are based on the underlined verbs and verb phrases in the preceding lesson description.

STEP 1: UNDERSTANDING THE TASK

To size up the gap between the language demands of each task in the lesson and Edith's English proficiency, we first examine the degree of nonverbal communication (SLIDE), then analyze the ways Edith is required to listen, speak, read, and write (TREAD).

SLIDE ANALYSIS. The group has many hands-on tasks, including selecting and holding up a sphere, shining a flashlight on it, observing how much of the sphere is lighted, estimating and recording the amount on a chart, and seeing different times of the day on the globe. Edith will be able to participate in these tasks and develop conceptual knowledge from them.

TREAD ANALYSIS. The directions to the group are entirely verbal. Each group is expected to discuss why the portion of the sphere was lighted by the flashlight. Participating in this discussion requires the ability to form sentences using a cause-and-effect structure, which is beyond Edith's level of proficiency without support. The class discussion also involves answering "why" questions, so Edith will need support to comprehend. The quiz is entirely verbal and requires responses that are far more complex than Edith can write without support. Edith will need another way to demonstrate comprehension of the process of the earth's rotation.

STEP 2: UNDERSTANDING THE STUDENT

For a description of Edith's proficiency, Ms. Oliver consulted table 1.1, which shows that Edith can point to items, follow commands, give one- or two-word responses, memorize common phrases, and label, match, and list items.

PHASE II: Narrowing the Gap Between the Task and Edith

Based on the SLIDE and TREAD analysis, Ms. Oliver is now ready to pinpoint areas within the lesson where Edith may need additional support as well as how, when, and by whom it will be provided.

STEP 1: SUPPORTING INSTRUCTION

Ms. Oliver needs to determine the types of nonverbal and verbal support that Edith needs and that can be provided.

WHAT TYPES OF NONVERBAL SUPPORTS ARE NEEDED? Building background knowledge visually is essential for Edith. In her introduction, Ms. Oliver can show on a globe where New Delhi is as she tells the story. She can then rotate the globe to show India's location in reference to Harveston, Florida, where the class is, noting that the turning of the globe represents the earth's rotation.

When beginning the group activity, Ms. Oliver can model the directions for the class as she states them, breaking down each step and verifying that each group follows the modeling and directions correctly.

Whenever she addresses the entire class or checks in on Edith's group, Ms. Oliver should make a concerted effort to act out the earth's rotation, the way the light hits the globe, and so on to make the verbal information more visible.

WHAT TYPES OF VERBAL SUPPORTS ARE NEEDED? First language support, by providing either translated labels or labels Edith can look up in her bilingual dictionary, will help her connect to the topic. For example, asking the ELD teacher, bilingual aide, or a volunteer to prelabel a textbook illustration of the process of the earth's rotation and write simple sentences that use the content-specific words will help Edith by connecting the content vocabulary and sentence structure to the hands-on activities. This handout can be given to her as a supplement to refer to before and during the activity.

The simple sentences from the handout can then serve as the basis for sentence frames that help Edith participate during the group discussion. For example: "I think that _____ (half of, most of, a slice of, etc.) the sphere was lighted by the flashlight because _____ (light spreads to the widest part, light cannot bend around the sides, etc.)." As a beginner, Edith may not be able to state these sentences during the discussion, but she can refer to them as she listens to the others and can follow up with the teacher afterward.

During the class discussions, Ms. Oliver should label the displayed picture of the globe and the sun with *sphere, rotate, rotation, spin, axis,* and similar words to help all students learn the content-specific vocabulary, in addition to writing words such as *day, night, dusk, dawn,* and *twenty-four hours* that allow Edith to read, write, and/or discuss rotation in English. Additionally, she can check for understanding and give Edith the opportunity to pronounce the vocabulary without being singled out by asking all students to say aloud what she is pointing to on the picture of the globe. Last, by writing the different groups' hypotheses on the board, Ms. Oliver gives Edith the opportunity to copy the phrases for follow-up with the ELD teacher.

In lieu of asking Edith to respond to the quiz questions in writing, Ms. Oliver can ask her questions 1, 3, and 4 by using the globe, gestures, and other graphics to illustrate each question while stating it. While checking comprehension of the question, the teacher can paraphrase and offer prompts to clarify, such as with "How long is the earth's day?" If Edith's expression shows lack of comprehension, Ms. Oliver can restate the question as "How many hours are there in a day?" or "One day has how many hours?" (said while holding up one finger during "one day" and palms up with a questioning expression during "how many"). To show her understanding of question 2, regarding the causes of day and night, Edith can make a graphic/physical explanation of the process of the earth's rotation, using clip art, simple English, and Spanish where necessary.

STEPS 2 AND 3: USE, TIME, AND PROVIDER OF SUPPORTED INSTRUCTION

All suggested supports for Edith could be added for the whole class (universal) or provided alongside instruction (supplemental), so no alternative would be necessary for Edith during class time. Labeling the globe is a universal support that is especially helpful for Edith. As mentioned previously, Ms. Oliver could create a supplemental list of sentence frames for Edith to refer to so she can participate in the group discussion. Ms. Oliver has plans to follow up the earth's rotation lesson for Edith with technology, a bilingual aide, and a volunteer.

As a follow-up to the lesson, working with a bilingual aide, Edith can be directed to a YouTube video of the earth's rotation and can tell the aide in Spanish what is occurring and why. If no bilingual aide is available, Ms. Oliver can ask a community volunteer to sit with Edith while the other students work independently. By pointing to different sections of the picture the teacher used in the introduction phase of the lesson, the volunteer can ask Edith to say what they represent in Spanish. Alternatively, if neither a bilingual aide nor a volunteer is available, Ms. Oliver could cue up the YouTube video on an iPad for Edith to preview independently prior to the lesson to create context for the subsequent activity.

INSTRUCTIONAL SUPPORT FOR OTHER ENGLISH LEARNERS

Based on the SLIDE and TREAD analysis above, table 3.3 shows suggested support for assisting learners at an intermediate or advanced level of oral proficiency for this lesson.

TABLE 3.3

Support for Intermediate and Advanced Students

	Providing Nonverbal Support	**Providing Verbal Support**
Intermediate	• Make verbal content-specific vocabulary visible through gestures and by pointing to objects or illustrations.	• Provide a list of academic vocabulary that will occur during the first experiment to facilitate participation in group discussion and recording of findings. • Practice a sample sentence, such as "When it is _____ o'clock in New York, what time is it in _____?" to facilitate participation in the last exploration. • Consider reading the quiz questions to student. Accept short answers or incomplete sentence formation in questions 2 and 4.
Advanced	• No extra nonverbal support necessary	• No extra verbal support necessary, with the exception of the quiz, where allowance for grammatical errors should be made.

STOP AND REFLECT QUESTIONS

1. How can you engage your students in scientific inquiry while respecting their cultural beliefs about science, especially if their views rest on supranatural forces to explain scientific events? How would you approach the topic of scientific inquiry and the need for your ELs to participate in the activities? In other words, how would you begin the discussion on this topic?

2. We introduced the IRF (Initiation/Response/Follow-Up) approach. If you have never used it, what would impede you from trying it in your class (e.g., time required, fear of losing control of the class or having students add comments you may not be sure of, etc.). Write or reflect on anything that would stop you from implementing this approach. If you have used it, how did it encourage your students to engage in scientific discussions?

GO AND PRACTICE ACTIVITIES

1. Implement the IRF approach in your class. During the first two weeks of implementing this approach, keep a journal on how your ELs and native English speakers are responding to the use of IRF. Have you noticed more engagement in the lesson? Are your ELs trying to use the scientific vocabulary introduced to your science lessons? Write any observation notes that would allow you to assess the effectiveness of this approach.

2. To motivate your students toward scientific learning, you will need to conduct an informal study to determine their views on science. First, begin by exploring their attitudes toward science and how they define the study of science. Second, find out whether or not they want to work in a science-related area after high school or college. Do not accept yes or no answers; have them provide detailed answers. If your ELs are at the beginning or intermediate stages of language proficiency, you will need to ask the questions in the students' native language for full comprehension. Use the information obtained to modify your lessons to motivate your ELs toward science learning.

3. Click on the science lesson video links below and view the videos. Watch the language-intensive (TREAD-heavy) lesson first. Then watch the hands-on (SLIDE-dominant) lesson and compare how comprehensible the concepts are in each. What elements of the first lesson make it difficult for a beginning second language learner?

   (a) This lesson contains a lot of verbal elements (TREAD-heavy): http://engage.ucf.edu/v/p/h65d4ak.

   (b) This lesson offers a lot of nonverbal support (SLIDE-dominant): http://engage.ucf.edu/v/p/rra6jCM.

4. List any new questions and ideas you have developed based on the science lesson videos and the information obtained from the chapter. Bring those questions and ideas to your principal for possible professional development training for the science teachers at your school and/or district.

CHAPTER 4

Teaching Tasir to Map Data

Project-Based Learning and the Use of Technology

"Nope. That's not right! These things are for mines. Look at the Web site!" exclaimed Tasir. Ms. Parker could hardly believe it when she overheard Tasir's contribution to the group discussion. "Let me see, Tasir. What are you refer-ring to?" she asked as she leaned over the work sheet. "Oh, these V-shapes? What do the rest of you think they are? Are you sure? Well, if you're not sure, I suggest you look at the Web site Tasir found, and you can take the discussion from there," Ms. Parker said with a wink to Tasir as she walked over to the next group.

Before leaving for the day, Ms. Parker stopped by the media center to look for the English language development teacher. "Ms. Marlin, I'm glad I caught you. I wanted to let you know that I've seen some improvement in Tasir's level of engagement lately, especially since you encouraged me to try other forms of text with her. However, next Monday we start a new unit that requires the stu-dents to sift through a lot of online text and data. Could we possibly meet this week to discuss more strategies?"

This was a really busy week for Ms. Marlin, with several meetings and a baby shower she was hosting for another teacher, but she did not want to put her colleague off. Ms. Parker had been trying to differentiate her instruction for Tasir. So, Ms. Marlin asked Ms. Parker to e-mail her the lesson plans for the unit, promising that she would review them and get back to her in a few days.

Unlike chapters 2, 3, and 5, which focus on teaching academic subjects to English learners, this chapter integrates academic subjects in project-based, thematic instruction. Of course, where social studies, science, and mathe-matics are part of the project content, the same communication gap issues for English learners apply. Because Tasir is at the middle school level, and project-based learning is very suitable for grades 6 through 8, we made the integration of academic subjects through project-based learning and the use of instructional technology the focus of this chapter.

COMMUNICATION IN TEACHING AND LEARNING SOCIAL STUDIES, SCIENCE, AND MATHEMATICS THROUGH PROJECT-BASED LEARNING

Throughout this book, we have shown that it is possible for teachers to make academic subject classroom instruction accessible for English learners as long as they provide the necessary verbal and nonverbal support. In our work with English learners like Tasir, we have seen repeatedly that developing English language proficiency and literacy interacts with developing knowledge and skills in academic subjects. Consequently, one of the key aspects of helping ELs meet grade-level standards is for teachers to create the instructional conditions under which the students can learn language and use language to learn content.

While there are various ways of creating optimal environments for students to learn academic content and academic language simultaneously, we encourage teachers to consider using project-based learning as a framework for organizing, implementing, and evaluating instruction in the mainstream classroom with one or more English learners. Although at this point in time there is limited research that focuses explicitly on the benefits of project-based learning in teaching ELs, research conducted over the past two decades strongly suggests that this instructional model can yield similar results for ELs.

Let us first consider project-based learning approaches from a broad point of view. Project-based learning both enhances students' achievement and engagement in learning[1] and offers an avenue for differentiation and student choice, which leads to increased intrinsic learner motivation.[2] It also provides an excellent means of integrating the teaching of language, literacy, and content in the classroom because the learners engage with other students in a wide range of activities, often through the use of technology, while working on an authentic learning task that leads to the completion of an end product.[3] Project-based learning thus integrates various important twenty-first-century skills such as teamwork and problem solving.[4] Teachers act as facilitators of learning rather than purveyors of knowledge, paying particular attention to scaffolding instruction in support of learners' investigations. All these points, in particular the integration of skills in real-world problem-solving scenarios as opposed to practice of isolated skills, are highly beneficial for English learners. When implementing project-based learning with English learners, teachers should keep one main consideration in mind—ELs may need access to a different set of resources than native English speakers because the way the information is organized and conveyed has to be compatible with their English proficiency levels.[5]

An additional advantage to project-based learning for English learners is that it lends itself to the use of thematic units. A thematic unit is defined as effective instruction that is organized around a central topic, idea, or theme and uses related activities and experiments across two or more content areas. When they are exposed to a topic in different subject areas, English learners are afforded longer exposure to the academic content, and they profit from the in-depth learning experiences because an integrated curriculum brings various aspects of the academic content into meaningful association.[6] Furthermore, the topic-specific academic vocabulary is repeated across the content areas, which gives the English learners more time to recognize and practice using it than would be possible in a single content-area unit.

As we discussed in chapter 1, learning through language and learning language occur during meaningful interactions with content and with others. We submit that thematic units and project-based learning are particularly well suited for English learners for this very reason. Content and academic language skills are naturally integrated, and students have to interact with the content through exploration rather than having it presented to them. This requires them to sift through textual information and evaluate its usefulness for the task at hand, leading them to employ higher-order thinking. Because many projects are completed in collaborative groups, English learners are also exposed to substantial amounts of academic language while interacting with a small number of peers, reducing the affective filter they often experience in whole-group discussions. They get to practice their listening and speaking skills, and get to collaborate with more advanced users of the target language when writing a report or making an oral presentation that represents the group's end product.

The Use of Technology in Project-Based Learning

In today's economically developed societies, technology abounds. Most people use and depend on all kinds of technological tools as they go through each day. Effective classrooms are no different. One of the many benefits of incorporating technology in teaching and learning is that it allows teachers to design learning experiences in multiple modalities and at different levels of complexity, thus creating conditions in which their students' diverse needs can be met.[7] For example, the teacher can assign an English learner to regularly complete grammar-based modules on the computer that are designed to address the particular developmental needs of the student at her proficiency level. The teacher can also use a number of apps on mobile devices to provide on-the-spot tutoring, also geared toward the English learner's particular language or background needs.

Students are intrinsically motivated to use technology in learning. When they can explore a topic on the Internet rather than reading a "boring" textbook or newspaper, or are tasked with creating a wiki or a blog in which they show what they have learned about an academic topic, they are more likely to become active learners and critical thinkers. Whereas most teachers feel comfortable delivering lessons with PowerPoint or Prezi and many regularly utilize the Internet to download pictures, graphs, or videos to provide visual enhancements for their lessons, newer communication technologies offer vast opportunities for students to search for and interpret information and produce solutions. For instance, experts can be brought in through videoconferencing (e.g., a physicist can demonstrate how a Tesla coil produces high-frequency, alternating-current electricity or a civil rights leader can tell his experience in attending rallies), or classes across the nation (or internationally) can be connected through social media as they report observations of bird migration. The use of authentic sources and materials, as well as the interactions with academic content and language that are made possible through information technology, creates rich contexts that facilitate second language acquisition. In one of the investigations on the use of technology for project-based learning, teachers saw value in pairing English learners with English-proficient students because the ample opportunities for interaction led to increased curriculum-related conversation. Students became "language models and language brokers with their peers, relying on each other for help in revising and polishing."[8]

When considering the inclusion of technology in academic-subject classes with one or more English learners, teachers should keep in mind the distinction between synchronous and asynchronous technologies. Synchronous communication can be enticing for students because it involves direct social interaction with others through, for instance, a chat room or videoconferencing. English learners at beginning levels are unlikely to benefit from these interactions because they require quick comprehension of what is said and equally quick language production in response. English learners at higher levels, while more able to participate, may still feel reluctant to engage because the immediacy of the interaction does not allow them to carefully plan their responses so as to avoid miscommunication and errors. Asynchronous modes, such as e-mail or the construction of a blog or a wiki, remove the need for immediate reaction and language production, which can lower anxiety.

In chapter 1 we discussed optimal conditions for second language acquisition, referring to comprehensible input, interaction, and output. Within this framework, in table 4.1 we categorize some of the more common technological tools (by no means a complete list) that content-area teachers can consider.[9] Teachers should keep in mind, however, that the selection and implementation of the technology tool need to be based on the English learner's level of English proficiency.

TABLE 4.1

Useful Technology Tools for Content Instruction

Input	Interaction	Output
• Audio—lecture or read-aloud by teacher • Smartboard (with audio, glossaries, etc.) • PowerPoint, Prezi • Internet	• Wiki, Web site • E-mail • Videoconferencing • Digital storytelling • Smartboard	• PowerPoint, Prezi • Wiki • Blog • Video demonstration • Digital storytelling

✦ CLASSROOM APPLICATION ✦

The district seventh-grade benchmark test results were low. The principal called an emergency meeting with all department chairs, instructional coaches, and guidance counselors. "I'm not interested in placing blame for these disappointing results. That won't change the reality that our seventh graders are not learning enough. All I am saying is we have GOT to try something different NOW. We can't afford to continue like this," said Mr. Phillips. After a deep breath, he stretched his arms out, holding them just above the tabletop, palms up, and continued, "I'm open to suggestions. Any and all ideas will be considered, as long as there is some evidence that whatever we're going to do has had success in other schools." After a long silence, a few ideas were brought up. An hour later, the team had reached consensus on what should and could be done, but only after Mr. Phillips promised that he would support the changes by freeing up the seventh-grade teachers on a regular basis to collaborate on planning. Their goal: thematic units across the content areas.

Excited, yet equally unsure about how the switch to an integrated thematic instructional model would work out, the seventh-grade team chose the theme of renewable energy to start out. They settled on three essential questions: (1) How do households use renewable and nonrenewable energy sources? (2) How can the physical environment impact resource use? and (3) How does energy use impact economic decisions? Since all teachers were new to thematic units across a grade level, the team decided to implement individual smaller projects for each content area, each of which would inform at least one other area, rather than trying to produce one large project. The following list describes the main objectives for the project in each content area. The social studies/geography unit is then described in detail in the next section.

- Science—Identify renewable energy sources for noncommercial use.
- Social studies/geography—Investigate geological formations and climate conditions, as well as energy consumption of rural and urban centers in the United States through GIS mapping.
- Mathematics—Considering the cost of original investment and cost recovery, develop a budget for a household of five that converts to renewable energy.
- Language arts—Write a persuasive essay to a city council, county commission, or state legislature supporting or opposing incentives for converting to renewable energy sources (to be highlighted in chapter 10).

GIS MAPPING LESSON DESCRIPTION

Since attending a professional development workshop two years ago that introduced her to GIS (Geographic Information Systems) mapping, Ms. Parker has used the new tool just once in the past year to show her students the difference between traditional maps and GIS. This is the first time her students are going to create their own maps using this technology. Cognizant that general reading and communication skills are necessary to complete the project, she decided to investigate both content-specific standards and appropriate literacy standards.

Geography Standards:[10]

G.1.7.4: Interpret specific types of charts, maps, and graphs showing weather patterns, climate, population, and other specific topics.

G.1.7.5: Compare a variety of regions to determine suitability for growth (e.g., climate, landform, vegetation regions).

G.1.7.6: Compare and contrast the tools used by geographers, past and present, to develop maps and globes (e.g., astrolabe, compass, sextant, Global Positioning System [GPS], Geographic Information Systems [GIS], LANDSAT, Internet)

G.3.7.2: Investigate the infrastructure of population centers.

Literacy Standards for History/Social Studies:

CCSS.ELA-LITERACY.RH.6-8.1: Cite specific textual evidence to support analysis of primary and secondary sources.

CCSS.ELA-LITERACY.RH6-8.7: Integrate visual information (e.g., in charts, graphs, photographs, videos, or maps) with other information in print and digital texts.

OBJECTIVES

- The student will be able to research and collect data and visually display it through GIS mapping.
- The student will be able to identify and categorize existing or potentially available renewable energy sources based on geographic formations and locations.
- The student will be able to connect the availability of renewable energy sources to their utility for given population centers.

INTRODUCTION

Project a traditional street-level map of an area that has several lakes or rivers; ask what it is and what it is used for.[11] Then display side by side the same map, a satellite view of the area, and a GIS view with the area's flood zones, each with a caption explaining what it is. Solicit from students ways in which the maps are similar and different. Give an operational definition of GIS mapping, then tell the students to brainstorm what a GIS flood zone map could be used for. Inform the students that they will use GIS maps to investigate the current and potential future use of renewable energy in a county or city assigned to them.

DIRECTIONS

1. While completing a teacher-created WebQuest, students create a GIS map of an assigned area, using various interactive mapping tools developed by governmental entities.[12]

2. Explain the details of the project, including the presentation expectations.

3. Present the National Renewable Energy Laboratory Web site, spending some time on the Dynamic Maps, GIS Data, & Analysis Tools page.[13]

4. Assign a mix of rural areas and urban centers in the United States to groups of four students. Students design a plan for researching needed data points (e.g., energy consumption, existing options for renewable energy sources in assigned areas) and select information sources (e.g., Web pages, magazine articles) provided by the teacher.

5. Provide groups with needed support during data collection and map creation.[14]

6. Each group reports its findings and conclusion to the class through a PowerPoint, Prezi, or interactive whiteboard presentation.

EVALUATION

Rubrics for (1) accuracy and details of the produced GIS map and (2) presentation.

APPLICATION OF THE ACADEMIC SUBJECTS PROTOCOL
to the GIS Mapping Lesson

To meet Tasir's academic content and language needs, Ms. Parker first has to examine the lesson and then consider appropriate modifications.

PHASE I: Understanding the Task and Tasir

In this section we describe the nonverbal and the verbal elements of the lesson, which are based on the underlined verbs and verb phrases in the lesson description.

STEP 1: UNDERSTANDING THE TASK

TASK

To size up the gap between the language demands of each task in the lesson and Tasir's English proficiency, we first examine the degree of nonverbal communication (SLIDE), then analyze the ways Tasir is required to listen, speak, read, and write (TREAD).

SLIDE ANALYSIS. The visual components of this lesson consist of the use of maps, the teacher's modeling of how the GIS software works, and the students' construction of their own maps, as well as the production of the visual aspects of the technology-based presentation.

TREAD ANALYSIS. Although supported by the visual element of both GIS and traditional maps, the discussion of similarities and differences of the two map types is highly verbal. The main instructional steps entail heavy language demands, with discussions between the team members to design the research plan, which involves skimming though available resources. Furthermore, the students have to read, interpret, and discuss information and data both individually and within groups, and make decisions while creating the GIS maps. Last, they produce and deliver the presentation to the class, which involves writing and speaking.

Although Tasir's English proficiency is at the advanced level, which allows her to communicate quite fluently with her peers in social interactions, she is weak in reading and does not like to write. Therefore, she will need support to get through the reading-intensive portions and help her contribute to the writing of the presentation content.

STEP 2: UNDERSTANDING THE STUDENT

For a description of Tasir's proficiency, Ms. Parker consulted table 1.1, which shows that Tasir can use some academic language, participate in discourse and complete written compositions with some grammatical errors, and read passages with support.

PHASE II: Narrowing the Gap Between the Task and Tasir

Based on the SLIDE and TREAD analysis, Ms. Parker is now ready to pinpoint areas within the lesson where Tasir may need additional support, as well as how, when, and by whom it will be provided.

STEP 1: SUPPORTING INSTRUCTION

Ms. Parker needs to determine the types of nonverbal and verbal support that Tasir needs and that can be provided. Because Tasir is at the advanced level of English proficiency, she needs less support than students at the beginning or intermediate levels.

WHAT TYPES OF NONVERBAL SUPPORTS ARE NEEDED? Having recently experienced success in modifying text for Tasir at the ELD teacher's urging, Ms. Parker knows that she needs to keep the written information on the WebQuest as simple as possible so that Tasir can complete it without being turned off from GIS map creation before she even starts the project. However, the hands-on portions of the lesson with the map production provide ample opportunities to connect visuals to text.

WHAT TYPES OF VERBAL SUPPORTS ARE NEEDED? Ms. Parker should first of all assign Tasir to a group of students who model good reading strategies such as skimming, underlining, and finding support in the text. After the group has selected its resources, she should also go through the texts and highlight important vocabulary or phrases for Tasir to draw her attention to the portions of the text that she needs to comprehend and be able to discuss with her peers. By requiring all students to write bulleted summaries of their findings before they create the maps, she naturally gives Tasir the beginnings for written descriptions of important points for her contribution to the PowerPoint, Prezi, or interactive whiteboard presentation.

Before each group presents its map and findings, Ms. Parker decides to include a rehearsal of the presentation. While this benefits those students who don't like to present in front of the class, it will particularly help Tasir to prepare and rehearse a script of exactly what she will say. Because Tasir is at the advanced level of oral language proficiency, Ms. Parker expects her to explain an equal amount of the group findings and conclusions during the class presentation.

STEPS 2 AND 3: USE, TIME, AND PROVIDER OF SUPPORTED INSTRUCTION

All suggested supports for Tasir could be added for the whole class (universal) or provided alongside instruction (supplemental), so no alternative would be needed for Tasir during class time. The highlighted text is a supplemental support for Tasir, which Ms. Parker, the ELD teacher, or a bilingual aide could prepare in advance.

INSTRUCTIONAL SUPPORT FOR OTHER ENGLISH LEARNERS

Based on the SLIDE & TREAD analysis above, table 4.2 shows suggested support for assisting learners at a beginning or intermediate level of oral proficiency for this lesson.

TABLE 4.2

Support for Beginning and Intermediate Students

	Providing Nonverbal Support	**Providing Verbal Support**
Beginner	• Label social studies chart for climate conditions, geological formations, and energy consumption (with pictures) for student to refer to throughout project. • Point to maps and map features and use gestures when soliciting responses from students. • Provide illustrated instructions in chronological order for project (with screen shots of WebQuest).	• First language support through bilingual aide, if available. • Concept building: Video of alternative energy sources or teacher-created PowerPoint slides with pertinent vocabulary highlighted. Student then completes sentence frames, such as "Power from [water] is called [hydro]" as energy sources are explored. These sentences can then be used for presentation. • Simplified text (with pictures) provided for research. • Student is not expected to speak in full sentences during presentation.
Intermediate	• Same as first and second supports listed above.	• Graphic organizer to organize/condense information. • Paired writing.

STOP AND REFLECT QUESTIONS

1. What is your perception of project-based learning? Do you think it is an effective approach for teaching English learners or is it too heavily language based and time consuming to be implemented at the elementary or secondary levels?
2. What are the benefits of engaging students in activities to solve real-world problems?

GO AND PRACTICE ACTIVITIES

1. Go to a project-based learning site. Explore the various projects students are engaged in at the elementary or secondary levels or create one on your own. Once you have decided on the guiding question, identify the areas where your English learners might need verbal and nonverbal support. ELs should be encouraged to participate in any project, regardless of their English proficiency level.
2. Although many second language learners come from countries where technology (computers, iPads, iPhones, etc.) is not as readily available as in the United States, it is rather surprising that even with limited technological resources, ELs arrive in this country with a collection of technological knowledge and related language. In fact, many technology-related terms are in English and have been borrowed by many other languages. Naturally, many of these terms experience phonological and morphological variations when spoken in other countries, but the resemblance to English remains very clear. For example, in Haitian Kreyòl, *imèl* is the same as *e-mail*; Facebook enjoys the same spelling but the emphasis is placed on the second syllable instead of the first. Although minor differences in pronunciation exist, the words are easily understood by two speakers of English and Haitian Kreyòl. Therefore, your ELs may know a surprising amount about technology, the terms used to describe many devices, or how to interact with multimedia.

   To determine just how much they know, create a list of technology-related words used in English. Have your students circle the words that are familiar to them. Conducting this simple survey will allow you to assign tasks or assignments using technology with full confidence that your students know and understand those words and the devices.
3. Create a multimedia center in your class for English learners.
4. Create a list of Web sites of useful, grade-level resources that would assist ELs at varying levels of English proficiency. Provide at least two resources for each level.

CHAPTER 5

Teaching Edgar Algebra

The Challenge of Word Problems in Math

"Paige . . . Jared . . . Marquise . . . Edgar . . . Edgar, where's Edgar?" Mr. Leibniz peered over his reading glasses just as the door handle clicked. "Edgar. You're late." Engrossed by the impending confrontation, those in attendance watched the tardy student. "I just come from ELD. Ms. Myers want me for help new student." Edgar held up a folded slip of paper, set it on Mr. Leibniz's desk, and walked to his seat.

It wasn't the first time Edgar had been late, but not one second of the remaining forty-five minutes could be wasted on verifying the note. That would have to wait. Mr. Leibniz approached the whiteboard, uncapped a red marker, and began. "Bobby is four times as old as Sally. Twelve years ago Bobby was seven times as old as Sally. How old is Sally now?"

Edgar leaned toward his classmate in the next row, squinting to see what he was writing. "So what's the unknown?" Mr. Leibniz asked as he pointed to Edgar. "Let's hear from Mr. Punctuality. Yes, you, Edgar. What's the unknown?" "I dunno," said Edgar as the class started laughing. "I dunno what is unknow." Mr. Leibniz approached Edgar's desk. "Very funny, Edgar. But you'd better get serious about doing your homework, getting to class on time, and paying attention when you're here or you'll never pass algebra." Edgar looked straight ahead, silent and expressionless, lest he lock eyes with the math teacher instigating this confusing and aggravating exchange. "I can't waste any more time here," Mr. Leibniz said as he moved toward the front row. "Let's hear from someone who knows the unknown. Paige, what is it?" Edgar slid low in his chair, crossed his arms on the desk, and put his head down.

COMMUNICATION IN TEACHING AND LEARNING MATHEMATICS

In many ways, mathematics is a universal language; fundamental mathematical operations such as addition, subtraction, multiplication, and division are present in all languages regardless of culture or location. Even though fundamental principles may be universal, the way mathematics is taught and assessed varies widely across the globe. In many countries, subtraction is tested using simple math equations, such as 6 − 4= ___?

However, in the United States, math assessment relies heavily on word problems. Word problems are short passages containing a question that requires working with numbers provided indirectly, in the passage. In a study that looked at how language affects math problem solving, Walter Kintsch found that native English speakers performed 10 to 30 percent worse on mathematical tasks using words rather than numbers.[1] Scholars such as Huang and Normandia assert that the common practice of focusing on key words in word problems is inadequate because many problems lack key words, and for those that do include them, the actual meaning of the details that convey mathematical reasoning may be revealed through sentence structure and other grammatical features.[2] Let's look at a typical word problem for a tenth-grade student and then consider a few issues that teachers of English learners like Edgar should keep in mind when they teach how to translate word problems into equations.

> If a tire rotates at 500 revolutions per minute when the car is traveling 81 km/h, what is its circumference?

First, to be able to solve this word problem, English learners must be able to comprehend most if not all the words that make up the mathematical statement. Moreover, words often have multiple meanings, and ELs must grasp the precise meaning used in the problem. EL students know that they must be able to unlock the meaning of every key word, almost in a linear fashion, because there is little narrative context to help them figure it out. Therefore, unknown words will prevent ELs from putting ideas together to form a story line. For example, the key word in the problem is *tire*. Depending on their levels of language proficiency and reading ability, some ELs might be able to skip the unknown word and move forward in the problem, but most would lack the confidence to do this because they get hung up on the meaning of the word *tire*. The same applies to the other key words of the problem, *revolutions* and *circumference*.

Second, the question segment of the word problem itself (i.e., what is its circumference?) may be confusing to some EL students since the key word *tire* has been replaced by the possessive pronoun *its*. Most native English speakers will not even notice that *tire* is not present in the question, but some ELs might have to work a bit harder to puzzle it out. Finally, it is worth stressing that word problems are predominant in math assessments. For example, Coombe, Folse, and Hubley analyzed the 2005 Florida Comprehensive Assessment Test (FCAT) for grade 4 and found that none of the forty items were expressed as a simple numerical problem.[3] Additionally, 65 percent of the questions in the test were word problems accompanied by a map, a geometric figure, or a table of data. The other 35 percent of the questions were word problems without any nonverbal support.

Focus on Vocabulary

Experienced mathematics teachers of English learners know that words have multiple meanings, which ultimately impacts the teaching and learning of mathematics to all students, native speakers included. They know that the words used in mathematics are also found in everyday language and across other academic subjects such as science and social studies. However, when conveying mathematical concepts, these polysemous words have specialized meanings that must be taught in the context of mathematics. For example, words such as *combine, describe,* or *analyze* are used in various subject areas. On the other hand, mathematics involves words (e.g., *average, angle* or *number*) that are often but not exclusively associated with mathematics concepts. Still other words (e.g., *asymptote, logarithm,* or *cosine*) are technical terms that have specific meanings in mathematics.[4]

One additional complexity of mathematics vocabulary is that similar mathematical concepts may be taught and used in assessments in different ways. For example, ELs must know that the operation of addition can be signaled by any of these six words: *add, and, plus, combine, sum,* and *increased by*. EL students often have difficulty understanding the use of prepositions when solving math word problems—for example, *divided by* as opposed to *divided into*.[5]

Language experts Lily Wong-Fillmore and Catherine Snow identified words that are challenging for ELs.[6] These include terms that express various kinds of quantitative relationships as well as everyday words that provide logical connections in sentences found in typical math word problems. Words that indicate quantitative relationships include *hardly, scarcely, rarely, next, last, most, many, less, longer, older, younger, least,* and *higher*. Words that indicate logical relationships include *if, because, unless, alike, same, different from, opposite of, whether, since, unless, almost, probably, exactly, not quite, always,* and *never*. English learners need extra support in comprehending the various meanings of these words, which may be nuanced and even change depending on the context. As with discipline-specific terms in other subjects, many of these words have one meaning for general use and a specialized meaning in mathematics.

Complex math expressions often contain words with specific meanings. The phrase *least common multiple* is an example of a problematic math phrase that ELs might have difficulty comprehending. It is hard for ELs to grasp the specialized math meaning of the phrase if they attempt to process it word by word using a dictionary, as they would normally do for isolated words. In this case, the math instruction should treat the phrase as an indivisible "chunk," meaning that when ELs see it, they should not attempt to separate it into components and get the meaning of each element.

TEACHING ENGLISH LEARNERS MATHEMATICS

The above examples illustrate the important role vocabulary plays in understanding mathematics and in doing well in mathematics assessments, especially for students like Edgar, whose language proficiency is still developing. We suggest that a mathematics classroom can be a rich environment for learning language as well as math as long as teachers help ensure that EL students are supported with both nonverbal and verbal communication.

Clearly language is an essential part of mathematics. Even though, as we indicated in chapter 1, the primary goal of academic subject instruction for ELs is to master the content of the discipline, mathematics teachers play a critical role in ELs' language development through a focus on successful communication of mathematics. For instance, when teaching students to solve math problems using mathematical expressions that contain technical terms with specific meanings, teachers should provide verbal support that goes beyond word definitions. In fact, they can help make mathematical concepts much more comprehensible by incorporating nonverbal support such as visuals and by providing adequate verbal support to make oral presentations, reading materials, and other relevant media accessible to English learners. In addition, mathematics teachers can help English learners interact with the teacher or other students, fostering their verbal exchanges with nonverbal support and language adjusted to their English proficiency. Finally, teachers may want to engage students in assessment activities that will help determine whether they have actually learned the mathematical concepts taught, and to what extent they can solve the problems posed. These types of supported communication strategies are likely to advance students' mathematical knowledge while simultaneously improving their English language development.

✦ CLASSROOM APPLICATION ✦

After reviewing the results from the chapter test on multistep equations, Mr. Leibniz walked into the teachers' lounge. "What's up, Mr. Leibniz?" asked Mr. Otto, the science teacher. "You don't look particularly happy today." Mr. Leibniz let out a long sigh and started a rant: "My third-period kids are driving me nuts! They don't listen in class, they don't do homework. Heck, they don't even copy the solutions I write on the board. Look at these test results!" Mr. Leibniz held up a stack of papers. "Not even half of them are going to pass the end-of-course exam! Edgar in particular is a problem. Even when he does show up on time, he disengages the moment I start talking. And the attitude of that kid . . . !" He saw his colleagues nodding with understanding. Only Mr. Otto, a second-year teacher who was new to Highpoint High, seemed doubtful.

Although Mr. Otto had his own struggles with Edgar's lack of enthusiasm for school, he felt for him. "Well," he said, "I don't know what Edgar's issues are in your class, but I had a pretty similar experience with him in the first few weeks of the school year. Then I started to break explanations, directions, and tasks into more digestible chunks." Mr. Leibniz turned toward his colleague. "Not only did several of my usual troublemakers start paying better attention," Mr. Otto continued, "but I've even caught Edgar making more of an effort. In my case, I found that direct instruction works quite well. I'm not sure, but maybe the regular comprehension checks keep them engaged. Maybe it'll work for you." With twenty years of teaching experience, Mr. Leibniz was tempted to disregard the unsolicited advice from a newcomer, but then he said, "Maybe you're right. Maybe it's worth trying something different."

ALGEBRA WORD PROBLEMS LESSON DESCRIPTION

After Mr. Leibniz decided to use a direct instruction model, he did more than simply redesign his original lesson. Instead, he decided to start as far back as explaining necessary vocabulary, such as *variable*, *algebraic expressions*, and *algebraic equations*. Let's see how Mr. Leibniz put Mr. Otto's suggestions into action.

Content Standards:

CCSS.MATH.CONTENT.HSA.CED.A.1: Create equations and inequalities in one variable and use them to solve problems. Include equations arising from linear and quadratic functions, and simple rational and exponential functions.

CCSS.MATH.CONTENT.HSA.CED.A.2: Create equations in two or more variables to represent relationships between quantities; graph equations on coordinate axes with labels and scales.

CCSS.MATH.CONTENT.HSA.CED.A.3: Represent constraints by equations or inequalities, and by systems of equations and/or inequalities, and interpret solutions as viable or nonviable options in a modeling context. For example, represent inequalities describing nutritional and cost constraints on combinations of different foods.

CCSS.MATH.CONTENT.HSA.REI.A.2: Explain each step in solving a simple equation as following from the equality of numbers asserted at the previous step, starting from the assumption that the original equation has a solution. Construct a viable argument to justify a solution method.

CCSS.MATH.CONTENT.HS.A-REI.B.3: Solve linear equations and inequalities in one variable, including equations with coefficients represented by letters.

CCSS.MATH.CONTENT.HS.A-REI.C: Solve systems of linear equations exactly and approximately (e.g., with graphs), focusing on pairs of linear equations in two variables.

Literacy Standard:

CCSS.ELA-LITERACY.RI.9-10.4: Determine the meaning of words and phrases as they are used in a text, including figurative, connotative, and technical meanings; analyze the cumulative impact of specific word choices on meaning and tone (e.g., how the language of a court opinion differs from that of a newspaper).

OBJECTIVES

- The student will be able to translate sentences into algebraic expressions with 85 percent accuracy.
- The student will be able to translate sentences into algebraic equations with 85 percent accuracy.
- The student will be able to correctly solve 4 out of 5 equations with two variables.

INTRODUCTION

Tell the students that because of yesterday's chapter test results, the class will have to repeat the entire chapter so that everyone can comprehend the material and clear up any misunderstandings.[7] Give the good news: by going back they will do better on the chapter test retake, and be better prepared to *successfully* move through the next chapters of Algebra 1.[8]

DIRECTIONS

1. Display important content vocabulary on a projector (e.g., *variable*, *algebraic expressions*, *algebraic equations*, *formula*, *solve*, *evaluate*, *proof*).
2. Ask the students to define/explain the terms, elaborating upon their responses, correcting misconceptions, and explaining any terms the students don't know.
3. Show several sentences (e.g., "five times a certain number," "five more than a certain number") and translate them into algebraic expressions.
4. Assign sentences similar to those in step 3 and direct students to translate them into algebraic expressions.
5. Tell the students to compare responses, then display correct answers.
6. Show what happens when the variable (e.g., x, y, n) is given a number (e.g., 11) with the algebraic expressions used in step 3.
7. Tell the students to work with their shoulder partner to solve the expressions first with 7, then with 23. Display the correct answers and discuss the results with the class.
8. Display several sentences (e.g., "9 less than a number equals 22", "the sum of 3 and a number is 34") and translate them into algebraic equations.
9. Assign ten similar sentences for students to translate as homework.

The reteaching of the chapter progresses in a similar manner for a few more days, moving from solving equations with one to equations with two variables, until the chapter is covered.

EVALUATION

Mr. Leibniz reviews daily homework for formative assessment and the chapter test as a summative assessment that is calculated into the final grade for his algebra class.

APPLICATION OF THE ACADEMIC SUBJECTS PROTOCOL
to the Algebra Word Problems Lesson

To meet Edgar's academic content and language needs, Mr. Leibniz first examines the lesson and then considers appropriate modifications.

PHASE I: Understanding the Task and Edgar

Based on the SLIDE and TREAD analysis, Mr. Leibniz is now ready to pinpoint areas within the lesson where Edgar may need additional support. The next sections describe the nonverbal and the verbal elements of the lesson, which are based on the underlined verbs and verb phrases in the lesson.

STEP 1: UNDERSTANDING THE TASK

To size up the gap between the language demands of each task in the lesson and Edgar's English proficiency, we first examine the degree of nonverbal communication (SLIDE), then analyze the ways Edgar is required to listen, speak, read, and write (TREAD).

SLIDE ANALYSIS. If Mr. Leibniz conducted a cursory analysis of the instructional actions in this plan by looking at verbs that fall in our SLIDE and TREAD categories, he would think that the content is quite comprehensible for Edgar since he notices the verb *display* four times and *show* twice. When looking more closely, however, he quickly realizes that none of these actions do much to decrease the language load of the lesson for Edgar. This is because whatever he displays or shows is either text by itself (i.e., the vocabulary, sentences) or is accompanied by a verbal explanation—for example, what happens when numbers are substituted for variables.

TREAD ANALYSIS. The lesson is largely conducted through spoken and written language, as became clear during the SLIDE analysis. A few examples illustrate this finding: students read a displayed vocabulary term and attempt to verbally define it, with Mr. Leibniz adding to their thoughts; the students are shown how to translate sentences into equations and then practice doing so with more sentences. Faced with this fact, Mr. Leibniz starts to wonder whether it is even possible to convey algebra to students whose native language is not English and who have not reached advanced proficiency.

STEP 2: UNDERSTANDING THE STUDENT

For a description of Edgar's proficiency, Mr. Leibniz consulted table 1.1, which shows that Edgar can use novel phrases and simple sentences, can describe items in simple terms, and makes frequent grammatical and pronunciation errors.

PHASE II: Narrowing the Gap Between the Task and Edgar

Based on the SLIDE and TREAD analysis, Mr. Leibniz is now ready to pinpoint areas within the lesson where Edgar may need additional support as well as how, when, and by whom it will be provided.

STEP 1: SUPPORTING INSTRUCTION

Mr. Leibniz needs to determine the types of nonverbal and verbal support that Edgar needs and that can be provided.

WHAT TYPES OF NONVERBAL SUPPORTS ARE NEEDED? Is there anything Mr. Leibniz can do to lower the verbal demands of this lesson by adding nonverbal support? Of course there is! As a matter of fact, what he (rightfully) disregarded as SLIDE actions of his instructional plan in the analysis phase can easily be turned into nonverbal support. For instance, while rewriting or translating sentences such as "five times a certain number" into the algebraic expression $5 \cdot x$ or $5x$, Mr. Leibniz should indicate through the use of colored pens or circles and arrows that "times" means multiplication and "a certain number" is the same as a variable—thus x, or whatever letter is given to the variable. He can apply the same strategy as he demonstrates the steps to solve an equation after a number has been substituted for a variable. Although this use of graphics is accompanied by academic talk, it provides Edgar with a visual frame of reference.

WHAT TYPES OF VERBAL SUPPORTS ARE NEEDED? One general recommendation we give secondary content-area teachers is to visit a primary school classroom in order to reacquaint themselves with the rich visual support that is closely tied to the development of academic language. For his algebra classes, Mr. Leibniz could create posters with "signal" words typically found in word problems that relate to addition, subtraction, multiplication, and division (see table 5.1). Ideally, Mr. Leibniz would start this list with his students each year, with the class adding to it whenever a new word that fits one of the categories appears in a word problem.

To provide substantial verbal support for this specific lesson, Mr. Leibniz does not have to look far. One of the advantages of direct instruction is its scripted nature. By thinking about what he will say at each step of the lesson, he can identify places where the students should repeat the vocabulary or restate what he just illustrated. He can also ask Edgar questions that allow him to respond in a short sentence or even a sentence fragment that shows he understands the process.

Since Edgar has to pass state end-of-course exams or other standardized tests, he needs to be able to solve the same word problems in the chapter test as the mainstream students. However, while Edgar practices the translation of word problems into algebraic equations, Mr. Leibniz may want to give him the option of completing fewer homework problems. This nod to Edgar's special circumstance would place less pressure on him and might reduce his frustration level to a point that leads him to give homework a try.

TABLE 5.1

Signal Words in Word Problems

Operation	Signal Words
Addition	Increase, more, sum, combine, total, altogether
Subtraction	Less, fewer, minus, reduce, decrease, difference
Multiplication	Double (2x), times, triple (3x), quadruple (4x), product
Division	Divided by/into, split, per, share

STEPS 2 AND 3: USE, TIME, AND PROVIDER OF SUPPORTED INSTRUCTION

All suggested supports for Edgar could be added for the whole class (universal) or provided alongside instruction (supplemental), so no alternative would be necessary for Edgar during class time. Mr. Leibniz's addition of the colored arrows and symbols is helpful for all students. The table of signal words in word problems is something that Mr. Leibniz or the ELD teacher could pre-teach and could also reteach as a follow-up, giving Edgar extra practice.

While Edgar may not require the assistance of a same-language peer in this lesson due to his intermediate proficiency level, he would benefit from specific language-related instruction. Mr. Leibniz should consult with an English language development specialist regarding grammatical features of English that typically cause English learners difficulty. Being at an intermediate proficiency level, Edgar may not have fully mastered comparatives and superlatives (i.e., *older*, *oldest*, *more*, *least*), for example. This can cause him to overlook or misinterpret important information in word problems, leading to him to incorrectly translate sentences into algebraic expressions or equations. Whether this instruction can be assumed by the ELD specialist during the sheltered language arts class or needs to be assumed by Mr. Leibniz himself naturally depends on the school's ELD programming resources.[9]

INSTRUCTIONAL SUPPORT FOR OTHER ENGLISH LEARNERS

Based on the SLIDE and TREAD analysis, table 5.2 shows suggested support for assisting learners at a beginning or an advanced level of oral proficiency for this lesson.

TABLE 5.2

Support for Beginning and Advanced Students

	Providing Nonverbal Support	**Providing Verbal Support**
Beginner	• Frequent pointing to posters when referring to key vocabulary terms or explaining solutions. • Diagrams/charts of word problems in simplified language, with pictures.	• Offer first language support through bilingual aide, if available. • Provide handout of important content vocabulary for use; translate terms, if possible. • Provide written first language translations of a few word problems, if available. • Allow students to write answers on individual whiteboard instead of asking them to vocalize answers.
Advanced	• No additional nonverbal support needed beyond what is supplied for intermediate-level student.	• Include leveled questions to confirm students' understanding.

STOP AND REFLECT QUESTIONS

1. As you know, math is a discipline that builds on prior knowledge of concepts. This could be problematic for some English learners who have not learned certain concepts in earlier grades or in their native countries. Rather than describe students as having low math skills, have you considered assessing them to determine whether or not a gap exists between their background knowledge and the concepts you will be teaching in your math unit?

2. Reflect on the ELs in your math class. How often do they readily contribute to the classroom discussion when presented with word problems? Observe and describe their behaviors. Do they appear to be engaged in trying to solve the problems individually, or are most engaged only when working with classmates?

GO AND PRACTICE ACTIVITIES

1. Explore how English learners solve word problems. Group your ELs together and, with the assistance of the ELD specialist at your school, conduct an informal study to determine the process by which the English learners solve word problems. Instruct your students that they will engage in a think-aloud protocol so that you can understand how they solve the word problems and the difficulties they might be experiencing. Begin by giving your students five to ten word problems and allow them to discuss among themselves, in English or their native language, the process they use to solve the problems. (Some students may be able to read the problems but not discuss them in English.) Let them know that you will be recording their verbal exchanges and not participating in the discussion. After examining the results, you and the ELD specialist will meet with the students individually to discuss their specific difficulties identified and to provide them with strategies to implement as they work on word problems. For example, what strategy would you recommend to a student who consistently demonstrated difficulty understanding conditional phrases in word problems? How would you help your student to change the question to make it more comprehensible?

2. Research how math symbols, calculations, and word problems are done in your students' native countries. This background information will help you understand how your English learners have been taught math in their respective countries.

3. Review the word problems in your math unit prior to teaching the unit. Select the words you believe are unknown to your ELs and review them with your English learners within the context of the problem to be solved. As stated in this chapter, teaching math vocabulary words in isolation does not help English learners understand their definitions or the concepts. (And do not rely on the vocabulary word list provided by the textbook publisher, as it is most likely a general list and may not include words unfamiliar to English learners.)

4. Have your English learners create a list of math concepts that they believe to be represented in many different ways in their math textbooks and/or practice tests. For example, addition operations are signaled in many ways: *add*, *plus*, *combine*, and so on. Allow them to work as a group on this project. Once completed, review the list with your English language development specialist and add any missing concepts you believe they should know. Last, review the list with your English learners. Tell them they may refer to the list when needed.

PART II

Teaching Language Arts and Literacy to English Learners

CHAPTER 6

Targeted Language Arts and Literacy Instruction

In chapter 1, we defined communication and described how it includes both verbal and nonverbal symbols to share meaning.[1] Throughout part I, we looked at communication broadly, considering its central role in the teaching and learning of academic subjects. In part II, we zero in on the language side of communication, exploring how language, and more specifically a second language, is learned and taught.

Just as with academic subjects, our focus in describing the difference in language arts and literacy instruction for English learners is the gap between their English proficiency and grade-level classroom communication. Distinct from how we approach academic subject instruction for English learners, however, we show how language arts and literacy instruction needs to be aimed at each English learner's more precise proficiency levels in listening, speaking, reading, and writing.[2] Our term for this goal is *targeted language instruction*. In this chapter we discuss the research and theory behind this approach, and in chapters 7 through 10 we provide practical examples and guidance to achieve this targeted goal for English learners at different grades and proficiency levels, explaining and applying our Language Arts Protocol through the classroom lenses of Gero, Edith, Tasir, and Edgar.

DEVELOPING COMPETENCE IN SPOKEN AND WRITTEN COMMUNICATION: LANGUAGE ARTS AND LITERACY INSTRUCTION

It is difficult to overstate the importance of the role of language in teaching and learning. Yet, for educators and students alike, language can be the most imperceptible aspect of the classroom. Paraphrasing Marshall McLuhan, communication scholar James Carey once noted that just as the one thing of which the fish is unaware is water, for human beings, language and other symbolic systems of meaning comprise the very environment of our existence. But these systems of meaning do not grasp our attention. Regular conversations, instructions, and other routine forms of communication become so familiar, so mundane and devoid of mystery, that they may no longer be perceived.[3]

Classroom Communication in Language Arts and Literacy Instruction

Most people typically don't know much about the form and structure of their own first language.[4] They can understand and use the language, but they don't normally know how to explain its rules. For example, most native speakers of English don't know why they can say, "He gave me a dollar," but not, "He gave me a money," when both *dollar* and *money* are nouns. Native speakers of English don't need to consciously learn rules to understand *count* and *noncount* nouns.[5] They just "picked up" how to use them and never thought about how and why.

The same goes for how and why verbs should be sequenced in a sentence. For example, native speakers of English know the correct order of words in the sentence, "You are not playing here!" but probably were never taught the rule as *You* + second person singular form of the present tense copula [*are*] + not + present participle form of the main verb [*playing*] + *here*! Nor did they practice using that sentence in dialogue exercises with a classmate after having already learned and practiced conjugating present tense sentences using the verb *be*. When native speakers first utter that type of sentence, most likely the only instruction they receive is some type of correction from an adult (if they had said, for instance, "You not playing here!").

Because they acquired spoken language in a natural setting, without formal instruction, native speakers are often unable to explain the form and structure of their language.[6] As with Carey's assertion that the communicator is unaware of language just like a fish is unaware of water, we are often unaware of the rules for the language we grew up speaking. Native speakers develop an ear for what sounds right, but a second language learner is still developing that ability to hear correctness versus error in grammatical forms and structures. Native speakers may not be able to explain the rules, but that doesn't stop them from understanding and using "correct" English.

The variety of the English language that is used and taught in the language arts classroom is known as *Standard English*. This is a prestigious variety of English that is spoken and written in many social as well as academic contexts. In fact, Standard English is a given in academic language of all types. For children whose language environment outside of school closely matches that in school, there is a small to nonexistent gap between their own language use and grade-level classroom language use. When a real gap exists, such as with English learners who are still acquiring oral proficiency in English, it becomes more important to explicitly teach and practice using the form, structure, and conventions of the language these students are expected to use at school.

In any classroom the job of language arts and literacy teachers is to make the hidden nature of language visible and the pathway to skillful language use accessible for all students. As we said in chapter 1, unlike with academic subject instruction, teaching language arts and literacy is focused primarily on what Halliday termed *learning the language* and *learning about the language*.[7] In learning the language, language is the *substance* of what is being learned. In learning about the language, language is studied as an *object* so that the learner can understand how it works. With academic subject instruction, communication that uses means other than language can enable English learners to master the course objectives; however, in language arts and literacy instruction, understanding and using language *is* the objective.

The traditional divisions between instruction in academic subjects and in language arts and literacy are softening, however.[8] Many academic subject teachers we know are now including some degree of focus on the language of their disciplines, and language arts and literacy teachers are moving beyond teaching mostly literary texts and language skills in isolation. In many cases this is advantageous for English learners, but just as with any other instructional practice that is appropriate for native speakers, different needs or issues may exclude English learners from gaining the same benefits. Multiple, complex factors are at play, perhaps the greatest of which is proficiency in the second language (English). We now turn to how it is learned, taught, and defined.

INSTRUCTED SECOND LANGUAGE ACQUISITION

Maybe you or someone you know learned another language by moving to a country or community where it is spoken. After being immersed in the new language environment for a period of time and having a need or desire to communicate, it's possible to pick up enough of the language to get by. Alternatively, maybe you or someone you know learned another language by studying it at school. Taking four or eight or twelve years of foreign language classes can lead to a basic ability to communicate as well.[9] Thus, unlike most other school subjects, a second language can be learned through informal or formal instruction. For language learning to occur in either case, the three essential elements of accessible input, interaction, and output must be present. However, formal instruction offers something more: it provides practice with and explanation of grammar.

Acclaimed second language acquisition researcher Rod Ellis terms informal and formal second language learning *naturalistic* and *instructed second language acquisition*, respectively.[10] Typical foreign language classes, for example, are designed to provide *instructed second language acquisition*. Unlike a naturalistic learning environment, an instructed learning environment is structured around *teaching the language* but includes *teaching about the language*. This usually means that elements of language are isolated and taught in a variety of spoken and written exercises and activities. In addition, the complexity of language is gradually increased in the course sequence, beginning with simple grammar forms such as present tense and moving to more complicated constructions.

What Does Instructed Second Language Acquisition Look and Sound Like?

A common format for instructed second language acquisition is to begin a lesson with a dialogue or reading passage that uses a particular verb tense. You might remember dialogue from your middle or high school classes that goes something like this:

MIGUEL: Hola. *(Hello.)*
MARIA: Hola.

MIGUEL: ¿Donde está la biblioteca? *(Where is the library?)*

MARIA: La biblioteca está a la derecha. *(The library is on the right.)*

This dialogue uses the present tense of the verb *to be* and a noun that is common to students the world over *(library)*. This is not real communication, as would occur in the naturalistic learning environment. It is contrived to include only the language that the foreign language student can learn at the beginning level. The technical term Ellis uses for a course organized by complexity of grammar points, such as the example above, is a *focus on formS*. Focusing on forms takes the overwhelming task of learning a foreign or second language and divides it into small, sequential pieces that become increasingly more complex. All exercises and activities are then based on the grammar point (also referred to as the form or structure) of focus.

The other hallmark of instructed second language acquisition Ellis refers to as a *focus on form* (using the singular term *form* rather than the plural used above, *formS)*, which can also be considered learning about the language. This simply means that the course includes an explicit presentation of a grammar point, either deductively, by stating the rule and giving examples, or inductively, by presenting examples and requiring students to figure out the rule. A focus on form could also occur in different language teaching approaches, such as one that is organized by language functions (asking permission, giving directions, and so on) or one that is known as content-based language learning, where second language students learn language and learn about language through using and analyzing leveled discourse and academic subject texts. No matter the language teaching approach that it is part of, a focus on form indicates that some part of the language used in the lesson will be highlighted and analyzed, whether or not technical grammar terms, such as *antecedent*, are mentioned. There will likely also be an exercise for students to practice using the form of focus correctly.

The preceding Spanish dialogue example illustrates a lesson that is part of a focus on formS. Let's look at how a focus on form could be added to a lesson. Since the verb used is the present tense of *to be*, the lesson might give an initial explanation that in Spanish there are two forms of the verb *to be*. To simplify the distinction, the lesson could explain that *ser* tells what something is and *estar* tells what something does or is at the moment. Then the lesson could provide a table that conjugates the verb *estar* (as in table 6.1).

TABLE 6.1

Conjugation of the Simple Present Tense of the Verb *Estar*

Person	Singular	Plural
1st	yo estoy	nosotros estámos
2nd	tu estás	vosotros estáis
3rd	él, ella, usted está	Ellos, ellas, ustedes están

Remember those verb tables? You might have even been asked to memorize them and fill in empty cells on a quiz. Here's something else you might remember. One other characteristic of instructed second language acquisition is a focus on language skill development—activities that focus on listening, speaking, reading, or writing, using the grammar and vocabulary of the lesson. For example, a short audio file of two Spanish speakers using the form of focus (the verb *be*) might be played in class, and students would be expected to answer multiple-choice questions (without the English translations presented here) about the details of the dialogue:

MIGUEL: ¿Como estás? *(How are you?)*
MARIA: Estoy cansada. *(I'm tired.)*
MIGUEL: ¿Porque? *(Why?)*
MARIA: Porque mi clase es muy difícil. *(Because my class is very difficult.)*

The multiple choice question might be:

¿Porque María está cansada? *(Why is María tired?)*

    a. Porque come mucho. *(Because she eats a lot.)*
    b. Porque su clase es difícil. *(Because her class is difficult.)*
    c. Porque no duerme mucho. *(Because she doesn't sleep much.)*

This activity helps develop listening skills in a second language, isolating details that come from spoken discourse or text. The dialogue presents language that is pitched to or just beyond the learner's current level of proficiency, primarily in terms of grammatical competence, meaning the degree of complexity of the forms and structures that the learner knows and can use.

Do these exercises sound familiar? They remind many of us of our own instructed second language learning experiences with Spanish, French, German, or another foreign language. They are common practices in foreign language classes. Often these same techniques are used as part of teaching ELs English language arts and literacy in an English-speaking environment, typically in what is called English language development (also known as English as a second language) classes. In English language development (ELD) classes, students do typically practice dialogues with formulaic language or use sentence frames focused on the give-and-take of academic subject–related conversations to improve their oral proficiency, especially at the beginning levels.[11] They also often study the form and structure of English and practice their listening, speaking, reading, and writing skills in English. Other things are going on in ELD classes, however, in addition to these stalwarts of foreign and second language instruction.

English language development teachers know a lot about their students' developing grammatical competence, having specialized degrees and years of experience teaching and conversing with newcomers, exited English learners, and everyone in between. Over time, these teachers also develop an ability to detect and match the communicative and grammatical pitch of their students' comprehension and expression in English.

When they teach a student at a particular level of English proficiency (i.e., instructed second language acquisition), they engage them in understanding and using language at, and slightly above, the student's current grammatical competence.[12] These ELD specialists are, in other words, attuned to their English learners' language and literacy development needs. They regularly collect and reflect on their students' spoken and written language samples, pace their instruction appropriately, select the right amount of language to focus on, and add any support needed, be it grammatical, cultural, or anything else, to develop language skills and clarify meaning.

Being attuned to the pitch of their English learners' communicative competence also enables ELD teachers to lead *instructional conversations*.[13] From the term itself, it is probably obvious that instructional conversations are more than haphazard, inconsequential chatter. Instead, they are very purposeful and powerful forms of language instruction, using conversations about the subject of focus or activity taking place (i.e., a real, rather than contrived or scripted, dialogue) to model and elicit forms and structures that a student is in the process of acquiring. Doing this allows ELD teachers to incorporate instructed second language acquisition into any subject or type of lesson. Using students' communicative and grammatical errors as cues for instruction, ELD teachers can recast errors with the correct wording and phrasing, giving the students new language input that is accessible through this interactive process. It takes an expert in second language acquisition to make these conversational moves instructional, but these intermittent, impromptu teachable moments can make a great difference in English learners' language development.

Why Do English Learners Need Instructed Second Language Acquisition and When Do They Need It?

Although it is possible to learn a language solely naturalistically, instructed second language acquisition has a number of documented benefits. Studies show that those who take part in instructed second language acquisition are better able to avoid making developmental errors permanent (known as *fossilization* or *stabilization*) and to reach higher levels of proficiency.[14] For example, for some English learners (especially adults who learned the language through exposure only), certain grammatical errors, such as "Why she couldn't come?" may persist even though the learners continue to be exposed to standard English vocabulary and grammar through accessible communication. It is becoming increasingly clear that instructed second language acquisition can complement naturalistic second language acquisition, and that preK–12 students, particularly at the secondary level, can benefit from the former.

You might be wondering how researchers track progress or measure language development in English learners. According to Ellis, second language acquisition can be considered as acquiring the form and structure of a language (among other aspects of language and its functions).[15] An important area second language acquisition researchers examine is the order in which learners acquire language forms, such as the added *s* on present-tense verbs, and the sequence of stages in acquiring a particular structure—such as the sentence structure of negative statements, beginning with placing *no* at the beginning of a sentence (No you talk here) and moving eventually to using *do* with the main verb (They didn't like the noise). Progression through these orders and sequences is constrained by various factors, many of which are considered developmental. This means that the developmental patterns are common to learners from different first language backgrounds, rather than determined by the influence of the learners' first languages, and should be expected for most students. Ellis surveyed a wealth of research showing that an explicit focus on these forms (for example, the added *s* on present tense verbs) can accelerate learners' rate of development and elevate their ultimate level of attainment of second language proficiency. There is less clear research, however, on the best way to sequence and teach the forms and structures. So, what do teachers have to go on in making those decisions?

Ellis points to Pienemann's Processability Theory as a successful attempt to predict the grammar development experienced by learners of a second language, beginning with single words or chunks, followed by simple subject/verb/object sentences and other structures, and moving eventually to embedded statements (e.g., "I see the spider suspended in its self-woven web").[16] Pienemann's theory can offer guidance for teaching and correcting learners' grammar since it has shown that certain forms or structures must be acquired before a given form or structure can emerge. For example, using the indefinite article *a* can occur only if the learner has moved beyond the one-word-phrase stage. This finding has important implications for teaching. It shows that correcting an English learner's grammatical error is important for future acquisition of the form or structure since the error can only be produced if the learner has developed some of the forms or structures required to utter it. However, most likely the English learner will not use the corrected form accurately in spontaneous speech until later, since it may be beyond processability for his stage of English development.

What this means for teaching English learners is that although some aspects of language can be taught without prerequisite knowledge or skills specific to the second language (for example, spelling in English for adolescents or adults who can write in a language that uses the Roman alphabet—they don't need to learn how to spell *cat* before they can learn to spell *catastrophe*), some have to be learnable before they can be teachable (for example, complex verb tenses—a learner won't be able to spontaneously produce *Why couldn't she have been fleeing from the scene at the time of the crime?* if he or she hasn't acquired the ability to say *Why is she running?*).

How Do Individual Factors Affect Instructed Second Language Acquisition?

We just spoke about developmental errors in second language acquisition, but they are not the only source of nonstandard (or incorrect) uses of English. A major source of influence for second language development is the native language of English learners. In many instances, English learners use expressions or grammatical structures from their first language when they speak in English. For example, Edith, a native speaker of

Spanish, may say, "I live in a house white" because in Spanish, the adjective may come after the noun, not before, as with English. In this case, first language interference may make the English expressions ELs produce difficult to understand. It's important to note that this interference is more common at the early stages of second language acquisition and decreases as the English learner becomes more proficient. This sort of influence from the first language can intermingle with the normal developmental patterns that English learners from various language backgrounds go through on their way to full proficiency. The spontaneous spoken and written utterances of English learners moving through the second language acquisition process follow a sequence and pattern of increasing complexity and common developmental errors.

There's a huge upside to native language influences on second language development, however. The transfer between two languages doesn't always cause grammatical or pronunciation errors. If the first language and English have similar features, ELs might benefit from the transfer of knowledge from the first to the second language. One example is cognates, words in two languages that share a similar meaning, spelling, and pronunciation. Thirty to 40 percent of all words in English have a related word in Spanish, which makes cognates a great tool for Spanish-speaking ELs. The similarity between the first and second language, including the number of cognates, affects the amount of exposure and study required to become proficient. Of course, the number of cognates varies greatly, depending on the second language. All things being equal, a speaker of Chinese, which has a totally different writing system and grammatical structure from English and shares virtually no cognates, would require more instructed second language acquisition and exposure to English than a speaker of Italian.[17]

It helps to see ELs' developing grammatical competence in English as *learner language* or what is termed *interlanguage*, a dynamic, internalized learner language that reflects the ELs' underlying developing knowledge of English, while still containing aspects of their native language.[18] Students' interlanguage may appear as error-filled spoken and written language. However, ELD specialists view these errors as typical stages that are replaced with correct forms as the learner becomes more proficient in English. In other words, the interlanguage produced by learners in the early stages of acquiring English can reflect the sentence structure, vocabulary, and pronunciation patterns of their native language. These patterns then become increasingly similar to accurate forms of the second language, as the learner gains more experience hearing, speaking, reading, and writing it using already known vocabulary and sentence structure.[19]

In a review of decades of research on instructed second language acquisition environments, Ellis found that younger children, such as Gero and Edith, normally acquire a second language without as much need for instructed second language acquisition, in particular the part that organizes instruction by learning grammar (focus on formS).[20] However, instructed second language acquisition is especially beneficial for secondary students such as Tasir and Edgar and, according to Ellis, has been shown to improve the rate of acquisition and the ultimate level of proficiency in the second language. This is certainly an important goal. Everyone wants EL students to reach grade-level proficiency in English listening, speaking, reading, and writing as soon as possible. It's not a simple one-to-one prospect, though. Quadrupling the amount of instructed second language acquisition doesn't guarantee reaching a language milestone in one-fourth the amount of time it takes to get there without instruction. But the positive effects of instructed second language acquisition are well established by research, and English learners in mainstream classes do benefit from this way of learning language. Even though research indicates greater benefits of instructed second language acquisition for older children, we have found it to be beneficial to some degree for ELs of all ages. So even simply pointing out the *s* on the end of present tense verbs for *he, she,* or *it*—reminding Gero and Edith to pronounce and write that final letter—can help them acquire accurate forms and structures in English, and perhaps do so a little more quickly.

When Does Instructed Second Language Acquisition Occur for English Learners in the Mainstream Environment?

We know that instructed second language acquisition is important for English learners, especially for those in middle and high school grades. So, when do preK–12 English learners take part in instructed second language acquisition? Although it might seem logical that they would spend the day in an instructed second language acquisition environment, some parts of their day at school may foster more naturalistic second language acquisition, such as when they are learning academic subjects with a mainstream teacher who provides accessible input, interaction, and output. Other parts of the day, however, may be more instructed. The focus on grammar that characterizes instructed second language acquisition might be offered through structuring the content of the English language development curriculum and instruction by using increasingly complex word forms and sentence structures, or through explicitly teaching about the forms and structures of the language. The ELD classes that Gero, Edith, Tasir, and Edgar attend generally provide that instructed second language acquisition environment, targeted to their levels of English proficiency, with an increasing focus on grammar as they move up the grade levels.[21] However, under the right conditions, the instructed second language acquisition can be intermittently integrated into mainstream language arts and even occasionally into academic subject instruction, especially when ELD and mainstream teachers collaborate to support their English learners. We will see examples of this in chapters 7 through 10.

LANGUAGE FORM AND STRUCTURE IN SECOND LANGUAGE LITERACY

So far, we have discussed how becoming proficient in English involves the acquisition of words and grammatical forms and structures. Students acquiring English learn the meaning of the words, forms, and structures, as well as how each word is put together and the order in which words are assembled in phrases and sentences. Learning grammatical forms and structures is part of developing oral proficiency—using and understanding spoken English—and oral proficiency is a key factor in the ability to comprehend and compose written texts in English. We also know that being able to read and write in the native language means that an English learner won't need to learn how to read and write all over again when learning to read and write in English. Together, oral proficiency in English and first language literacy are powerful determiners of English learners' literacy skills in English.[22]

Learning to Read in English

The research available on English learners who are learning to read (that is, learning to read, for the first time, in their second language) is quite limited in comparison to the research on native speakers of English learning to read (for the first time) in English.[23] It is also worth noting that of the research conducted with English learners, the vast majority of studies have been conducted mostly with Spanish-speaking children in primary grades, with few studies of children in upper elementary grades. Nonetheless, research findings from these studies have provided valuable insights about the factors that influence language and literacy development across languages.

Studies comparing English learners' reading development in their second language to that of their monolingual peers have shown similarities and differences between the two groups.[24] For instance, in one major research study, Nonie Lesaux and her colleagues reported that primary grade EL and non-EL students typically perform at similar levels on measures of basic reading skills such as phonological processing, word reading, and spelling.[25] However, they conclude, "the findings of studies on reading comprehension paint a very different picture, yielding highly consistent results that, in comparison to their monolingual peers, reading comprehension is an area of weakness for language minority learners." They further report that in upper elementary grades, the effect of word reading skills on reading comprehension for English learners becomes increasingly weak, whereas the influence of other skills such as vocabulary, listening comprehension, and oral proficiency becomes increasingly strong.

As mentioned previously, there is less definitive research on English learners who are learning to read (for the first time) at the secondary level. Language arts and literacy teachers who have EL students in their middle and high school classrooms, where the language demands of reading steadily increase and comprehension becomes central to students' academic achievement, should use what is well established about learning to read in the first language. However, they should also carefully interpret those insights in light of teaching English learners, who vary a great deal in language proficiency, literacy development, and schooling. For instance, we know from available cross-language research that for most EL students, instruction in key components of reading, such as phonemic awareness, word recognition, vocabulary, reading fluency, and comprehension, is necessary, but not sufficient for teaching them to read and write proficiently in English. Cross-language research indicates that oral proficiency in English is equally important, but it is often overlooked in instruction. In addition, this research has further shown that the development of literacy in English is a process that is influenced by individual differences in oral language proficiency, age, previous schooling, and cognitive abilities, as well as similarities between a student's native language and the second language of instruction.[26]

How Vocabulary, Word Forms, and Sentence Structure Affect English Learners' Reading

Research has shown that language elements that are typically part of instructed second language acquisition are important to ELs' reading and writing ability in English. One area that is commonly taught is vocabulary. Research is confirming what seems self-evident—vocabulary knowledge contributes to English learners' reading comprehension. In a study of fourth-grade Spanish-English speakers, a high correlation was found between vocabulary knowledge and reading comprehension.[27] Evidence of the importance of vocabulary knowledge for English learners isn't limited to elementary age students, however. A study of eighth to tenth graders also showed a strong correlation between English vocabulary knowledge and reading comprehension. These findings indicate that given adequate word decoding skills, vocabulary knowledge is crucial for improved reading comprehension for English learners (similar to the results of many studies of the relationship between vocabulary knowledge and reading comprehension with native English-speaking students).

There is also research showing that understanding the form and elements of words impacts students' ability to read and understand what they read. In other words, readers who "know" the internal structure of words have a distinct advantage in vocabulary and comprehension. In their influential report *Preventing Reading Difficulties*, Catherine Snow and her colleagues maintain this type of knowledge is important because it helps readers connect word forms and meanings.[28] For example, children learn that past events use verbs with an -*ed* suffix. For children, awareness of these forms and elements of words may be an important support skill in reading and spelling.

A relatively small but growing body of research indicates that in addition to vocabulary and word formation skills, knowledge of other grammatical aspects of language contributes to proficiency in reading and writing in English. Recent language and literacy research suggests that while vocabulary knowledge deficits are at the core of reading problems among upper-grade students, deficits in skills such as understanding and using correct sentence structure likely play a larger role in reading comprehension than originally assumed.[29]

Finally, understanding how information is organized in different types of texts (referred to as discourse structure) has been found to impact English learners' reading (as well as native English-speaking students' reading) across various grade levels. Research in this area is quite extensive, documenting positive effects of understanding discourse structure on students' reading, writing, and learning from text.[30]

We've discussed how acquiring the forms and structure of a second language is a major part of becoming proficient in oral language and literacy. In the next section, we look at how these building blocks of language are assembled to describe how proficient English learners communicate in listening, speaking, reading, and writing.

DESCRIBING AND MEASURING ENGLISH PROFICIENCY

"There should be nothing on your desk except a number 2 pencil. You may not open the test booklet until I tell you to. You may not move to the next section until you are told. You may not. . . ." Testing seems to involve a lot of negatives, nothings, and nots. This testing was different, however, for Gero, Edith, Tasir and Edgar. It was English language proficiency testing time at their schools, and throughout the designated day, each English learner filed into the office where an ELD teacher led them through an oral proficiency interview. This was the type of test on which Gero, Edith, Tasir, and Edgar could feel successful, and its results gave their teachers great insights into their performance in language arts and literacy classes and their English language development. The ELD teachers carefully recorded and filed their test results, planning to meet with each English learner's mainstream teachers to share ideas for supporting their progress.

English proficiency is evaluated in different ways. We've seen how researchers study the process of second language acquisition in terms of language forms and structure, but proficiency is measured also by the ability to use spoken and written language accurately for real purposes. Standardized tests such as ACCESS for ELLs and the English Language Proficiency Assessment for the 21st Century (ELPA 21) are one way to place English learners' listening, speaking, reading, and writing skills at their appropriate levels, enabling teachers to provide the necessary targeted support.[31] These standardized language assessments correspond to national and state standards of English language development for ELs. We look at the most widely used standards and descriptors in the next section.

English Language Development Standards

There are currently two sets of national standards for English language development: the TESOL preK–12 proficiency standards and the K–12 English Language Development Standards published by the WIDA Consortium.[32] Each set of standards describes the process of language acquisition through multiple levels. Because learners go through predictable stages as they acquire English, there are many similarities between the two sets of standards, the only notable distinction being that WIDA uses six levels of proficiency (the sixth representing grade-level proficiency), and TESOL, five.[33]

WIDA LANGUAGE PROFICIENCY LEVELS

Related to these standards, which are organized by level of English proficiency, WIDA developed language proficiency level descriptors across the preK–12 grade continuum for their assessments of English proficiency. Because many states use this assessment to measure ELs' progress, we summarize these proficiency level descriptors in table 6.2.

Back in chapter 1 we introduced Gero, Edith, Edgar, and Tasir as English learners at beginning, intermediate, and advanced levels. We presented table 1.1 with specifics on their needs for communication support in learning academic subjects. As we look at teaching language arts and literacy to ELs, aiming to provide targeted instruction, we

TABLE 6.2
WIDA Language Proficiency Levels

Proficiency Level	Linguistic Complexity	Language Forms and Conventions	Vocabulary Usage
Level 1 Entering	• Words, phrases, or chunks of language • Single words used to represent ideas	• Phrase-level grammatical structures • Phrasal patterns associated with common social and instructional situations	• General content-related words • Everyday social and instructional words and expressions
Level 2 Emerging	• Phrases or short sentences • Emerging expression of ideas	• Formulaic grammatical structures • Repetitive phrasal and sentence patterns across content areas	• General content words and expressions • Social and instructional words and expressions across content areas
Level 3 Developing	• Short and some expanded sentences with emerging complexity • Expanded expression of one idea or emerging expression of multiple related ideas	• Repetitive grammatical structures with occasional variation • Sentence patterns across content areas	• Specific content language, including cognates and expressions • Words or expressions with multiple meanings used across content areas
Level 4 Expanding	• Short, expanded, and some complex sentences • Organized expression of ideas with emerging cohesion	• A variety of grammatical structures • Sentence patterns characteristic of particular content areas	• Specific and some technical content-area language • Words and expressions with expressive meaning through use of collocations and idioms across content areas
Level 5 Bridging	• Multiple, complex sentences • Organized, cohesive, and coherent expression of ideas	• A variety of grammatical structures matched to purpose • A broad range of sentence patterns characteristic of particular content areas	• Technical and abstract content-area language, including content-specific collocations • Words and expressions with various degrees of meaning across content areas
Level 6 Reaching	Language that meets all criteria through Level 5, Bridging		

need a more precise categorization of what they can comprehend and express in English. The WIDA Consortium language proficiency levels help us know what listening, speaking, reading, and writing behaviors to expect from a student at a given level, and by looking ahead, we can also see what we should be helping the student to reach as he or she progresses to the next level.

For example, we know that Edith, who is placed at the top range of level 1 (Entering), currently can use single words and short, common phrases in expressing everyday and general topics. We can see that as she progresses to level 2, she will use short sentences and common sentence patterns and expressions. Knowing this can help aim language arts instruction at or slightly above her current proficiency.

Based on the description of language proficiency levels in table 6.2, figure 6.1 shows where we could place our four English learners for the purpose of language arts instruction and evaluation.

FIGURE 6.1

Our English Learners' Placement on the WIDA Language Proficiency Continuum

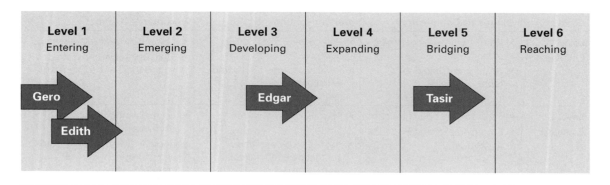

WIDA CAN DO DESCRIPTORS

In addition to proficiency level descriptors, WIDA provides a set of Can Do Descriptors (see table 6.3 for the preK–12 descriptors), which are viewed as a starting point for working with English learners and a collaborative tool for planning. This information can be used by language arts teachers to plan their instruction and to interpret the meaning of test results beyond the simple assignment of a number indicating language proficiency level.

For example, Ms. Oliver can design literacy development activities for Edith that are appropriate for her level. She can see that at level 1, Edith can match nonverbal symbols to words and phrases, label graphics, and write words and phrases.

When planning language and literacy lessons, language arts and literacy teachers can refer to the WIDA Language Proficiency Level and Can Do Descriptors documents appropriate for the English learners in their classrooms. In the Language Arts Protocol section of this chapter, we draw from these resources to develop language arts and literacy instruction for English learners.

With these more specific descriptors of English proficiency, language arts and literacy teachers can better support the listening, speaking, reading, and writing development of their English learners. When learning any subject in English, ELs face a gap between their English proficiency and mainstream classroom language use. For academic subjects instruction, we describe the teacher's goal in addressing this disparity as "narrowing the communication gap." For language arts and literacy, we describe the teacher's goal in addressing the gap as "targeted language instruction," the topic of the next main section, "Targeted Language Arts Instruction for English Learners."

A NOTE ABOUT UNDERSTANDING ENGLISH LEARNERS' PROFICIENCY LEVELS

Although English language proficiency assessments used to satisfy state and federal mandates for English learners can tell you at which level(s) your ELs performed on the last test, we suggest that you also take student language samples when designing new

TABLE 6.3

WIDA Can Do Descriptors PreK–12

	Level 1 Entering	Level 2 Emerging	Level 3 Developing	Level 4 Expanding	Level 5 Bridging	Level 6 Reaching — Language that meets all criteria through Level 5 Bridging
Listening	• Point to stated pictures, words, phrases • Follow one-step oral directions • Match oral statements to objects, figures, or illustrations	• Sort pictures, objects according to oral instructions • Follow two-step oral directions • Match information from oral descriptions to objects, illustrations	• Locate, select, order information from oral descriptions • Follow multistep oral directions • Categorize or sequence oral information using pictures, objects	• Compare/contrast functions, relationships from oral information • Analyze and apply oral information • Identify cause and effect from oral discourse	• Draw conclusions from oral information • Construct models based on oral discourse • Make connections from oral discourse	
Speaking	• Name objects, people, pictures • Answer WH– (who, what, when, where, which) questions	• Ask WH–questions • Describe pictures, events, objects, people • Restate facts	• Formulate hypotheses, make predictions • Describe processes, procedures • Retell stories or events	• Discuss stories, issues, concepts • Give speeches, oral reports • Offer creative solutions to issues, problems	• Engage in debates • Explain phenomena, give examples and justify responses • Express and defend points of view	
Reading	• Match icons and symbols to words, phrases, or environmental print • Identify concepts about print and text features	• Locate and classify information • Identify facts and explicit messages • Select language patterns associated with facts	• Sequence pictures, events, processes • Identify main ideas • Use context clues to determine meaning of words	• Interpret information or data • Find details that support main ideas • Identify word families, figures of speech	• Conduct research to glean information from multiple sources • Draw conclusions from explicit and implicit text	
Writing	• Label objects, pictures, diagrams • Draw in response to a prompt • Produce icons, symbols, words, phrases to convey messages	• Make lists • Produce drawings, phrases, short sentences, notes • Give information requested from oral or written directions	• Produce bare-bones expository or narrative texts • Compare/contrast information • Describe events, people, processes, procedures	• Summarize information from graphics or notes • Edit and revise writing • Create original ideas or detailed responses	• Apply information to new contexts • React to multiple genres and discourses • Author multiple forms/genres of writing	

instruction. You can gather important information about your English learners' proficiency through collecting spoken and written language samples repeatedly throughout the school year. Sitting together and discussing daily routines as well as academic topics with your English learner is a great way to get started, recording the conversation with a smartphone or tablet for later analysis. While listening to the recording, you can take notes on the words and phrases your English learner uses and how well she can understand and contribute to the conversation. If you're feeling ambitious, or if you have a classroom helper, you can even transcribe the conversation so you have an exact, written document of your English learner's speech at a given time in the year. When you examine the transcript, you can compare the student's English to descriptions of English language development, identifying where you think your student is on the oral proficiency (listening and speaking) continuum.

Giving your student recurrent open writing prompts can provide the same type of language samples (without your having to transcribe them), placing her written skills on the writing proficiency continuum. Having these sources of student language can give you a more complete understanding of where she is than a mere categorization from a standardized test. We will show what the combination of these two types of data looks like in practice in chapters 7 through 10.

TARGETED LANGUAGE ARTS INSTRUCTION FOR ENGLISH LEARNERS

Picture an archer at a competition—her left hand gripping the arc of the bow, all four bent fingers of her right hand at eye level, pulling the bowstring taut. Directly ahead of the bow stands a target, perfect concentric circles of red and white. The archer tilts her chin and left hand up slightly, releases the string, and the arrow shoots skyward, its trajectory rising well above the target, and ending far beyond it.

Why would an archer miss the point of her goal, you might wonder? Why wouldn't she attempt a direct hit? Just think how odd it would be to hear her explain, "I was told to aim high. Anything less would not be acceptable." How useful would it be to aim high if this were nowhere near the goal?

So it is with language arts and literacy instruction for English learners. Their proficiency in English listening, speaking, reading, and writing is at a temporary place, a momentarily stable (yet incrementally rising) level of second language development. But just imagine that every time the target is hit, every time instructed second language development occurs, the target moves ahead, getting closer and closer to its ultimate destination—grade-level proficiency in listening, speaking, reading, and writing. Instructed second language development, what we call *targeted language instruction*, is a mark that any language arts teacher of an English learner needs to hit for that learner to progress steadily, promptly, and accurately toward grade-level proficiency in spoken and written English. What if the targeted proficiency for an English learner is way below grade level? Some might say that's aiming too low. However, we believe it serves no purpose to insist that all students should meet grade-level language arts and literacy standards within a given lesson if some of them are still developing basic English proficiency. Setting the target high above English learners' proficiency, just to require the same rigorous standards of all, misses the point. In discussing the English language arts standards of the Common Core State Standards (CCSS), many English language development scholars have pointed to the benefit for English learners because the explicit instruction in the four skill areas, as well as the incorporation of a focus on form, can greatly aid the second language acquisition process, as discussed earlier. Although we agree with this view, we do need to point out that these benefits disappear if the classroom communication involved in curriculum, instruction, and assessment is beyond the English learner's proficiency level.

If, for example, a lesson on embedded phrases (e.g., "the person whose money was stolen") were part of language arts instruction in Edith's mainstream fourth-grade class, Edith could not process it—as a beginning English learner, she produces only single words and chunks in English. As we discussed earlier, Pienemann's research about the internal processing constraints on the acquisition of language features shows that Edith would still need to acquire a number of grammatical forms before she could internalize the complex structure involved in embedding.[34] If she were participating in this fourth-grade language arts lesson, Edith could copy examples of embedded sentences that were being taught in the mainstream class, but exposure to, and even explicit teaching of the grammatical features of embedded phrases, would not prompt immediate acquisition. The grade-level language arts instruction would benefit Edith very little, if at all, because the gap between her proficiency in listening, speaking, reading, writing, and grammar and the demands of grade-level communication is substantial.

If language arts and literacy instruction were designed and offered exclusively for the needs of English learners (for example, a fourth-grade EL like Edith, who is at level 1), it would likely include instruction specific to each of the six language skill levels in the WIDA ELD standards (often offered in multilevel ELD classes). Examining this second language instruction on the preK–12 continuum, a gap exists between the grade-level expectations in language arts and literacy and the instruction that is targeted to the English learner. This fits one defining characteristic of an English learner—assessed English language skills that are below grade level.

Because the purpose of language arts and literacy instruction is to develop language skills in English, instruction must be targeted to the individual's precise level of proficiency in each skill area. This is quite different from the general approximation that suffices in teaching academic subjects, where learning the academic subject is primary and the associated language is secondary. With language arts instruction, learning the language is the point, and given the constructive, incremental nature of second language acquisition and the potential variation in proficiency across the different skill areas (listening, speaking, reading, and writing), teaching aspects of language that are well above the individual level of proficiency is not productive. Rather, accessible language arts instruction meets an English learner just at or beyond his current level of proficiency—targeted language instruction—and moves the target incrementally upward toward the grade-level language standards.

This is illustrated in figure 6.2, with Edith as an example. When Edith entered fourth grade, she was assessed at level 1. As she progresses, on track, to more advanced levels of proficiency, something is holding her back from reaching grade-level expectations. At the same time she's advancing, the language demands are rising by grade level. To enable her to reach the challenging grade-level standards that prepare her for college or career, her teachers need to provide targeted language instruction so she can proceed as swiftly as possible.

As seen in figure 6.2, language arts and literacy teachers have to hold in mind two opposing forces when making decisions about the right degree of challenge for English learners. This is especially true for ELs at the intermediate level, such as Edgar. On one end there are developmental constraints to the student's ability to rise to grade-level language and literacy tasks. On the other end is the urgent need to move the English learner forward and upward on the language development continuum. If the English learner is put in a position where the classroom language instruction is well beyond his current English proficiency, no learning of consequence occurs. Conversely, if the English learner stays at his level, asked only to do what he can do effortlessly, or if his teachers accept language use that doesn't improve in complexity or accuracy, the student may plateau at a level of English that won't reach college and career readiness. That is not acceptable for Edgar, or for any English learner.

FIGURE 6.2

Edith's Current (4th grade) and Projected (through 12th grade) English Proficiency Levels Compared to Grade-Level ELA Instruction

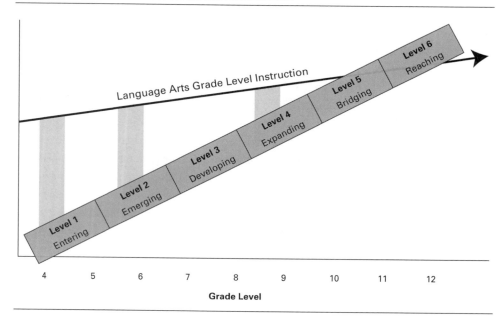

Similarities and Differences Between First and Second Language Arts and Literacy Instruction

Can targeted language instruction for English learners take place together with native speakers? That depends on a number of factors, most important of which is likely grade level. Figure 6.3 shows how the targets for English learners and native speakers could be close together or far apart. In this diagram, first language instruction (noted as L1, the light gray circle) is contrasted with targeted second language instruction (L2, the dark gray circle).

Let's take a closer look at the diagram, starting with the kindergarten side and then moving to the right for twelfth grade. In kindergarten, an advanced English learner would need targeted language arts and literacy instruction that is overwhelmingly similar to grade-level language arts and literacy instruction for native speakers. In this case, it is possible for the specific needs of this hypothetical advanced EL to be met through scaffolding in the same classroom (although some research shows that separate ELD programs for ELs even in early grades leads to greater gains in English oral proficiency).[35] You can see in the diagram that the L2 target, which represents what would occur in instructed second language acquisition (or ELD) for that level of English proficiency, overlaps significantly with grade-level first language arts and literacy instruction (represented by the L1 target). However, at the opposite end of the spectrum in twelfth grade, instruction for beginning-level English learners would have nothing in

FIGURE 6.3

Native Language (L1) English Language Arts Instruction Compared to Second Language (L2) English Language Development Instruction at Kindergarten and Twelfth-Grade Levels

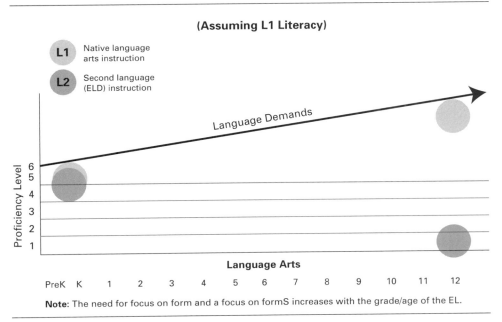

Note: The need for focus on form and a focus on formS increases with the grade/age of the EL.

common with grade-level L1 instruction, illustrated by the wide divide between the L1 and L2 instruction circles.

Why English Language Development Classes Are Important for English Learners

Unlike formal instruction for English learners (which at beginning levels resembles what would be taught in a foreign language class), language arts and literacy classes for native speakers of English typically focus primarily on developing skills in reading and writing. The assumption is that these students already possess oral English skills—they can comprehend spoken language and express themselves through speech. Teachers then help build literacy skills on students' already established oral language. But for English learners, oral language in English may be absent or much less developed due to second language acquisition processes and influences from the students' native languages.

In other words, the progression in the preK–12 language arts and literacy curriculum is based on the norm for native speakers. Grade-level expectations indicate where the average native speaker should be at a certain point in time, given grade-level oral language proficiency upon entering preschool (or kindergarten) and adequate yearly progress in language arts and literacy. English learners, however, can enter preschool with no oral proficiency in English or with less oral proficiency than native speakers. And preschool or kindergarten is not the only point of initial access to school conducted in English. An English learner with no oral proficiency in English may enter school in any grade—kindergarten, fourth, seventh, or tenth.

English learners entering any of these grades may have already developed grade-level literacy in their native languages. Or they may have no literacy whatsoever. Clearly, first language literacy skills help English learners develop literacy skills in English, but their oral language still needs to be developed for them to participate meaningfully in language arts and literacy instruction.[36] And if literacy needs to be developed for the first time in any language, in tandem with developing English oral proficiency, the English learner has a much more challenging course to follow.

Teaching language arts to English learners should be more akin to an instructed second language learning environment through targeting a focus on form (and, where possible and necessary, a focus on formS) to the English learner's proficiency level. When the target can't be reached in the mainstream classroom because of a large gap between grade-level expectations and the English learners' proficiency, then the English learner should be learning language arts with an ELD specialist (similar to a second language acquisition environment for a foreign language). In a synthesis of research on the value of ELD classes for preK–12 English learners, Saunders and colleagues note that there is evidence for continuing this form of instructed second language acquisition from beginning through advanced levels of English proficiency.[37] He also asserts that ELD instruction should be provided daily and be offered by proficiency levels, explicitly teach language structure and form, focus on academic and conversational English, emphasize listening and speaking in addition to reading and writing, balance a focus on meaning and form, provide corrective feedback on form, and include carefully planned interactive activities.

Other than the optimal learning environment of bilingual or dual language programs, instructed second language acquisition that takes place in separate English language development classes taught by ELD specialists is the gold standard for meeting English learners' language arts and literacy instruction needs. But teachers know that optimal environments and gold standards aren't the norm everywhere. What can language arts teachers do if ELD isn't provided at their school or if its scheduling doesn't coincide with their language arts block? When we know we can't give our students what's absolutely best for them, we don't have to be resigned to giving them nothing at all. We do our best with what we have to give our English learners as much as we can. The Language Arts Protocol is a tool to help make this happen.

THE LANGUAGE ARTS PROTOCOL

We've discussed what second language acquisition research and theory tells us that English learners need in language arts and literacy instruction. So how do we provide that instruction in the mainstream classroom? Many teachers might respond, "Scaffolding!" But what does it mean to scaffold language arts and literacy instruction for English learners? And if we do this for one or two ELs in a class filled with native speakers, how do we know if we're reaching them? Does the scaffolding we provide for native speakers hold up for English learners as well?

It's easy to assume that language arts and literacy teaching techniques are universal. Articles in professional journals for ELD specialists often include descriptions of teaching techniques and activities that are quite familiar to any language arts teacher, not just those who teach English as a second language. The steps might be the same, but something major is different. For English learners, it's not *what* you do (the technique or strategy), it's the *way* that you do it (and *why*).

The Language Arts Protocol is a tool to help determine the way and the why of scaffolding language arts and literacy instruction for English learners. It is not designed to plan English language development instruction—ELD specialists know full well how to do that. It is intended, instead, to help mainstream language arts and literacy teachers determine how (and in some cases, *if*) they can address the EL's language and literacy development needs within a lesson intended for native speakers. Real teachers in real schools can use this tool to do the best they can with the circumstances and resources available to them and their students. At schools with lots of English learners and plentiful resources to offer adequate ELD and bilingual instruction, the Language Arts Protocol would guide mainstream language arts teachers right to the ELD and bilingual classes. In schools without these resources, or for the single English learner from a less-common first language background, the mainstream classroom might be the only place he has to go.

LANGUAGE ARTS PROTOCOL

PHASE I: Understanding the Needed Language Skills and the Student

STEP 1: Identifying the Language Skills Needed to Complete the Lesson

- Listening
- Reading
- Speaking
- Writing
- Language conventions

STEP 2: Understanding the Student

- What is the student's proficiency level in listening and reading? (English Proficiency Descriptors)
- What is the student's proficiency level in speaking? (English Proficiency Descriptors)
- What is the student's proficiency level in reading? (English Proficiency Descriptors)
- What is the student's proficiency level in writing? (English Proficiency Descriptors)
- What is the student's proficiency level in using language conventions?

PHASE II: Targeted Language Instruction

STEP 1: Scaffolding Language Arts Instruction

- Can the pitch be adjusted?
- Can the pace be slowed?
- Can the portion be reduced?
- Can the perspective/point be added or changed?

STEP 2: Use of Scaffolding

- Can scaffolding be used for the whole class? (universal)
- Can scaffolding be provided alongside instruction? (supplemental)
- Is a different instructional approach needed for this student? (alternative)

STEP 3: Time and Language Arts Scaffolding Provider

- When should scaffolding be provided?
  - Pre-teach
  - Teach or co-teach
  - Post-teach (follow-up)
- Who should provide the scaffolded instruction?
  - Classroom teacher
  - Bilingual paraprofessional
  - ELD/bilingual specialist
  - Volunteer
  - Technology-based resource

The purpose of the Language Arts Protocol is to help teachers provide targeted language instruction for English learners by (1) identifying the gap between grade-level language arts and literacy instruction and corresponding descriptors of English proficiency for English learners; (2) addressing the gap through four criteria for scaffolding language arts for English learners; and (3) determining if any or all of the necessary scaffolding criteria can be provided as part of grade-level English language arts instruction, either by the classroom teacher alone or with support from other school professionals, or if they can only be provided in a separate ELD venue, based on school resources and collaborators.

Because the available ELD class doesn't always coincide with the EL's language arts block, and because some schools don't have the minimum number of English learners to provide separate ELD instruction, we emphasize providing targeted language instruction through scaffolding in the mainstream classroom, led by the classroom teacher or another school professional or volunteer. For cases where there is no real possibility of doing this (as with Edgar in chapter 10), we show what would be done in the separate ELD class and how the ELD teacher could support Edgar's mainstream teachers.[38]

Now it's time to take a closer look at the steps of the Language Arts Protocol. Summarized visually at the end of the chapter and in appendix B, the protocol is divided into two phases. Following instructional design principles, phase I starts with an analysis of the task, the student, and the gap between them, whereas phase II involves instructional decision making. The box provides an outline of the upcoming section, which describes each part of the protocol.

PHASE I: Understanding the Needed Language Skill and the Student

In phase I you need to consider two things—what language skills are needed to fulfill the tasks of your language arts or literacy lesson and which tasks your ELs are able to complete. The chart presented in figure 6.4 can help organize this comparison.

STEP 1: IDENTIFYING THE LANGUAGE SKILLS NEEDED TO COMPLETE THE LESSON

The first column identifies the language skills as well as any language conventions (grammar points). The second column leaves space for you to describe in what ways your lesson will require all students to understand and use each language skill. When gauging the gap between the English learner's proficiency level and the language demands of the lesson, it helps to begin with a review of the lesson steps *from the perspective of the student*. Once you identify the specific skill use and development requirements of your lesson, you can then compare them to each English learner's proficiency.

STEP 2: UNDERSTANDING THE STUDENT

In the third column you include descriptors for the English learner's proficiency levels in listening, speaking, reading, and writing. We suggest you begin with the WIDA

FIGURE 6.4

Comparison of Language Skills Needed and EL's Proficiency

Language Skill	Lesson Steps (designed for all students)	English Proficiency Descriptors
Listening		
Speaking		
Reading		
Writing		
Language Conventions		

Proficiency Levels and Can Do Descriptors for listening, speaking, reading, and writing because of their clarity and simplicity, but you can use whatever descriptors your school, district, or state has adopted.[39]

Because the analysis of the lesson steps applies to all students, it needs to be completed only once per lesson. However, you will likely need to complete the individual English proficiency descriptors for each English learner in your class. This is because language arts instruction must be targeted not only to five levels, but also to each EL's specific language skill proficiency. In other words, an EL's instruction may need to be targeted to WIDA's listening/reading Can Do Descriptors at the Bridging level, but aimed at the speaking/writing Can Do Descriptors at the Expanding level. Therefore, it is unlikely that all of your ELs fall at the same proficiency levels. To streamline this analysis portion of the Language Arts Protocol, we recommend that you duplicate the list of WIDA Can Do Descriptors (or any other set of descriptors you plan on using) for each student, updating it only when the English learner progresses to the next proficiency level of the listening/reading or speaking/writing skills areas, and paste it next to the lesson steps column for each lesson plan you analyze.[40]

For example, let's look at a lesson in Gero's language arts class. Ms. Levin planned a lesson that expects her kindergarten students to:

1. Listen as the teacher reads a big book—*Brown Bear, Brown Bear* (by Bill Martin and Eric Carle).
2. Match printed words from the story to their pictures in the book.
3. Answer questions about story details, such as "What was the second animal Brown Bear saw?"

Looking at WIDA Language Proficiency and Can Do Descriptors for Gero (level 1), we see he: (1) understands and uses general and everyday single words and chunks of language and (2) can match visual representations to words and phrases. So, after watching and listening to Ms. Levin, Gero can participate in the matching activity. However, the next task, answering story detail questions, is a level 2 descriptor for reading (identify facts and explicit messages) and speaking (restate facts), so we know that Gero will need support. We'll see how Ms. Levin plans to provide it in phase II.

PHASE II: Targeted Language Instruction

We have worked with mainstream language arts and literacy teachers for many years, and one of the biggest areas of confusion we've seen is what is different about teaching English learners, especially since a lot of the same terminology and techniques are used. As we have discussed in this chapter, what we think is most different, or what makes a real difference for English learners, is instructed second language acquisition, or what we refer to as targeted language instruction in the mainstream preK–12 environment. In targeted language instruction, typically offered in ELD classes, teachers design language skill-building activities, facilitate instructional conversations, and focus on grammar at the level of English proficiency of their students. Teachers can provide these types of language development support, or scaffolding, in various settings. We identified qualities of scaffolding that set the instruction of English learners apart from that of native speakers.[41] We termed these qualities of scaffolding for English learners *pitch*, *pace*, *portion*, and *perspective/point*. These qualities are the focus of the next part of the Language Arts Protocol, step 1.

STEP 1: SCAFFOLDING LANGUAGE ARTS INSTRUCTION

The first step in this phase of the Language Arts Protocol presents the four scaffolding criteria for providing targeted language instruction in relation to the grade-level language arts instruction as a way to identify whether scaffolding instruction in the English language arts mainstream classroom (the L1 context) is feasible. Combining our analysis of ELD teachers' language use and instructional practices in targeted language instruction for English learners, we developed the mnemonic device of the *four Ps*, which represent the language arts and literacy scaffolding qualities of **p***itch*, **p***ace*, **p***ortion*, and **p***erspective/* **p***oint*. Let's look at what they represent.

Pitch

Pitch pertains to classroom language use and its complexity, accuracy, and familiarity. In targeted language instruction, the pitch of classroom language is addressed at or just beyond the ELs' level of English proficiency. For example, ELD teachers use the approach to developing composition skills known as process writing, but gear it to their English learners' level of vocabulary and sentence structure. ELD teachers know what their ELs' learner language, or interlanguage, should be at their specific level of English proficiency, so they work with that learner language to strategically correct each student's errors, focusing on those that are typical at the given level. Working with each EL's learner language where it is enables ELD teachers to lead the student through the steps of process writing, but the language they use and the language they expect their students to use will be different.

ELD teachers also adjust their pitch in their presentations and instructional conversations, using "foreigner" or teacher talk that involves careful selection of words, sentence structures, and nonverbal connections to promote comprehension. Similarly, students' oral language reflects their levels of proficiency, and teachers understand and expect corresponding second language developmental patterns.

Let's look at Ms. Levin's *Brown Bear, Brown Bear* reading lesson to see how or if she needs to adjust her pitch to Gero's level.[42] Fortunately, the pitch of the language doesn't need much adjustment for Gero, as the text is repetitive and uses simple words and formulaic phrasing, and it provides accessible (comprehensible) input through nonverbal support (pictures, gestures, facial expressions, and so on). On the other hand, if Ms. Levin led her students in reciting the nursery rhyme "The Old Lady Who Swallowed a Fly," expecting them to participate in a faster and faster call and response, the pitch of the language would be too advanced for Gero to comprehend or produce.

Pace

Pace refers to the rate of instructional practice, which is dependent on language. In targeted language instruction, the rate of instruction is slower, with more comprehension checks, expansion, and elaboration. For example, in a directed reading lesson, the teacher would rephrase and extend much of the language presented in the text or produced by the students, asking questions to ensure comprehension was achieved. Because English learners often need more time to phrase an answer in their second language, wait time can be longer than for native speakers. There is also more interaction around language, with instructional conversations between teacher and student, using language pitched to their levels and frequent expanding and rephrasing of the EL's learner language. More interaction between students, with opportunities for negotiating meaning, is an important part of targeted language instruction for English learners.

Ms. Levin's lesson allows for a slowing of pace to check Gero's comprehension without slowing it too much for her native speakers. She uses leveled questions to enable him to respond successfully. Even though other children might be asked details that Gero can't yet comprehend or express in English, Ms. Levin focuses on what Gero *can* do. Instead of asking, "What animal was looking at the redbird?" Ms. Levin asks him to point to the redbird in a group of pictures of the book's characters. She keeps Gero engaged by checking his comprehension frequently, allowing him to respond both verbally and nonverbally.

Portion

Portion is the amount of spoken or written content in a lesson. In targeted language instruction, reading materials and other media beyond (even well beyond) the English

learner's proficiency level are used, but the amount of content is reduced, enabling unpacking for issues relevant to each English learner at his or her level of proficiency. For
example, ELD teachers often use a listening activity with a brief audio or video file and
go through it sentence by sentence, even word by word, to clarify meaning. Extracting a
smaller portion from an "authentic source" rather than one designed for a specific level
of second language proficiency is a technique that has been used successfully in English
language development classes.

In Ms. Levin's lesson, the repetitive nature of the *Brown Bear* storybook keeps
its content from being overwhelming to Gero. It is a short story, with little variation
in wording from page to page. This gives Gero a manageable amount of language to
take in.

Perspective/Point

Issues of focus for English learners, or the points of instruction, often differ from what
would be emphasized with native speakers. For example, targeted language instruction often includes a presentation of first and second language form or structure contrasts and similarities, using the students' first language as a resource but also pointing
out when miscommunication or errors can occur in English because of language differences.[43] Another illustration of difference in perspective or point is when the class tells
a story based on a shared experience and the teacher records it on chart paper. With native speakers, it is common for the teacher to write what they say and to focus on the
spelling and composition of the dictated passage, primarily to help develop emergent
reading and writing skills. For example, "Yesterday we went on a field trip to the science
museum. We saw the planets in the planetarium." In contrast, English learners can benefit from a literal transcription of their speech for teacher-led reflection on the grammatical accuracy of the sentences, with the teacher writing them as spoken but then
correcting them together with the class. They might dictate, "Yesterday, we go to field
trip at science museum. We see the planet in planetarium." Using these written sentences, the teacher would begin by asking, "Yesterday, we GO, is that correct?" leading
the children to reflect on the verb and its tense. The issues of perspective/point that are
generally different for English learners tend to address *meaning* (extra support for infrequent or unusual terms, such as idioms, needs to be provided), *language form and structure*
(a focus on form or forms that are appropriate for the English learner's level can clarify
meaning or help develop accuracy of expression), and *cultural background knowledge* (English learners often lack background knowledge related to culture, such as references to
baseball or American history).

Gero could use a little extra language support for this lesson, so Ms. Levin stresses
and points out the *do* when saying, "What *do* you see?" She could even extend that a bit
for Gero, changing it to, "What do you hear?" or "What do you like?" to help him acquire the sentence structure for "What do you _____?" It will be a little while before Gero will acquire the form *do*, so making its use apparent and frequent in stories
and instructional conversations should help that process. The vocabulary in the book
is frequently used, the subjects and actions of the book are represented in pictures that

closely correspond to the text, and the simple story requires no special cultural background knowledge to comprehend.

The examples of Ms. Levin's lesson show how the four Ps can be adapted in whole-class instruction, and how mainstream language arts and literacy teachers can attune the four Ps of targeted language instruction to each English learner's proficiency level during an individualized process of scaffolding referred to as collaborative dialogue and instructional conversations.[44] When working one-on-one with an English learner, or with pairs or small groups of ELs at the same levels of English proficiency, teachers can carefully lead the conversation by prompting students to respond to questions and tasks that are appropriate for their English proficiency. They can extract a short segment of text or audiovisual media to unpack. They can also teach a mini grammar lesson on a point of relevance that is learnable at the students' current proficiency level.[45]

At other grade levels, English learners in mainstream classrooms may not be afforded instruction that includes these qualities of scaffolding during teacher-led classroom communication. Obviously, for the teacher to present new information using instructional or "foreigner talk" and reading materials whose pitch is geared to the proficiency of a beginning English learner would not be ideal for the native speakers in upper grades. Likewise, a pace and portion of instruction adjusted for the English learners would be too slow and cover too little for native speakers. And the entire perspective/point of a lesson for English learners could be completely different from what native speakers need. To help determine how scaffolding can be provided under these circumstances, we move to step 2.

STEP 2: USE OF SCAFFOLDING

As with the Academic Subjects Protocol, step 2 involves assessing the type of support needed (which of the four Ps you need to adjust for English learners) and whether that scaffolding can be provided for all students (universal), can be applied as a supplement, or should be an alternative to the mainstream English language arts instruction.

In Gero's case, much of the scaffolding he needs is universal, such as the general pitch of the language in the lesson, while some is supplemental, such as the instructional conversations Ms. Levin has with Gero individually.

STEP 3: TIME AND LANGUAGE ARTS SCAFFOLDING PROVIDER

The timing of targeted language arts instruction will likely be affected by available personnel and resources. The people best suited and available to scaffold instruction are to a large extent dictated by the resources at your school, the EL program model used, and the degree of collaboration that instructional and other school professionals practice. We designed the Language Arts Protocol to be used in collaboration, wherever possible.

A Note About Using Technology for Scaffolding

Technology can be a great way to provide the specific scaffolding that English learners need. Tools such as grammar apps and online tutorials, and practices such as creating and sharing podcasts and videos, allow for individualization that can provide any of the four Ps that would not be feasible to provide otherwise. For instance, Gero might benefit from using an iPad or other electronic tablet to develop basic concepts of print, decoding, and word identification skills. Gero, Edith, Edgar, and Tasir can use iPads to listen to stories through e-books, thus seeing the print being read, which can improve their word recognition as well as reading fluency skills. They can also monitor and improve their reading fluency by listening to themselves reading, by using the voice-over function to record themselves reading a book and then replaying their recording. Recent research has shown that tablets have the potential to reduce many social and behavioral barriers by providing tools and applications that allow students with and without learning difficulties to communicate and learn.[46] Adolescent English learners like Tasir and Edgar who are developing reading skills in English might benefit from text-to-speech software that enables them to simultaneously read and listen to any kind of digital or scanned printed material, as well as provides a host of online reference and study tools, such as online bilingual dictionaries, to strengthen listening, speaking, reading, writing skills. Finally, students with advanced oral proficiency in social language but below grade-level proficiency in academic language and literacy, like Tasir, can benefit from Web-based instruction aimed at enhancing new literacy skills and strategies such as asking questions, locating and synthesizing information, and communicating information to others.

Don't worry if the Language Arts Protocol is still a bit abstract at this point. Take a look at the infographic of the protocol on the next page (for easy reference, it also appears as appendix B), and know that as you read chapters 7 through 10, the protocol's specifics will become more concrete. Each chapter shows samples of and more details about each of our four English learners' developing listening, speaking, reading, and writing skills in English. We will also discuss research and theory on second language acquisition issues related to each English learner's language development and the grade level he or she is placed in. And on the very practical side of the upcoming chapters, we will show four different language arts and literacy lessons and how we used the Language Arts Protocol to provide targeted language instruction for Gero, Edith, Tasir, and Edgar. Once you get to the conclusion, you'll see what targeted language instruction for English learners looks, sounds, and feels like.

LANGUAGE ARTS PROTOCOL

PHASE I
UNDERSTANDING the Needed Language Skills and the Student

Language Skill	Lesson Steps (designed for all students)	English Proficiency Descriptors
Listening		
Speaking		
Reading		
Writing		
Language Conventions		

PHASE II
TARGETED Language Instruction

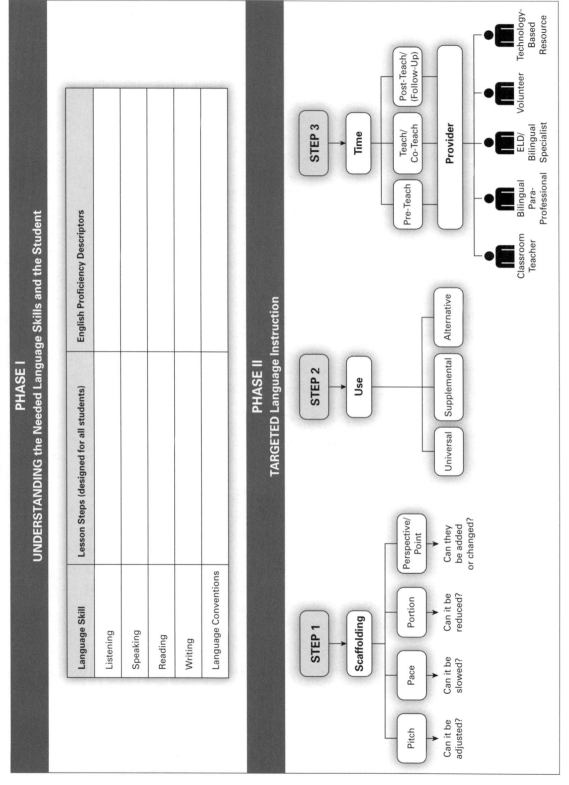

STEP 1

Scaffolding

- Pitch — Can it be adjusted?
- Pace — Can it be slowed?
- Portion — Can it be reduced?
- Perspective/Point — Can they be added or changed?

STEP 2

Use

- Universal
- Supplemental
- Alternative

STEP 3

Time

- Pre-Teach
- Teach/Co-Teach
- Post-Teach (Follow-Up)

Provider

- Classroom Teacher
- Bilingual Para-Professional
- ELD/Bilingual Specialist
- Volunteer
- Technology-Based Resource

STOP AND REFLECT QUESTIONS

1. It is grammatically incorrect to say, "between you and I." Why does this rule exist? Test yourself: without consulting a grammar book, list at least five rules of English grammar. How many were you able to identify? How comfortable do you feel with your knowledge of English grammar?

2. What activities do you use to support the native language of the English learners in your class?

3. How important are listening activities in second language acquisition? What specific role do they play in assisting learners to acquire a language?

4. Review WIDA's Language Proficiency Continuum http://wida.us/standards/eld.aspx (table 6.2). Identify where your EL would be placed on this continuum. How can you help your learner progress to the next level?

5. How would you describe the development of your ELs' writing skills? How are they demonstrating progress?

6. If two languages are similar in structure, would it be easier or harder for a speaker of one of the languages to acquire the other language? Explain your answer based on the information provided in this chapter.

GO AND PRACTICE ACTIVITIES

1. Devote a class session to listening and recording verbal interactions among your ELs. You should record interactions between ELs and/or between ELs and native speakers of English. Analyze the interactions. How are your ELs demonstrating progress toward obtaining oral academic language proficiency?

2. In this chapter, we discussed the ability of native speakers to develop an ear for what "sounds" right in their language. Organize activities to help English learners develop the ability to hear correct forms of the English language while acquiring the structure of the language. How can you assess whether or not they have acquired this ability?

3. Develop a plan to sequence the teaching of affixes to your ELs. Review your list. Is your sequence for affixes in line with current research on this topic? Review at least three research-based articles on the teaching of morphological development of English learners.

4. Share with another teacher or student any new insights you have gained on second language literacy acquisition from observing an English learner. Clearly describe the ways in which the learner demonstrated progress toward increased reading comprehension skills.

CHAPTER 7

Teaching Gero to Write About "My Favorite Pet"

Language and Literacy in the Primary Grades

"Krik!" exclaimed Grand-mère, the burst of the final *k* shaping her smile. "Krak!" replied Gero, ever ready for the call to respond. *[In Kreyòl]* "Grand-mother, tell us another story about Bouki and Malice!" Grand-mère continued *[In Kreyòl]*, "One day, Malice . . . " Grand-mère spoke slowly, pausing at dramatic turns. Her voice, throaty for Malice and creaky for Bouki, carried clear into the living room, where Gero's mother and father had sought quiet to read. Gero, along with his brothers and sister, stayed at the table, sweet-talking Grand-mère into one more tale of the notorious characters' antics.

Every evening Gero and his family sat snug around the dinner table, nimbly moving from French to Haitian Kreyòl and back.[1] As they ate, Papa singled out the children, round-robin style, until everyone answered each of his daily questions. *[In French]* "Gero, what was your favorite part of school today?" Gero loved telling about Ms. Levin's storybooks and bulletin boards. *[In Kreyòl]* "I learned about *kayiman*. In English it's al-li-ga-tor." Mama clapped her hands together and said, *[in French]* "Gero, it's alligator in French, too! So you know how to say alligator in three languages!" Gero turned toward his older brother, who nodded in agreement. *[In French]* "Ms. Levin will be so happy when I tell her all the ways I can say alligator!"

Before Gero began kindergarten, his first school had been their home, filled with picture and chapter books and weighty discussions, in both Haitian Kreyòl and French. Outside of school, Gero continues to converse with adults and is building emergent literacy and conversational skills in his home languages. At school, Ms. Levin knows the importance of using these skills in developing Gero's literacy in English, and she is quickly learning how to teach to his unique language and literacy needs.

GRADE-LEVEL EXPECTATIONS FOR LANGUAGE AND LITERACY IN KINDERGARTEN

Ms. Levin's class has implemented the Common Core State Standards (CCSS), which means that by the end of kindergarten, her students are expected to meet the new rigorous English language arts standards. The following sections outline the language demands these expectations establish for reading, writing, speaking, listening, and language and also summarize their degree of accessibility for Gero.

Reading

In developing specific skills for reading, kindergartners are taught how to follow words on a page, name all upper- and lowercase letters of the English alphabet, identify syllables in spoken words, isolate and substitute sounds in one-syllable words, and read high-frequency words such as *the*. As they develop the broader skills involved in comprehending texts, kindergartners are taught how to identify details, main topics, and major events; connect illustrations and the text they correspond to; identify book components such as the cover, author, and illustrator; and read grade-level texts with purpose and understanding.

The following passage gives a sense of grade-level text for kindergarten:[2]

I went to a pet store. I saw big dogs. I saw little dogs. I saw dogs with long hair. I saw dogs with short hair. I got a little dog.

Writing

In the related area of writing, kindergartners can draw, dictate, or write their opinion on a book topic or a series of events. The language category includes many skills that are necessary for writing (rather than drawing or dictating), such as printing upper- and lowercase letters, capitalizing the first word in a sentence, knowing letters for most consonant and short vowel sounds, and spelling simple words phonetically.

Speaking, Listening, and Language

Speaking and listening are part of all language use, so kindergartners are taught to converse about grade-level topics and texts, confirm comprehension of others' speech, and describe people, places, things, feelings, and thoughts. Similar to the speaking and listening standards, language standards apply to all other language skills. This involves using frequent nouns and verbs, adding -*s* or -*es* to make spoken words plural, using prepositions, and expressing thoughts in full sentences.

This brief overview summarizes the general expectations in language and literacy for kindergarten students who are native speakers of English. It is also important to understand which parts of these grade-level expectations an English learner at Gero's level of proficiency can reach—the topic of the next section.

LEVEL 1 ENGLISH LEARNERS' LANGUAGE AND LITERACY IN KINDERGARTEN

The following English Language Proficiency (ELP) standards, established by the Council of Chief State School Officers, represent the forms and functions ELs in kindergarten know and can perform in English by the end of level 1 of English proficiency, Gero's current level.[3] They were developed to show English learners' effective language use during their progress toward expected language proficiency targets in grade-level curriculum, instruction, and assessment.

Gero's teacher can refer to these standards to better understand where the gap is between his English proficiency and the CCSS language arts and literacy standards that his class is expected to meet by year's end. Comparing them to the CCSS standards can highlight where extra support and time may be required in instruction and assessment.

Language Forms

After attaining level 1 language proficiency, the English learner will be able to demonstrate the knowledge, skill, or ability described in the standard, using gestures, a few frequently occurring words, simple phrases, and formulaic expressions.

Language Functions

The following language function descriptors begin with a CCSS grade-level standard, followed by its adaptation for English learners at level 1 of English proficiency (the *italicized* descriptor after the colon).

A level 1 English learner in kindergarten can:

- determine the meaning of words and phrases in oral presentations and literary and informational text: *with prompting and support, recognize the meaning of a few frequently occurring words in simple oral presentations and read-alouds about familiar topics, experiences, or events, using context and visual aids (including picture dictionaries).*
- extract evidence from grade-appropriate oral presentations and literary and informational texts through close listening or reading: *with prompting and support, identify a few key words in read-alouds and oral presentations (information or stories presented orally).*
- speak and write about grade-appropriate complex literary and informational texts and topics: *communicate simple information or feelings about familiar topics or experiences, using a combination of a few words, gestures, and labeled pictures or other visual aids.*
- construct a grade-appropriate oral or written claim and support it with reasoning and evidence: *express a feeling or opinion about a familiar topic, using a few frequently occurring words and drawings, illustrations, or other visual aids.*
- participate in grade-appropriate oral and written exchanges of information, ideas, and analyses, responding to peer, audience, or reader comments and questions: *participate in short conversations about familiar topics and respond to simple yes/no questions.*

- research and/or obtain, evaluate, and communicate grade-appropriate oral and written information in a clear and effective response to a defined task and purpose: *with guidance and support from adults, recall information from experience or from a provided source, and label information using a few frequently occurring words and drawings or illustrations.*
- use grade-appropriate standard English forms to communicate in speech and writing: *recognize and use a small number of frequently occurring nouns and verbs, and understand and respond to question words.*

The description for language form shows that Gero, as a level 1 English learner, is moving toward expressing himself in English with a few frequently occurring words, simple phrases, and formulaic expressions. Since he is not yet at the upper end of level 1 proficiency, he still uses a lot of nonverbal communication as well as his two home languages, Haitian Kreyòl and French, to express himself.

A quick look at the CCSS English language arts standards for kindergarten indicates a number of outcomes that Gero's English proficiency, as described by the ELP language functions above, may preclude him from reaching by year's end. For example, if he is expected to retell stories, describe relationships between two text elements, compare and contrast experiences of characters in a story, and do so in complete sentences, then his developing ability to form words correctly and put them together in complex sentences in English may not enable him to meet the mark. Ms. Levin needs to keep Gero's developmental pathway in mind when designing daily lessons and tasks. The ELP standards reflect the general route English learners commonly follow toward the end goal of grade-level mastery in language arts and literacy. By aiming toward the spirit of the year-end CCSS standard—for example by recognizing that full sentences may not be the only way an English learner can retell, describe, and compare and contrast—Ms. Levin can keep Gero moving in the right direction as his English proficiency catches up with grade-level instruction and standards.

On the other hand, a number of CCSS outcomes do not depend on the progression of Gero's interlanguage (the merging of his first language and English) toward native-speaker proficiency. For example, Gero can certainly be expected to print upper- and lowercase letters, which would not depend on his developing capacity to understand and produce complex, novel sentences in English. He could also learn to capitalize the first word in a sentence, even if he didn't fully understand the meaning of the sentence. Likewise, he could recognize and name end punctuation. The application section of this chapter presents a lesson showing the precise types of scaffolding necessary to target instruction to Gero's English proficiency level.

RESEARCH ON TEACHING LANGUAGE AND LITERACY TO ENGLISH LEARNERS IN PRIMARY GRADES

Some children arrive in kindergarten with the crucial set of skills needed to begin reading. Other children may not have been taught those skills in preschool or at home.

Children who routinely observe literary practices at home, such as parents reading the newspaper, leaving notes on the refrigerator door, and making grocery lists, have already become socialized into literacy. Those who haven't developed these understandings of literacy need to be taught them. Research has shown, however, that with English learners, the teaching of foundational literacy skills, while necessary, is insufficient because oral language proficiency influences the ability to learn to read and write.[4] This finding is important for two reasons. First, learning to read in a second language depends on having good oral language proficiency in that language, a key point that will be discussed in the following section. Second, it echoes a crucial disclosure contained in the National Literacy Panel Report,[5] which asserts that research available on acquiring literacy in English as a second language is quite limited in comparison to the vast research available on learning to read in English as a first language.[6] These findings suggest that when teachers read about best practices in teaching literacy skills, they should not assume that the same practices work equally well or should be implemented in the same way for ELs. However, research does indicate that primary-grade EL and non-EL students typically perform at similar levels on measures of basic reading skills such as processing sounds, word reading, and spelling.[7] As will be discussed in more depth in chapter 8, the greatest differences in English learners' reading performance pertain to reading comprehension.

Of the research conducted with English learners, the vast majority of studies have been conducted with Spanish-speaking children in the primary grades, with few studies representing upper elementary grades. Nonetheless, research findings from these cross-language studies have provided valuable insights about the factors that influence language and literacy development across languages. Given these caveats, there are key findings from the National Literacy Panel that can help guide teachers of English learners in primary grades:

- Instruction in the five areas described by the National Reading Panel—phonemic awareness, phonics, fluency, vocabulary, and text comprehension—benefits English learners.[8]
- Instruction in oral proficiency for English learners is critical for their acquisition of literacy skills.
- Oral proficiency and literacy in the native language can facilitate literacy development in the second language.
- Individual differences such as general language competence, age, cognitive abilities, previous learning, and similarities between the native language and English greatly affect English literacy development.
- Home language experience can positively affect literacy development.

Oral Proficiency in English

One accommodation that research has found effective for expanding literacy in ELs is developing oral proficiency in the "context of literacy instruction."[9] Children whose oral language is limited in their second language, and whose literacy in any language is emergent, lack the ability to self-monitor and self-teach because they may not comprehend the meaning of words they decode.[10] Catherine Snow explains that learning to read (for the first time) in a second language is different from learning to read a second language (after learning to read in at least one other language) and suggests that more research is needed to illuminate the different processes involved. Snow agrees with other researchers that "language and literacy skills in either the first or second language have a transactional relationship with one another: The development of each depends on and contributes to the other."[11]

Transfer of Basic Literacy Skills and Strategies from the First Language

There is a general consensus among researchers that once a learner has acquired a given level of phonemic awareness in one language, it is possible to transfer that understanding to any other language. Research has shown, for instance, that in kindergarten and first grade, students' ability to isolate initial sounds in their first language significantly predicted their ability to do the same in the second language.[12] Children learning languages whose spelling systems have close and consistent sound/symbol correspondences (called transparent orthographies), such as Spanish, Greek, Finnish, German, Italian, and Haitian Kreyòl, rapidly acquire phonemic awareness. On the other hand, children learning nontransparent orthographies, where the same sound can be represented by many different symbols and spelling patterns, such as English, Danish, and French, are slower in acquiring phonemic awareness. [13]

Other literacy skills and strategies transfer from first to second language reading and writing. The greater the similarity in the writing systems of the two languages, the

FIGURE 7.1

Transactional Relationship of L2 Literacy Development

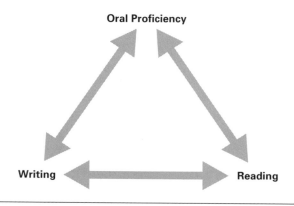

Oral Proficiency

Writing ⟷ Reading

greater the degree of transfer, thus reducing the time and difficulties involved in learning to read the second language.[14] Through our experiences as teacher educators, we have concluded that the more teachers are aware of the students' underlying interlanguage as well as the common contrasts between students' first and second languages, the better prepared they are to address their language and literacy needs.

In Gero's case, it would help Ms. Levin to be aware of contrasts between Haitian Kreyòl, French, and English.[15] For example, in Haitian Kreyòl, nouns are not feminine or masculine, as they are in French. In French, *le livre* (*the book*) is masculine, but in Haitian Kreyòl, *liv la* is gender neutral. In English and French, nouns carry an -*s* to demonstrate plurality. In contrast, Kreyòl uses *yo*; for example, *the books* would be *liv yo*. Furthermore, in English, both the definite (i.e., *the*) and indefinite (i.e., *a/an*) articles precede the noun. In Kreyòl the indefinite article precedes the noun and definite articles follow the noun.[16] These are but a few contrasts that could affect Gero's understanding and use of English.

◆ CLASSROOM APPLICATION ◆

My favorite anim an a ligator. It HA sHrp tetH ta Lev In tagwater.

"Do you like alligators, Gero?" asked Ms. Levin. Gero smiled as he looked down at the ruled paper, the tops of his scribbled letters just clearing the bold lines that alternated with the dotted ones. "Look at that word, *favorite*. You copied it perfectly, and you wrote the letters so neatly." Gero looked up for a second. Ms. Levin bent down next to him. "Favorite means the one you like the most. My favorite animal is a rabbit. A bunny rabbit," Ms. Levin made bunny ears with her index and middle finger, hopping back and forth across the table.

"Let's look at the word you wrote after *favorite*. I see A-N-I-M, and that sounds like *an-im*, but there is something missing at the end. How do we say that word, Gero?" She waited, and waited some more. "Gero, finish this word, *an-im*. . ." "ahl! ah-nee-máhl!" Gero exclaimed. "An-i-mal, right, animal!" confirmed Ms. Levin. "So, how do we write the whole word? How do we write the missing letters? A-N-I-M-*uhl*. Can you write the letters for the sound *uhl*?" She pointed to the chart paper on the whiteboard, and read its first two sentences, "My favorite animal is an alligator. It has sharp teeth and lives in the water." Ms. Levin pointed to a poster behind them, an alligator lounging on a riverbank. Gripping the number 2 pencil with his thumb and all four fingers, Gero wrote *al* to the right of the letter *m*.

ANALYZING GERO'S CLASSROOM LANGUAGE SAMPLES

Gero is working hard to print. Although some of the letters are the wrong case and are not written neatly on the lines, he is doing very well. In Haiti, students are not taught to print. It is believed that very young children begin to write by drawing scribbling lines and round shapes with one consistent line. Therefore, Haitian educators see no need to break up this skill by introducing print during the early grades and then reintroducing cursive after the primary grades. Haitian students begin to use cursive writing as soon as they enter school, even as prekindergarten students, and by the fourth or fifth grade they have perfect penmanship. Knowing that printing is very new to Gero, Ms. Levin plans to provide him with many opportunities to practice.

Gero is using inventive spelling to spell the words unfamiliar to him. He is also using his understanding of the sound system of the English language, an indication of his developing phonemic awareness in English. Since Haitian Kreyòl enjoys a one-to-one sound-to-letter correspondence, Gero is also transferring his limited knowledge of spelling of Haitian Kreyòl to writing in English. Gero knows that words are written left to right, he has a general idea of word boundaries, and he knows some sight words in English. Ms. Levin is ready and willing to provide him with the support he needs to assure success in writing.

One aim of early writing is to develop the ability to form the letters and order them properly. For example, by copying sentences, Gero is learning and practicing writing letters, words, and words in a sentence. A second aim of early writing is to list, restate, or paraphrase information rather than express original thoughts. These two goals are not considered composition. In Gero's writing sample above, his only original contribution to the writing is selecting the animal in the first sentence; he copies the second sentence, which describes a physical feature and habitat of the animal.[17]

Gero is progressing well in all language arts and literacy skills, having been assessed at level 1 a few weeks earlier by the district ELD testing supervisor. Ms. Levin took Gero's test data into account, along with her observations of his performance in class, her spoken interactions with him, an informal reading assessment she conducted, and samples of his writings in and out of class. These various types of data have informed her approach to scaffolding instruction so that it is targeted to Gero's needs at his current level of English proficiency.

Ms. Levin's Writing Lesson

Ms. Levin likes to introduce writing to her kindergartners by getting them to put their thoughts on paper first; she then helps them make their text better by modeling how to improve their spelling through the same phonic skills the children have been using to decode text when reading. She often uses shared writing experiences to accomplish this. Therefore, while she makes sure to include teaching language conventions, she anchors much of her instruction at this point in the school year in two Common Core English Language Arts Standards for kindergarten writing:[18]

Literacy Standards:

CCSS.ELA-LITERACY.W.K.2: Use a combination of drawing, dictating, and writing to compose informative/explanatory texts in which they name what they are writing about and supply some information about the topic.

CCSS.ELA-LITERACY.W.K.5: With guidance and support from adults, respond to questions and suggestions from peers and add details to strengthen writing as needed.

OBJECTIVE

Ms. Levin's objective for this lesson is for students to explain through descriptive writing why their chosen animal should become the class pet.

LESSON DESCRIPTION

Ms. Levin plans to meet her lesson objective through the following tasks:

1. Display the books on animals the class has been reading, then ask the students to share with their shoulder partners what they remember about these animals.
2. While students report out from their pair discussion, list the animals mentioned on the whiteboard (leave room for a second column).
3. Pick an animal and elicit from the students how they would describe it (e.g., furry, soft, cute). Add a column labeled *adjectives* next to the list of animals, and write down these words.
4. Assign specific animals to pairs of students, who must then come up with at least four new adjectives that describe them.
5. As students report back to the entire group, write the adjectives in the column on the whiteboard.
6. Explain the writing prompt (What animal the class should get as the class pet, and why) and reveal the sentence frame "A/An [animal] because it is _____." Point to an animal and an adjective, and ask students to say the completed sentence frame out loud, writing as they say the sentence. Remind students to use the lists of animals and adjectives both for ideas and for spelling. Allow ten minutes for writing a draft, then give five minutes for drawing a picture that represents their text.
7. Give students an opportunity to tell a partner what they wrote, without reading the draft. Collect the papers.
8. The next day, discuss editing by using a previous year's first draft. Model how the writing can be improved through adding more adjectives (expand the sentence frame to "A/An [animal] because it is _____ and _____") and by checking for spelling mistakes (encourage students to say each word out loud as they re-read their text).
9. Pairs of students conduct conferences in which they read each other's opinions and make suggestions for editing.

EVALUATION

As with most assignments, Ms. Levin uses this "My favorite animal" drawing and writing sample as a formative assessment that informs her future instruction.

APPLYING THE LANGUAGE ARTS PROTOCOL
to the Writing Lesson

Scaffolding language arts and literacy education for Gero requires a clear understanding of his precise English proficiency level in relationship to each task required of him in curriculum, instruction, and assessment. The Language Arts Protocol leads language arts teachers through a series of analyses and decisions to mediate the gap between successful participation in grade-level language arts and literacy activities and an individual English learner's current ability to listen, speak, read, and write in English. The protocol is intended for use with daily lesson or unit plans and offers an in-depth look at exactly what scaffolding is needed and how it can be done given the resources and personnel available at the school.

PHASE I: Understanding the Needed Language Skills and Gero

The first column in table 7.1 identifies the specific language domains for language arts and literacy instruction. In the second column, Ms. Levin broke down each step of the lesson, noting how all students are expected to use listening, speaking, reading, writing, and knowledge of language conventions to participate successfully. The third column includes descriptors of the EL's English proficiency level, in this case filled out for Gero. Based on his current proficiency level, it indicates that, other than being able to follow one- or two-step commands, he is very much limited to recognizing and producing familiar words and phrases.[19]

When Ms. Levin looks at the selected CCSS and lesson objective, she knows that a "combination of drawing, dictating, and writing to compose informative/expository texts" aligns with what an English learner at level 1 of English proficiency can do. However, once she compares the language demands of the lesson tasks (column 2) to the English proficiency descriptors (column 3), Ms. Levin starts to notice gaps she will need to consider when adapting the instruction for Gero.

Ms. Levin realizes that when she makes a connection from oral to written language (which she does for all students), her transcription of what Gero dictates will be different from what his native English-speaking peers produce. For native speakers, the main issue in this writing lesson is making a connection from oral to written language, but they are able to form complete sentences in English. Gero, on the other hand, will require additional scaffolding before he can dictate his thoughts in English. For example, he will need prompting to come up with adjectives that describe his chosen pet because most of the adjectives offered by his peers will be unknown vocabulary for Gero. Ms. Levin will also have to pay close attention to Gero's syntax as he formulates his

TABLE 7.1

Language Demands and EL Proficiency Analysis for Writing Lesson

Language Skill[1]	Lesson Steps (designed for all students)	English Proficiency Descriptors[2]
Listening	• Listen to directions on tasks. • Listen to partner's choice and description of the animal.	• Follow one- or two-step commands. • Recognize a few frequently used or recently understood new words.
Reading	• Complete the reading required to copy correctly (see writing row below).	• Recognize a few frequently used words.
Speaking	• Discuss with shoulder partner and report out to class.	• Produce simple two- or three-word phrase responses on familiar topics (e.g., I like dog, dog cute).
Writing	• Complete sentence frame on whiteboard with chosen nouns and adjectives. • Expand original text.	• Express an opinion in simple phrases while heavily relying on displayed words/phrases.
Language Conventions	• Correct spelling mistakes.	N/A

1. We acknowledge that these skills do not always occur separately, but for ease of outlining this lesson, we list them individually.

2. For the sample lessons showing the application of the Language Arts Protocol in chapters 7–10 , we adapted and augmented the appropriate WIDA Can Do Descriptors and state English language proficiency standards. We recommend that language arts teachers check with their ELD specialists to obtain the appropriate descriptors for their location. The WIDA Can Do Descriptors can be downloaded at http://www.wida.us/standards/CAN_DOs/.

sentences. Another consideration is that he will not be able to provide suggestions for improving the writing of a peer, again due to his low oral proficiency in English, but he can listen to the other descriptions and share his own.

PHASE II: Targeted Language Arts Instruction for Gero

This section shows how Ms. Levin plans to provide Gero with the scaffolding he needs to successfully complete the writing lesson and to move forward in his English language and literacy development.

STEP 1: SCAFFOLDING LANGUAGE ARTS INSTRUCTION

The distance between the CCSS English language arts standards and Gero's English proficiency is small enough that Ms. Levin should be able to scaffold her instruction through the four Ps without need of separate ELD instruction.

STEP 1

Scaffolding

PITCH. As explained in chapter 6, pitch involves the complexity, accuracy, and familiarity of the language used or studied in a lesson. Generally speaking, the language kindergarten teachers use with native English-speaking students is similar in the simplicity of the word choices, grammar structures, and discourse features to what is appropriate for English learners at level 1 of language proficiency. Therefore, Ms. Levin does not need to adjust her own language in making her lesson comprehensible to Gero.

PACE. Pace involves both the teaching and the learning process. Because of Gero's low proficiency level, more instructional conversations between teacher and student are needed. Ms. Levin needs to include more comprehension checks with Gero during the whole-class portions of the lesson to make sure he stays engaged. She also needs to use frequent repetition when she works with him. In addition, because Gero has to mentally translate many of the words he dictates to her, she needs to allow greater wait time after questioning.

PORTION. Portion is connected to the teaching and learning process represented by pace, but it centers around the amount of language input given and output expected for English learners. Ms. Levin only needs to make a small portion adjustment for language input because her lesson does not require students to read or listen to long passages. She is aware that because Gero is a level 1 English learner, he cannot yet produce sentences as long as those of native speakers when he spontaneously dictates his thoughts. In other words, she does not expect the same amount and complexity of output.

PERSPECTIVE/POINT. Perspective involves the specific knowledge and skills that need to be taught to English learners that native speakers would already know explicitly (for example, the meaning of a spoken word or phrase or cultural background knowledge, such as how many bases there are in baseball) or implicitly (for example, the order of multiple adjectives, as in a *big, red balloon*). Although Gero's background knowledge would not include the notion of a classroom pet, Ms. Levin doesn't need to teach the concept. Explaining how some classrooms in the United States have class pets wouldn't help Gero write his opinion of a good pet and support this opinion with details. Understanding that he has to write about a pet is information enough.

Knowing that joining two sentences is a difficult task for a level 1 English learner, Ms. Levin spent a little extra time on explicitly teaching *because* and helping Gero combine the first two sentences. She gave examples of well-formed sentences using *because* and then removed certain words to allow Gero to supply a word or short phases to complete them. In attending to meaning, Ms. Levin focused on providing contextualized examples, so once Gero had told her that a kitten was his favorite class pet, she showed pictures of a kitten to provide nonverbal cues to point to when eliciting his description of the cat's qualities as a class pet.

STEP 2: USE OF SCAFFOLDING

Because the targeted instruction and assessment are very close to what is done for all students, there is no need to provide alternative tasks or materials for Gero.

STEP 3: TIME AND PROVIDER FOR SCAFFOLDING

TIME. Ms. Levin did not need to pre-teach or post-teach anything to meet Gero's needs. Because much of the lesson was appropriate for Gero's level of English proficiency, Ms. Levin was able to integrate scaffolding seamlessly. However, because she has two native English-speaking students who struggle with writing, Ms. Levin pulled Gero and these two students into a small group where she worked with them while the rest of the class worked quietly on their first draft. Based on the Common Core State Standard listed earlier that uses dictation as a prompt for writing, Ms. Levin gave each child a turn at dictating his thoughts to her. She opted to have Gero go last so he could listen to her prompting the other students, providing him both with extra thinking time and a model.

PROVIDER. Ms. Levin was able to address the four Ps with Gero on her own through her organization of class activities. While she worked with Gero's small group, the other students were engaged in learning centers and with technology.

STOP AND REFLECT QUESTIONS

1. Do you know whether rhyming activities or songs are common educational practices in the cultures of your English learners? Speaking with a bilingual aide or a parent volunteer could help bridge your English learners' first language educational practices with common practices in your classroom.
2. Do you simply correct the writings of your ELs, or do you analyze them to identify areas of strength and/or weakness? If you mainly correct, you might consider keeping a running list of errors by student so you can begin to select areas on which to focus.

GO AND PRACTICE ACTIVITIES

1. List at least five activities you have created or designed to specifically focus on oral language development of your English learners.
2. Meet with the speech-language pathologist at your school and explore appropriate assessment instruments that may be used to test the phonemic awareness of your ELs in English and in their native language. Use the results to develop a plan geared toward improving phonemic awareness of your English learners.
3. Obtain a copy of the English Language Proficiency standards and the Common Core State Standards. Evaluate both documents and determine how the ELP standards will assist English learners to meet the CCSS.

4. Read the literature on literacy socialization of native speakers of any language. According to research on this topic, children are first socialized into literacy within their home environments. Ask parents to share with you some of the literacy practices they use at home. Then find ways to bridge the home practices with those used in your classroom.

Teaching Edith About
Roots, Prefixes, and Suffixes

Language and Literacy in the Intermediate Grades

Some time had passed since Ms. Oliver first sat down to talk with Edith. Knowing Edith had difficulty participating in Wednesday's science lesson, Ms. Oliver thought it would be helpful to get a better understanding of Edith's reading and writing skills in English—maybe even in Spanish. The test scores in Edith's folder didn't explain much, so Ms. Oliver invited Edith to be this Friday's weekly "Lunch with Ms. Oliver" companion.

"I can already see that your English is better than when I met you," said Ms. Oliver, slowly and clearly, as she opened her lunch bag. "I'm happy you can understand more now." Edith nodded, and poked a straw into her juice box. Taking a sip, she looked around the room, empty chairs pushed under scratched and dented tables, no one else for Ms. Oliver to pay attention to but Edith. It felt like her birthday.

After they finished eating, Ms. Oliver handed Edith a blank page and a pencil. "Edith, would you write something for me in English? Would you please write two or three things about yourself?" "I no . . . I no . . . ," Edith whispered. "Edith, it's just for me. Write what you can. Tell me about yourself." "No puedo escribir en ingles," Edith explained. "Just two or three things," Ms. Oliver gently pleaded, "English or Spanish." Edith took the pencil, and began:

Ma na se Edith. [My name is Edith.]

I es 10. [I am 10.]

I ly uno peja ocer. [I like to play soccer.]

llo vien de Mexico [I come from Mexico.]

mi comida feborita es la pizza [My favorite food is pizza.]

"Thank you, Edith," Ms. Oliver said as she reached for the paper. "For our next lunch, I'll bring a pizza."

GRADE-LEVEL EXPECTATIONS FOR LANGUAGE AND LITERACY IN FOURTH GRADE

Since her school recently implemented the Common Core State Standards (CCSS), Ms. Oliver has been adjusting the curriculum for her fourth graders. The following sections summarize the language demands established by these expectations, and explain their accessibility for Edith.

Reading

By fourth grade, students are expected to have developed most of the specific skills required for reading. These include comprehending most prefixes and suffixes, decoding multisyllabic words, and reading fourth-grade words with irregular spelling. More emphasis in now given to comprehending and explaining texts, both literary and informational. Drawing inferences from details in the text, students are also expected to summarize the theme or main idea, describe key elements in detail, and refer to the structure of various types of texts when discussing their differences. In addition, they are required to integrate information from two texts on the same topic.

The following passage gives a sense of grade-level text for fourth grade:[1]

> Outside of the station, the astronauts have to wear special suits because there is no air to breathe in space. But inside the space station people can breathe because there is air. People stay at the station and do experiments. Some of these experiments show how plants grow and act in space. Staying at the space station can be fun. It can also be dangerous.

Writing

At this grade students are expected to develop written compositions that include multiple sections and paragraphs. They develop arguments based on facts and reasoning, using precise language. In addition, students are expected to write narratives that include descriptions of situations, narrators, and characters as well as dialogue. The language category includes many skills that are specific to writing, such as avoiding fragmented and run-on sentences and correctly using homophones such as *to*, *too*, and *two*. They are also expected to accurately use punctuation and capitalization for quotes and compound sentences, spell grade-appropriate words, and use terms and punctuation to convey ideas precisely.

The following paragraph provides a sense of the expectations for satisfactory writing at the intermediate grades. It is an excerpt from a fourth-grade writing sample graded a 4 on a 6-point scale:[2]

> I love this kind of weather because sometimes my grandma picks me up and we go somewhere together. She has a blue convertible and in the summers I ask her, "Can you put the top down?" and then she says, "No, because it is too hot and I don't

want the hot blazing sun beating on my body." Then I say, "OK." Then when it is cool outside I ask her and she says, "Sure." So when I am sitting in her convertible I feel the coolness racing around me. I can hear the wind swishing around me, swish-swish-swish. I can also see the wind blowing my hair up, down, and all around.

Speaking, Listening, and Language

In preparation for speaking, students are expected to read texts on topics of discussion. They ask and answer relevant questions, paraphrase information, and explain their ideas in relation to key points. They are expected to use formal register (how they would speak with adults in authority) when appropriate, and be able to paraphrase orally presented information. They also use descriptive details in telling stories and recounting experiences.

Language skills are implicit in reading, writing, speaking, and listening, requiring students to correctly use *who*, *whose*, *whom*, *which*, *that*, *where*, *when*, and *why*; past, present, and future progressive verb tenses; and auxiliary verbs such as *can*, *may*, *must*, *might*, and *could*; to order adjectives properly in a sentence; and to use prepositional phrases. Additionally, they are able to use context, common Greek and Latin prefixes, suffixes, and roots, and reference materials to understand a term; explain the meaning of simple similes, metaphors, common idioms, adages, and proverbs; and relate words to their antonyms and synonyms. There are also language skills that are primarily used in writing, which were noted in the writing section above.

LEVEL 1 ENGLISH LEARNERS' LANGUAGE AND LITERACY IN FOURTH GRADE

To understand the gap between the grade-level expectations and what a typical English learner who was assessed at level 1 can understand and express, it is helpful to examine the descriptors for this proficiency level in detail. The following English Language Proficiency (ELP) standards, established by the Council of Chief State School Officers, represent the forms and functions English learners in fourth grade know and can perform in English by the end of level 1 of English proficiency, Edith's current level.[3] They were developed to show English learners' effective language use during their progress toward independent participation in grade-level curriculum, instruction, and assessment.

Teachers can refer to the following ELP standards to better understand where the gap is between their students' English proficiency and the CCSS language arts and literacy standards that their classes are expected to meet by year's end. Examining them in comparison to the CCSS standards can highlight where extra support and time may be required in instruction and assessment.

Language Forms

After attaining level 1 English language proficiency, the English learner will be able to demonstrate the knowledge, skill, or ability described in the standard, using gestures, a few frequently occurring words, simple phrases, and formulaic expressions.

Language Functions

The following language function descriptors begin with a CCSS grade-level standard, followed by its adaptation for English learners at level 1 of English proficiency (the *italicized* descriptor).

A level 1 English learner in the fourth grade can:

- determine the meaning of words and phrases in oral presentations and literary and informational text: *recognize the meaning of a few frequently occurring words, phrases, and formulaic expressions in simple oral discourse, read-alouds, and written texts about familiar topics, experiences, or events, relying heavily on context and visual aids (including picture dictionaries).*
- extract evidence from grade-appropriate oral presentations and literary and informational texts through close listening or reading: *identify a few key words and phrases in read-alouds, simple written texts, and oral presentations.*
- speak and write about grade-appropriate complex literary and informational texts and topics: *communicate simple information about familiar topics, events, or objects in the environment, using a few frequently occurring words, drawings, illustrations, and other visual aids.*
- adapt language choices to purpose, task, and audience when speaking or writing: *not applicable at this proficiency level.*
- construct a grade-appropriate oral or written claim and support it with reasoning and evidence: *express an opinion about familiar topics, using a few frequently occurring words and formulaic expressions.*
- participate in grade-appropriate oral and written exchanges of information, ideas, and analyses, responding to peer, audience, or reader comments and questions: *participate in short conversational and written exchanges about familiar topics, listening to others and responding to simple yes/no questions.*
- research and/or obtain, evaluate, and communicate grade-appropriate oral and written information in a clear and effective response to a defined task and purpose: *recall information from experience or gather information from a few provided sources and label some key information, using a few frequently occurring words, illustrations, diagrams, or other graphic forms.*
- analyze and critique the arguments of others orally and in writing: *identify a point an author or a speaker makes, using a few frequently occurring words and phrases.*
- use grade-appropriate standard English forms to communicate in speech and writing: *recognize and use a small number of frequently occurring nouns, noun phrases, and verbs, and understand and respond to question words.*
- create clear and coherent grade-appropriate speech and text: *combine high-frequency words and formulaic phrases, using simple conjunctions to link events and ideas.*

The description for language form shows that level 1 English learners generally use gestures, a few frequently occurring words, simple phrases, and formulaic expressions.

They rely on their native languages when they need to express themselves in situations that require greater proficiency in English than they currently have attained.

Comparing the CCSS English language arts standards for fourth grade with Edith's assessed level of English proficiency (level 1), as described by the ELP language forms and functions above, indicates a number of outcomes that Edith may not reach by year's end. For example, if she is expected to explain or draw inferences from a grade-level text in English, her knowledge and use of frequent words, simple phrases, and formulaic expressions would not yet equip her to comprehend complex sentences or verb tenses. The ELP language functions give reasonable suggestions on addressing a CCSS standard given the level of English proficiency. They do not, however, provide specifics on how to teach lessons addressing those standards for English learners. Of course, as Edith's English language proficiency develops, she will be able to comprehend and express concepts with more complex language.

CCSS grade-level descriptors that Edith can meet, even with her level 1 proficiency, include comprehending common Latin prefixes, roots, and suffixes; using technology for writing; following the writing process of planning, revising, and editing with guidance and support; adding media and graphics to oral presentations; and using some auxiliary verbs, such as *can* and *may*, as well as simple prepositional phrases. Although there are some CCSS English language arts standards that fourth grader Edith can achieve without modification, in contrast with Gero's experience in kindergarten, she is faced with more CCSS standards that require a much higher level of English proficiency. In the Classroom Application section, we present our Language Arts Protocol, which provides guidelines for teaching English language arts to Edith based on formal and classroom assessments of her oral proficiency and literacy skills in English.

RESEARCH ON TEACHING LANGUAGE AND LITERACY TO ENGLISH LEARNERS IN INTERMEDIATE GRADES

Even though children's reading competency develops throughout the school years, a critical period in reading development seems to occur between the third and fifth grades. An emergence of comprehension difficulties around the middle of this period is sometimes referred to as the fourth-grade slump.[4] Key factors contributing to the reading difficulties faced by children at this age are related to changes in reading requirements around the third- and fourth-grade levels, where students are increasingly asked to read not just for pleasure, but to learn from texts. During this time, they are exposed to increasingly difficult texts and, perhaps for the first time, expository texts. This is important because third- and fourth-grade students face critical comprehension challenges from expository texts, particularly those covering scientific material. An English learner in the fourth grade could be affected by this shift in reading requirements in different ways, especially given the student's level of English proficiency. An English learner who enters the U.S. school system in the fourth grade has a decidedly different climb to grade-level reading comprehension than a fourth-grade English learner who entered U.S. schools in kindergarten.

Oral Proficiency in English

In addressing Edith's language needs, it is evident that oral language is a significant barrier for her learning. Language learners like Edith need to hear and speak language before reading and writing it. EL students typically experience limited oral language practice in the mainstream classrooms.[5] Most English learners need more extensive oral language practice with subject-specific concepts to help them progress toward using the more formal language of academic texts. Current school practices typically have little effect on oral language development during the elementary school years. Because the level of language used is often limited to what the children can read and write, there are few opportunities for language development in primary classes. Thus, early delays in oral language come to be reflected in low levels of reading comprehension, leading to low levels of academic success. If we are to increase children's listening, speaking, reading, and writing ability, we have to enrich their oral language development during the early years of schooling. Teachers can support the oral language development of second language learners by developing lessons that include small-group discussions and/or report presentations that use academic vocabulary. Teachers can scaffold these activities by giving the EL students a list of words or possible sentences they may select from in order to participate in these discussions. These are just a couple of examples; schools could do much more than they do now to foster the language development of less-advantaged children and children for whom English is a second language.

To succeed at reading, a child must be able to *identify* or "read" printed words and to *understand* the written text composed of those words. Both identifying words and understanding text are critical to reading success. For many children, increasing reading and school success will involve increasing oral language competence in the elementary years.[6] Research on children's reading development has shown that in primary grades English learners usually process sounds, decode words, and spell with the same accuracy as native speakers. However, when examining children's reading comprehension, we find that English learners, particularly in intermediate grades, perform significantly worse than native speakers. Studies show that at the fourth- to fifth-grade level, oral proficiency has the greatest effect on reading comprehension for English learners, and is an even stronger influence on reading performance than word reading skills.[7] In addition, studies that looked at listening comprehension found it to be the strongest influence on reading comprehension.[8]

Transfer of Basic Literacy Skills and Strategies from the First Language

Language arts and literacy teachers know a great deal about children's language and literacy development in naturalistic as well as in instructed second language acquisition settings. When adapting curriculum, assessment, and instruction to address the language and literacy needs of elementary grade English learners, it is helpful to keep in mind established research, policy, and practice insights in relation to language and literacy development across languages.

First language reading ability influences students' learning to read in a second language. Elizabeth Bernhardt, a prominent second and foreign language researcher, developed a compensatory model of second language reading proposing that readers use all the resources available to them in their first language and literacy to compensate for any deficiencies in their second language reading.[9] She maintains that 50 percent of second language reading ability is attributed to second language knowledge and first language reading ability. However, much remains unknown about what contributes to second language reading. Recently, McNeil proposed an extension of Bernhardt's model, suggesting that the remaining 50 percent of reading ability is due to readers' strategic knowledge and background knowledge.[10] Strategic knowledge requires readers to deploy cognitive and metacognitive actions to plan, adjust, and monitor reading comprehension processes. Bernhardt's compensatory theory of second language reading is one of the most thorough and comprehensive models that attempts to clarify and build understanding of the complex ways in which first and second language reading processes interact and support each other.[11] Bernhardt's model suggests that there are fundamental similarities between first and second language skills, and that these skills are linguistically interdependent and supportive of each other. In other words, second language reading processes involve the interplay of two sound systems (phonology), two word formation systems (morphology), two sentence structure systems (syntax), and two meaning systems (semantics). When reading academic texts in a second language, those who are literate in their first language should have access to their first language, and many use their first language knowledge and skills to support their understanding of second language materials.

There are well-established contrasts between English and other languages, and these contrasts affect how well children learn to read across these two languages.[12] For instance, common cross-language interference errors that many native speakers of Spanish make when learning English include, but are not limited to, use of articles, gender, number, personal pronouns, prepositions, question formation, verb tenses, word order, and false cognates. A native speaker of Spanish might make errors in the use of the definite and indefinite articles in English since in Spanish the definite articles *el* and *la* are used with possessive pronouns, while the indefinite articles *un*, *uno*, and *una* are not used before nouns describing profession, occupation, or social status. With these contrasts in mind, the appropriate instructional strategy for an English learner depends on his or her age, level of English proficiency, and reading ability.

✦ CLASSROOM APPLICATION ✦

To get a general sense of Edith's reading and writing ability, Ms. Oliver asked Ms. Montilla, the ELD specialist, whether she could come observe the two of them one day while the school's writing coach led the mainstream class for her daily twenty-minute instructional session. Ms. Oliver sat nearby as Ms. Montilla handed Edith a book entitled *The Book About Me*, asking her in Spanish to read the book for her. Edith spoke very softly, slowly, and hesitatingly, watching for cues and confirmation from both adults.

EDITH: I em [pauses] em [hesitates]

MS. MONTILLA: Sound it out.

EDITH: D . . . [hesitates] d . . . er [hesitates] dring [pauses] drin . . . k

MS. MONTILLA: ing [pronounces emphatically]

EDITH: drink

MS. MONTILLA: drinking

MS. MONTILLA AND EDITH: [very slowly] drinking

MS. MONTILLA: I am

EDITH: drink . . . ing

MS. MONTILLA: Perfect! I am drinking. Do you know what that means?

EDITH: [hesitates] Um . . .

MS. MONTILLA: What? In Spanish. Pero, dímelo en español.

EDITH: Um . . .

MS. MONTILLA: ¿Estoy que?

EDITH: Uh . . . Tomando.

MS. MONTILLA: ¡Tomando! ¡Perfecto! OK.

EDITH: I . . . I . . . ea . . . [hesitates] um . . . ea . . .

MS. MONTILLA: Same ending. I am eat [exaggerates the *t* sound at the end of the word while Edith softly repeats *eat*] ing. I am eating [pronounces normally]. What's that?

EDITH: Come [in Spanish].

MS. MONTILLA: Está comiendo. ¡Perfecto!

EDITH: I am try—

MS. MONTILLA: *Talk* [emphasizes this syllable] ing.

EDITH: Talking.

MS. MONTILLA: ¿Que es eso?

EDITH: Habla.

MS. MONTILLA: Hablando. OK. ¿Ves todas las palabras con *ing*? Talk—ing, cry—ing, laugh—ing. ¿OK? So let's see what the next one is.

ANALYZING EDITH'S CLASSROOM LANGUAGE SAMPLES

The dialogue presented in this transcript as well as in the previous sample of Edith's writing show that conversations between Edith and Ms. Montilla have been steadfast, yet strenuous, with each grasping for words that make sense to the other. It is easy to see that while Edith seemed to understand most of what Ms. Montilla was saying, her limited language proficiency prevented her from expressing herself and eventually from learning through language.

ELP standards for listening, speaking, reading, writing state that students at level 1 of English proficiency, such as Edith, are expected to process and produce simple sentences or questions, basic grammatical constructions and sentence patterns, and general content words and expressions. The text Ms. Montilla chose, a book that students wrote and illustrated as a group project in last year's ELD class, meets all these parameters. The sentences are short, simple vocabulary is used, and there is a lot of repetition of the very basic grammatical feature present progressive (I am _____ing). The selected book would be too easy for fourth-grade students, yet Edith clearly struggles to read and fully comprehend its content.

After quickly reading "I em" (her pronunciation reflecting her native language) Edith has difficulty to decode the last word of the sentence. It takes her several tries to say the word *drink*, at which point she stops reading. The fact that she does not produce the *-ing* can be explained in two ways. First, Edith probably recognized the verb after decoding *d-r-i-n-k* and stopped to translate the meaning of the sentence back to Spanish. Second, the grammatical feature of *-ing* added to a verb is unfamiliar. Even after Ms. Montilla supplies the ending and asks Edith to repeat *drinking* after her, Edith hesitates to put the verb and the ending together. She has not yet acquired the *-ing* tense in spoken English. However, even though she struggles to read these verb patterns, because they are only slightly above her current proficiency, repeated exposure will help accelerate their acquisition.

Edith's challenges in decoding are evident in her difficulty reading *Eat* and *talk* because the irregular spelling of English does not allow her to consistently pronounce each letter to form words as is possible in Spanish, the language in which Edith learned to read when she was in first grade. As you learned in the introduction, Edith began learning to read in Mexico, but her schooling was interrupted, and as a result her reading skills in Spanish are below grade level. Ms. Montilla's classroom has a set of academic subject texts provided by the Mexican National Commission of Free Textbooks, so Edith has been able to access reading materials in her native language.[13] Now, as she is developing proficiency in English listening, speaking, reading, and writing, she will be expected to read fourth-grade texts in English. Her lack of oral proficiency in English is likely the greatest deterrent to her comprehension of the more complex texts required in intermediate grades.

Edith's writing sample combined her first language, Spanish, with her developing English vocabulary. Beginning English learners often shift to their native language when they are required to express something in English that is beyond their current capacity. For example, Edith mixes Spanish and English in simple sentences, such as "I es ten," and she uses Spanish sentences exclusively for more complex expressions, such as "Mi comida feborita [sic] es la pizza." Her spelling in Spanish shows an understanding of its sound/symbol correspondences, with errors where two different symbols could represent the same sound (the letters *b* and *v*, as in *feborita*). She knows the formulaic phrase in English, "My name is . . ." but she hasn't yet learned the spelling of the individual words, and writes "Ma na se Edith." She is using inventive spelling according to her developing understanding of the sound/symbol correspondences in English, such as "I ly" to represent "I like." As her English develops from one-word expressions and formulaic phrases to more complex sentences, she will need to learn English spelling conventions to write accurately and precisely.

At this level of English proficiency, students need a great deal of verbal, visual, graphic, and interactive support, which will enable them to process and produce the language needed for effective listening, speaking, reading, and writing. Edith's and Ms. Montilla's exchanges began to form an initial strong basis for tailoring instruction to Edith's language and literacy learning needs. From interactions such as these coupled with information gathered from other assessment data, educators working with English learners in mainstream classrooms can gain an understanding of what a beginning English learner like Edith can say and do in a second language.

MS. OLIVER'S PREFIX-ROOT-SUFFIX LESSON

Ms. Oliver strongly believes in teaching word attack strategies as a means to foster her students' self-efficacy as they increase their sophistication in comprehending various texts and in producing academic writing. Noticing that the use of morphology not only is featured as a foundational reading skill but also appears under the language category of the CCSS, she decided to set aside small blocks of time for morphology instruction.

> **Literacy Standards:**
>
> **CCSS.ELA-LITERACY.RF.4.3.a:** Use combined knowledge of all letter-sound correspondences, syllabication patterns and morphology (e.g., roots and affixes) to read accurately unfamiliar multisyllabic words in context and out of context.
>
> **CCSS.ELA-LITERACY.L.4.b:** Use common, grade-appropriate Greek and Latin affixes and roots as clues to the meaning of a word (e.g., telegraph, photograph, autograph).

OBJECTIVES

Her objectives for this lesson are for her students to (a) indicate the difference between the terms *prefix* and *suffix* and (b) to identify prefixes, suffixes, and root words in appropriate examples across content areas.

LESSON DESCRIPTION

Ms. Oliver started her lesson planning by selecting a number of root words, prefixes, and suffixes that are developmentally appropriate for her grade level. She then broke them up into digestible groups to be taught over the course of the next grading period. What follows is an example of the individual instructional tasks in the introductory lesson:

1. Display the first page of an interactive flip chart with about a dozen words distributed around an empty center frame.

2. Ask the students to discuss with a shoulder partner whether they can see a pattern.

3. In the empty frame, draw as many boxes as the students say there are groups of verbs and invite students up to move the words into the appropriate boxes.

4. Ask students if they know what a prefix is, then have a volunteer click on the definition icon to reveal the definition and discuss.

5. Point to the group of words that contain the prefix *pre-* and ask students to come up with their shoulder partner with further examples. Write them on the chart during reporting out. Discuss the meaning of the prefix *pre-*.

6. Reveal the next page of the chart, which contains a three-column table with headings of *pre-*, *mis-*, and *re-* and a verb bank at the bottom. Pick a number of verbs and copy them into the appropriate column, as directed by students. Discuss why some of them (e.g., *search*) fit only into the *re-* column, whereas others (e.g., *read*) can go in all three columns.

7. Discuss the meaning that the three prefixes carry, writing down the definition of the newly formed verb.

8. Direct the students to complete their handout, which is a copy of the flip chart page, checking with their partner every now and then.

9. Debrief on the flip chart, encouraging students to copy words or definitions they missed or got wrong.

10. The next day, as a class, construct a list that shows the prefix (or suffix), the definition/meaning, an example, plus a drawing/symbolic representation of the meaning.[14]

Ms. Oliver's intention is to repeat steps 5–10 in a similar fashion once or twice a week until all chosen root words, prefixes, and suffixes are acquired by the class.[15] Furthermore, referring back to the second lesson objective, she implements a competition in which students could earn points for identifying root words that contain the covered affixes when they encountered them in content-area text. This way, she feels, she can wrap this explicit vocabulary instruction into other instructional events across different subjects. At the end of each day, these words, with definitions and drawing/symbolic representations, will be added to the class list that will remain displayed for everybody's use for the remainder of the grading period. Ms. Oliver also plans to wrap up this instructional sequence with a class project in which the students will produce a summary of the displays to make room for future vocabulary instruction, while providing a review of the concept.

EVALUATION

Ms. Oliver plans to formatively assess the students' understanding of the concept by checking the worksheets each evening and incorporating occasional quizzes that require the students to match prefixes and suffixes with their associated root words and use the word in a sentence.

APPLYING THE LANGUAGE ARTS PROTOCOL
to the Prefix-Root-Suffix Lesson

Fourth-grade-level language arts instruction is obviously built upon previous grade-level instruction, and thus requires far more language and literacy skills than kindergarten, which we described in the previous chapter. Therefore, fourth-grade teachers should expect to detect a larger gap between the language demands of English language arts instruction and the linguistic ability of a student at a level 1 English proficiency than kindergarten teachers typically find. This hypothesis is put to the test with Ms. Oliver's prefix-root-suffix lesson, which will need to be adapted for Edith's specific needs.

PHASE I: Understanding the Needed Language Skills and Edith

As Ms. Oliver listed each step the students would be expected to follow (presented in table 8.1), she quickly noticed how the students would need to use each of the four language skills, and that there was not always a direct relationship between students having to "listen" and "speak." In other words, she realized that there are times when she simply expects students to comprehend her verbal instructions and follow through with actions. Other times she expects students to comprehend a concept that is explained orally or through writing and then depends on language to determine the students' understanding. This realization made her curious as to how much of a gap there might be between the language demands of her expectations for native English-speaking students and what Edith can comprehend and express given her level 1 English proficiency (see English proficiency descriptors in table 8.1).

When she compares the grade-level expectations in the middle column of the table to the English proficiency descriptors for a student at Edith's level, Ms. Oliver makes an unexpected discovery. For this lesson, the English language arts Common Core State Standards refer to using knowledge of roots and affixes to read unfamiliar words and using common Greek and Latin affixes and roots to guess word meaning. The descriptors for Edith's level of proficiency in reading make it clear that Edith is able to recognize cognates from her first language. It is therefore reasonable to assume that she should be able to follow much of the prefix-root-suffix lesson designed for native speakers. This will not only facilitate the comprehension of the concept of root words and affixes, but with a little bit of additional prodding by Ms. Oliver following the lesson, Edith can learn to conscientiously use cognates as a strategy for reading comprehension when she comes across unknown words.

The English proficiency descriptors also signal that Edith should be able to follow some of Ms. Oliver's directions, such as moving verbs into appropriate columns on the flip chart, as they are supported by modeling. However, the verbal instructions of sharing observed patterns and ensuing conversations or Ms. Oliver's explanations of the meaning of the prefixes and new meanings of the verbs are out of Edith's reach. This is where the use of Spanish would be needed to deepen Edith's understanding.

TABLE 8.1

Language Demands and EL Proficiency Analysis for Prefix-Root-Affix Lesson

Language Skill	Lesson Steps (designed for all students)	English Proficiency Level Descriptors
Listening	• Follow directions on tasks. • Listen to partner's description of pattern and proposed verbs. • Comprehend teacher's explanations.	• Comprehend one- and two-step directions and simple instructional commands such as *discuss, write, tell me*. • Recognize frequently occurring words.
Reading	• Read word banks and completed columns. • Decode and comprehend definitions of derived verbs.	• Point to words used in instructions. • Recognize cognates.
Speaking	• Exchange verbs with peer during sharing. • Respond to teacher-produced questions.	• Answer yes/no or choice questions. • Use single words, recalling information from frequently occurring words. • With support, use words beyond highly familiar ones.
Writing	• Form new verbs using roots and prefixes listed on the flip chart. • Write definition of derived verbs.	• Copy words and sentences.
Language Conventions	N/A	N/A

Last, the English proficiency descriptors also indicate that Edith can only copy words, and although she should be able to create the new verbs, she won't be able to come up with the definition of the new verbs in English by herself.

PHASE II: Targeted Language Arts Instruction for Edith

Depending on the resources and scheduling at the school, the targeted language instruction for Edith could be provided by Ms. Oliver with different arrangements, as described in the following section.

STEP 1: SCAFFOLDING LANGUAGE ARTS INSTRUCTION

PITCH. The actual content and outcome of the lesson, to identify prefixes, suffixes, and root words, should be accessible to Edith with the right adjustments. By isolating word elements as the focus of instruction, Ms. Oliver's lesson is less sensitive to pitch than a broader application of listening, speaking, reading, or writing skills, such as a guided reading lesson. Many of the word roots, prefixes, and suffixes are likely to be similar in Spanish and thereby offer a reference point that Edith is already familiar with.

The pitch of the language used in explaining the word elements will be too complex for Edith to fully comprehend. Instructional language that might be inaccessible could include the teacher's opening question (Do you know what a prefix is?), the shoulder partner's examples and Edith's ability to supply prefix, root, and suffix examples for the shoulder partner, and the class and pair discussion of new word meanings.

PACE. The pace of the lesson should be appropriate for Edith given the factual, knowledge-level nature of the topic. With support, Edith should be able to keep up with the main points of instruction during all lesson phases; she will miss some details but this shouldn't impede her meeting the standard.

PORTION. Because the word elements follow a straightforward pattern and many are similar to their Spanish counterparts, the portion of instructional content should be appropriate for Edith. No additional unpacking should be necessary to convey the main points.

PERSPECTIVE/POINT. As with any lesson for English learners, establishing meaning is critical. Whereas for native speakers the meaning can be explained through discussion, for Edith meaning can be supported through visuals and through her native language. Spanish cognates provide a gateway to clarifying the meaning of word elements. In terms of form and structure, additional emphasis linking the spelling and pronunciation of the word elements would help Edith learn the new word-building blocks. For example, it would be helpful to reinforce that *pre* is pronounced "pree" (or "pruh" if unstressed) rather than "pray," as it would be if read in Spanish. Cultural background knowledge could be a factor in some of the words that use any of the three prefixes, such as the concept of a *preteen*.

STEP 2: USE OF SCAFFOLDING

USE. The scaffolding necessary to provide targeted language instruction for Edith can be a supplement to whole-class instruction. This support can be supplied through curriculum (materials) and instruction.

STEP 3: TIME AND SCAFFOLDING PROVIDER

TIME. An ELD or bilingual education teacher can provide instructional support by pre-teaching the Spanish cognates of the prefixes, roots, and suffixes and their English counterparts. In this case, the teacher would also prepare a supplemental handout with word elements supplied for Edith's reference as she participates in the pair activities and discussion.

The ideal circumstance would be to have this co-teaching support during the lesson. During the class discussion and pair activities and discussion, Edith could work independently with the ELD or bilingual education teacher, or if there were other beginning English learners in the class, they could be gathered in a small group for this portion of instruction.

PROVIDER. Assistance from the ELD or bilingual education teacher in a push-in arrangement or through pre-teaching the concepts would help engage Edith. If this is not possible, a bilingual aide or volunteer could help Edith if the classroom teacher prepared the supplemental instructional materials in advance.

STOP AND REFLECT QUESTIONS

1. Reflect on the conversations of your English learners. Do you recall any evidence of your learners using multiword chunks? If so, when did they use them? Were they speaking with you, other teachers, with native English-speaking classmates, or with other English learners? Remembering the interactions can suggest who they feel comfortable with to try out their new expressions.

2. Do you have a general idea of the grammatical structures of the different languages spoken in your class?

GO AND PRACTICE ACTIVITIES

1. Make a list of the formulaic language expressions that you would like your English learners to know and use. Create sentence strips of those expressions and share them with your learners. Allow them to practice the expressions with classmates as well as other school personnel to help build their confidence when speaking with others. Remember, if they are still in the "silent stage" of language acquisition, do not force them to speak. Simply explain that when they are ready, they can use the expressions. No pressure!

2. If you do not know the grammatical structures of the non-English languages spoken in your class, then complete this activity. Select a piece of writing from one of your ELs and analyze the types of errors being made. From your preliminary analysis, can you guess what the grammatical structure of his/her language might be? Your hypothesis may be incorrect but simply engaging in the activity will provide some insight as to possible grammatical features you need to be aware of in the student's native language.

3. Google the different languages spoken in your class. Familiarize yourself with differences in grammatical structures between their language and English. Think of it as detective work—have fun with it! Your students will deeply appreciate your interest in their language.

4. In this chapter, we discussed skills required for students at the fourth-grade level. Create a list of skills required for a particular grade level. For example, by fourth grade, students are expected to know prefixes, suffixes, how to decode multisyllabic words, and so forth. Create a required skills list for ELs in your class. Which skills have they already mastered? Which ones have yet to be acquired? From your analysis of the skills, can you conclude that the English learners are on, above, or below grade level?

CHAPTER 9

Teaching Tasir to Write a Persuasive Argument

Language and Literacy in Middle School

"Listen carefully, Tasir. You wrote, 'That was so mean. How they *could* have *did* that?' Does what you wrote sound right? You just need to hear the sentences to know if they're correct."

"Sounds OK to me. I don't hear anything wrong." Tasir shifted to the right, moving about an inch away from Mr. Grant, who had bent down to the left of Tasir's desk.

"Really? Don't you hear it?" Mr. Grant raised his voice. "Don't you hear the mistakes?"

"I hear the words. I know what they mean. Everything's right." Tasir half-smiled and inched away a bit more.

As he stood up, Mr. Grant gripped the back of Tasir's chair. Once steady, he let go and rested his hand briefly on Tasir's shoulder. "That's OK, Tasir. That's OK for now. I'll correct it when you turn in the paper."

Tasir looked down at her composition, nowhere near the required five paragraphs. It told the story of her family's move to the United States, how her mother, father, brother, and sister boarded the plane with passports, visas, and their most valuable possessions. They packed what they could carry and shipped a few things they couldn't. But they left so much there.

Tasir's last recollection of Egypt was her grandmother's face, crestfallen and cradled in her hands. "But, Nanna, why can't you come, too?" "I tried, Tasir," her grandmother said. "I did everything I could, but my application was rejected. I can't come now, but don't worry. I promise I will join you soon." Tasir imagined her grandmother walking toward her at the airport terminal, picked up her pencil, and continued writing.

GRADE-LEVEL EXPECTATIONS FOR LANGUAGE AND LITERACY IN SEVENTH GRADE

Mr. Grant has faced some challenges in preparing his seventh-grade students to meet the expectations required by the English language arts standards of the Common Core State Standards (CCSS). The following sections summarize the language demands established by these expectations and explain their accessibility for Tasir.

Reading

By middle school, foundational reading skills are no longer addressed in the CCSS English language arts standards. Seventh graders are expected to use these skills in a variety of reading functions. They are required to cite evidence in analyzing and making inferences from a text; determine, analyze, and summarize a theme or central idea of a text; and analyze stylistic aspects of various text types. The language knowledge and skills pertaining to reading include using context, knowledge of synonyms and antonyms, Greek and Latin prefixes/roots/suffixes, and dictionaries to comprehend terms. Seventh graders are required to read and comprehend literature and informational text in the grades 6 through 8 band, with scaffolding at the high end of the range (eighth-grade text).

The following passage gives a sense of grade-level text for seventh grade:[1]

> The United States has lagged behind other countries in developing fast, convenient rail travel. Instead more attention has been given to travel by air and by car. The United States has one high-speed rail line, the Acela Express, which runs between Washington, D.C., and Boston via New York City. Although the Acela trains are capable of running up to 150 mph (241 km/h), they average around 78 mph. More rail lines need to be built in the United States to have high-speed trains. This is because passenger trains share tracks with freight trains and the tracks are too crowded to allow high-speed trains to run.

Writing

Seventh-grade writers are expected to introduce and support claims with logical reasoning, use words, phrases, and clauses for cohesion and clarification of relationships, use formal style, provide a conclusion supporting their argument, organize ideas using rhetoric, use transitions for cohesion, and use precise language. The language skills that pertain to writing include explaining the function of phrases and clauses, using compound and complex sentences to convey relationships, using phrases and clauses in sentences, avoiding dangling modifiers, using commas to separate coordinate adjectives, spelling correctly, and using language precisely and concisely, avoiding wordiness and redundancy.

The following paragraph provides a sense of the expectations for satisfactory writing at the middle school level. It is an excerpt from an eighth-grade writing sample graded a 4 on a 6-point scale:[2]

> The last place I will talk about is St. Augustine. St. Augustine is the oldest town in America and has a lot of sites and excursions to see like Ripley's believe it or not and the Fountain of youth. St. Augustine happens to be where my Grandparents live which is why I go there so much. This is a great town to go to if you want to know Florida's history. So if you want to learn visit St. Augustine.

Speaking, Listening, and Language

The speaking and listening requirements placed on seventh-grade students include reading to prepare for and participate in discussions, eliciting elaboration from others, acknowledging others' new information, analyzing main and supporting ideas and explaining how they clarify the topic being discussed, evaluating a speaker's argument, presenting claims using clear pronunciation, and adapting speech to contexts and tasks, demonstrating a command of formal English. The language standards address either reading or writing and have been summarized as part of both sections in this chapter.

LEVEL 5 ENGLISH LEARNERS' LANGUAGE AND LITERACY IN SEVENTH GRADE

To understand the gap between the grade-level expectations and what a typical English learner who was assessed at level 5 can understand and express, it is helpful to examine descriptors of level 5 proficiency in detail. The following English Language Proficiency (ELP) standards, established by the Council of Chief State School Officers, represent the forms and functions English learners in seventh grade know and can perform in English by the end of level 5 of English proficiency, Tasir's current level.[3] They show English learners' effective language use during their progress toward independent participation in grade-level curriculum, instruction, and assessment.

Teachers can refer to the following ELP standards to better understand where the gap is between their students' English proficiency and the CCSS language arts and literacy standards that their classes are expected to meet by year's end. Examining them in comparison to the CCSS standards can highlight where extra support and time may be required in instruction and assessment.

Language Forms

After attaining level 5 English language proficiency, the English learner will be able to demonstrate the knowledge, skill, or ability described in the standard, using a variety of words, phrases, and idiomatic expressions and simple, compound, and complex sentences.

Language Functions

The following language function descriptors begin with a CCSS grade-level standard, followed by its adaptation for English learners at level 5 of English proficiency (the *italicized* descriptor).

A level 5 English learner in the seventh grade can:

- determine the meaning of words and phrases in oral presentations and literary and informational text: *determine the meaning (including the figurative and connotative meanings) of idiomatic expressions and general academic and subject-specific words and phrases in texts about a variety of topics, experiences, or events, using context, reference materials, and knowledge of morphology.*

- extract evidence from grade-appropriate oral presentations and literary and informational texts through close listening or reading: *determine the central idea or theme in oral presentations or written text and explain how it is developed by supporting ideas or evidence, and summarize a text.*

- speak and write about grade-appropriate complex literary and informational texts and topics: *compose oral or written narratives or informational texts about a variety of topics and experiences, developed with relevant details, ideas, or information, using a variety of simple, compound, and complex sentences and general academic and subject-specific words and phrases.*

- adapt language choices to purpose, task, and audience when speaking or writing: *adapt word choices and style according to purpose, task, and audience with ease; use a large number of general academic and subject-specific academic words to express ideas precisely and maintain an appropriate and consistent style and tone throughout an oral or written text.*

- construct a grade-appropriate oral or written claim and support it with reasoning and evidence: *construct a claim about a variety of topics: introduce the topic, provide logically ordered reasons or facts that effectively support the claim, and provide a concluding section, using a variety of sentences and general academic and subject-specific words.*

- can participate in grade-appropriate oral and written exchanges of information, ideas, and analyses, responding to peer, audience, or reader comments and questions: *participate in extended conversations, discussion, and written exchanges about a variety of topics, texts, and issues; build on the ideas of others and express his or her own clearly; pose and respond to relevant questions; add relevant and specific evidence; and summarize and reflect on the key ideas expressed.*

- research and/or obtain, evaluate, and communicate grade-appropriate oral and written information in a clear and effective response to a defined task and purpose: *gather information from multiple print and digital sources, using search terms effectively; quote or paraphrase the data and conclusions of others, using a variety of sentence types and charts, diagrams, graphic organizers, or other graphics; and cite sources, using a standard format for citation.*

- analyze and critique the arguments of others orally and in writing: *analyze and evaluate the argument and specific claims in texts or speech/presentations, determining whether the reasoning is sound and the evidence is relevant and sufficient to support the claims; and cite textual evidence to support the analysis, using a variety of sentence types and general and subject-specific vocabulary.*

- use grade-appropriate Standard English forms to communicate in speech and writing: *use intensive pronouns and verbs in the active and passive voice; place phrases and clauses within a sentence, recognizing and correcting misplaced and dangling modifiers; and produce and expand simple, compound, and complex sentences.*
- create clear and coherent grade-appropriate speech and text: *narrate a complex sequence of events or present ideas and information, using transitional words and phrases to show logical relationships among events and ideas.*

The description for language form shows that Tasir, as a level 5 English learner, uses a variety of words, phrases, and idiomatic expressions and simple, compound, and complex sentences. In addition, the language functions for level 5 closely resemble the CCSS ELA standard they modify. This means that Tasir's general proficiency in English listening and speaking is close to that of native speakers. However, from samples of her reading and writing (presented in an upcoming section), it is apparent that she is still developing academic language and literacy skills in English and is not performing on grade level in those areas.

Looking at the gap between CCSS ELA grade-level expectations and the ELP standards for level 5, Tasir's continuing need for development in reading, for example, would not prevent her from meeting CCSS ELA standards such as citing evidence in analyzing and making inferences from a text. She would just need more scaffolding, by adjusting the pace, portion, and perspective of language arts and literacy instruction, when working with grade-level text. At the same time, because Tasir learned to read English in the third grade, after learning to read in Arabic previously in Egypt, she has some gaps in foundational reading skills in English that would have been taught in K–2 had she been schooled in the United States. In writing, Tasir is able to introduce and support claims with logical reasoning, but because her grammatical competence in English is still not fully developed, she has difficulty writing complex sentences using certain verb tenses or clause structures accurately. It is especially critical for Tasir to participate in form-focused, targeted language arts instruction so that these grammatical errors do not become intractable, or what is termed in the field of second language acquisition as fossilized or stabilized.

RESEARCH ON TEACHING LANGUAGE AND LITERACY TO ENGLISH LEARNERS IN MIDDLE SCHOOL

In describing our Language Arts Protocol in chapter 6, we noted that instruction in English language arts and literacy classes should focus primarily on developing EL students' language skills (i.e., listening, speaking, reading, and writing) in English. We suggested that given the dynamic, incremental nature of second language acquisition, and potential variation in proficiency across the different skill areas, instruction must be targeted to the individual student's precise level of proficiency in each skill area. In other words, the goal of second language instruction is to move the target incrementally upward toward the grade-level language standards. Common Core State Standards for English language arts call for new and more complex language demands, requiring significant shifts in instructing English learners.[4] The following findings are particularly relevant to middle school EL students, who vary in terms of language proficiency as well as first and second language literacy development.

First Language Influences on English Literacy

An interesting yet controversial issue related to EL students' writing relates to how different languages organize thoughts in writing. During the past several decades, a great deal of contrastive and error analysis research has focused on comparing and contrasting various aspects of language, reading, and writing across languages.[5] Teachers of English learners have used findings from this research to help anticipate areas of divergence across language systems, which are likely to cause English learners difficulty, and those of convergence, where one could expect positive transfer.

In an influential study, Robert Kaplan, a notable researcher in the field of rhetoric and composition, found that cultural differences in how languages tend to organize text structures (i.e., rhetoric) affect how students from different first language backgrounds compose written work in English.[6] Kaplan classified language groups according to cultural thought patterns. For instance, in Germanic languages such as English, German, Dutch, Norwegian, Danish, and Swedish, communication is direct and linear and doesn't digress or go off topic. In Semitic languages such as Arabic and Hebrew, thoughts are expressed in a series of parallel ideas, both positive and negative. In Asian languages, communication is indirect; topics are not addressed head on, but viewed from various perspectives, while in Romance languages such as French, Italian, Romanian and Spanish, communication often digresses to introduce extraneous material. In languages such as Russian, communication is often digressive and includes a series of parallel ideas. Finally, in Haitian Kreyòl, proverbs, which are inherently indirect, are added to communication to provide support or verbal evidence to strongly emphasize a particular point. For example, *"yon sel dwèt pa manje kalalou"* literally means that "one cannot eat okra with one finger," which in turn implies that people must work together to accomplish tasks.

The main premise behind Kaplan's assertions is that, in order to communicate effectively across cultures, one needs to understand the cultural thought patterns behind the language of communication. These thought patterns influence the way native speakers of a language express themselves. They will also influence how particular individuals expect to hear information presented. While this study has had a fair amount of positive and negative criticism, its insights have helped inform the teaching of reading and writing to EL students, especially at high school and college levels.

CONTRASTS BETWEEN ENGLISH AND ARABIC

There are well-established contrasts between Arabic and English, and these contrasts affect how well children learn to read across these two languages. For instance, common cross-language interference errors that native speakers of Arabic often make when learning English include, but are not limited to, use of articles, gender, number, personal pronouns, prepositions, question formation, verb tenses, word order, and cognates. A native speaker of Arabic might make errors in the use of subject-verb-object word order since Arabic sentences follow a verb-subject-object order. The more teachers are aware of cross-language contrasts as well as EL students' underlying interlanguage, the better they are prepared to address their language and literacy needs.

Teachers of English learners like Tasir, who is a native speaker of Arabic, a Semitic language, may or may not know that Arabic is quite different from English on several grounds. First, Arabic differs from English in terms of script, orthography, and directionality. The Arabic script is written from right to left in a cursive style. In most cases, the twenty-eight letters of Arabic transcribe consonant rather than vowel sounds. When transcribed, vowel diacritics (symbols similar to accent marks) are placed above and below consonants to indicate pronunciation and meaning differences. Because of redundancy in the language, vowels are rarely used in written Arabic texts above third-grade level. In most cases, starting in fourth grade, normally developing readers and writers are expected to be able to read and produce writing materials without vowel diacritics. Finally, teachers will find that in most types of academic writing, Arabic writers organize information in text differently than in English. Depending on the type of text used (e.g., textbook chapter, narrative, expository texts), these structures are more akin to the rhetorical structures described by Kaplan.

When teaching adolescents, like Tasir, to address language and literacy challenges, researchers and practitioners agree on a balanced approach, where instruction is focused on meaning with some degree of targeted attention paid to language form or discrete aspects of language development. When second language instruction is entirely communication-driven or meaning-focused, important grammatical or lexical features of the second language may not develop to targeted levels. Ultimately, those aspects of second language acquisition that learners need to notice, but for whatever reason do not, will need to be addressed through appropriate instructional intervention that meaningfully integrates the teaching of communication and language skills. (Anecdotally, when one of this book's coauthors, Kouider Mokhtari, was learning English as a foreign language, his language classes focused mostly on language forms. He had very limited opportunities to practice speaking inside or outside the classroom. Consequently, for some time, he reported feeling "grammatically competent" but "communicatively incompetent." His experience learning English in Morocco was markedly different from Tasir's experience learning English in Arkansas.)

Transfer of Basic Literacy Skills and Strategies

English learners may display difficulty in writing, especially in spelling, depending on the writing system of their first language. Various writing systems map out and represent spoken language in very different ways.[7] In alphabetic writing systems, such as

Korean, English, and Romance languages, letters must be arranged according to their individual sounds to form syllables. Conversely, in writing systems that use graphic symbols, such as Chinese, these symbols represent an entire unit of meaning (i.e., a word or part of word, such as *un*, that has meaning) and not just the symbol's sound.[8] Thus, research demonstrates that second language writers from first language writing systems like Chinese may not be as sensitive to sounds in the alphabetic system of English.[9] Therefore, the writing system of English learners' first language can have an effect on their spelling ability in their second language.[10]

Teachers of English learners need to understand the issues unique to second language writing and how to appropriately address them. Experts in reading and writing instruction for EL students note that high-stakes assessments for all students, including ELs, are moving beyond multiple choice formats to include short, extended, and essay-response questions, and therefore it is important for teachers to be able to identify and respond to errors made by EL students when learning to read and write in English.[11] These experts agree that errors are a normal part of language acquisition, that the acquisition of particular language structures may be delayed or even halted when ELs do not receive feedback and appropriate instruction, and that expert intervention can help these students improve their writing skills over time.

The types of errors EL writers commonly make range from improper use of parts of speech (e.g., use of articles, pronouns, and verbs) to errors in number (i.e., use of plural endings), word choice, and sentence structure (e.g., use of tenses, word order, and subject-verb agreement) and in language mechanics (e.g., use of punctuation, capitalization, spelling, and related conventions). For example, many of the mistakes involve sound/letter correspondences, more precisely concerning the "uh" sound, which can be represented by every letter vowel in English. In addition, mistakes are common with the letters *s* and *c*, and pronunciation mistakes often transfer to the written language, such as the Japanese use of the letters *l* and *r*.[12] For Romance and Germanic language speakers, pronunciation of the short *i* sound (bit) as a long *e* sound (beet) can cause errors in spelling and in reading. In particular, sound-linked errors may be more extensive since English learners' pronunciation may differ from that of native speakers in many ways. Thus, errors made by ELs often reflect their conceptual knowledge of the sound system of their native language, as letters with matching sounds are substituted and transposed, especially when English letter sounds and blends don't correlate or exist within the native language. For instance, beginning learners of English who are native speakers of Arabic often substitute the sound /b/ for /p/ in words such as *park* since the phoneme /p/ is not a phoneme per se in Arabic. Similarly, studies indicate that a large proportion of errors can be attributed to the user's native language phonological system.[13] Permissible combinations and variations in letter/sound placements may also be responsible for difficulties in pronunciation that can be reflected in student writing.

Experts recommend addressing these errors at beginning, intermediate, and advanced stages of writing development, focusing primarily on significant errors that are likely to pose reading comprehension problems. Teachers of EL students can and should integrate effective strategies for treating errors in writing. Depending on whether teachers provide error correction feedback to students individually, in small groups, or in classroom settings, instructional strategies might range from explicit and direct feedback (e.g., teacher corrects errors and explains the rationale for doing so) to indirect but guided input (e.g., teacher points out the error, asks student to make the correction, and assists as needed) to selective feedback focused on specific error types (e.g., teacher marks patterns of several specific error types by underlining or highlighting these errors). The work of Dana Ferris provides sound guidance on when and how to correct EL students' writing errors.[14]

As we indicated in previous chapters, because a majority of the research available pertains to learning to read in English as a first language, we urge middle-level teachers who have EL students to carefully interpret those insights in light of teaching English learners, who vary a great deal in age, gender, language proficiency, literacy development, and schooling. In other words, deciding what and how to teach ELs should be informed by the relevant research as well as the insights gained by working directly with these students.

✦ CLASSROOM APPLICATION ✦

"As she watched . . . the top of . . . of tall . . . sky . . . [sigh] scrappers
disappeared from view . . . and and . . . her mind began to
der [pause] derft . . . to the mountains . . . in . . . Montana.
Uh, Grandma [pause] and Grandfather lived . . . on the small ranch near
Great . . . Great Falls." Tasir paused for quite some time before going on to
read the following.

"The whole piece . . . of land . . . was actually . . . actually only ten . . . uh
uhsss [long pause] uh . . . curs [acres] but [flat intonation] . . . to . . . Melissa
[descending intonation as with ending a sentence] . . . who lived in [rising intonation as with beginning a sentence] in an apartment with her mother . . . it
was . . . as big as . . . Central Park . . . "

Tasir continued reading aloud in spurts, clear to the end of the story, alternating between word-by-word and small chunk bursts, sometimes expressionless and other times dramatically expressive. Mr. Grant was working
individually with his students, helping them with text-dependent questions.
"So, Tasir, what was the reason Melissa went to Montana?" "I think it was because she really missed her grandmother," Tasir replied. "Her grandmother
couldn't come to New York, so Melissa had to go to Montana." Mr. Grant
scrunched his eyebrows and pursed his lips. "Are you sure about that, Tasir?
Does it say that in the text?" "Yeah, I think so. Melissa is thinking about her

grandmother. She's far away, in Montana." Mr. Grant thought he had explained how to extract meaning from the text, but Tasir didn't seem to catch on. Getting his EL students used to the close reading required of the Common Core State Standards could take some time.

ANALYZING TASIR'S CLASSROOM LANGUAGE SAMPLES

A review of two informal measures of reading and writing conducted by Tasir's language arts teacher reveals much about her strengths and needs in these areas, which will in turn help in designing instruction to address these needs.

In the reading-aloud sample above, it is easy to see that while Tasir has near-native English conversation skills, she clearly had difficulty reading text with adequate fluency. We can see, for instance, that her reading is marked with frequent pauses, hesitations, corrections, repetitions, and mispronounced words. These fluency errors or miscues contribute to her speed, accuracy, and expression, which in turn affect her comprehension of what she reads. In other words, she appears to have some basic word decoding problems that force her to devote most of her cognitive resources to decoding and less of them to comprehension. Language arts and literacy teachers have an array of evidenced-based fluency-oriented reading strategies (e.g., repeated readings, reader's theater, echo-reading, etc.) for addressing reading fluency problems among first and second language readers, and they should integrate these strategies in the teaching of language and literacy for level 5 English learners like Tasir. Tasir's late start (third grade) in learning to read and write in English affected her composition skills. In the following writing sample, Tasir appears to have a few problems related to content, organization or ideas, and mechanics.

> "My gramna is the oldest person in my ralatives, she's nice and really cares about avery one she gives me prasnt and gets me out of trouble. She read to me and explains me averything. When i came to her house she cook food. When im not happy she trys to make me feel batter. I love my granma she is the Best Older Person in my family."

Knowing that Tasir is a native speaker of Arabic and that she has lived in the United States long enough to develop good oral language proficiency, it is easy to see that some of the writing difficulties are likely due to cross-language interference, awareness of audience, and general awareness of writing conventions in English. For instance, one problem native Arabic speakers often encounter when learning English is the use of prepositions. In Arabic there are about twenty prepositions but only five or six are used most of the time. For instance, Arabic uses the preposition *fii*, roughly the equivalent of *in* in English, in instances where English uses several other prepositions, such as *into*, *among*, *at*, *on*, and *into*. The use of the preposition *in* in the first sentence: "My gramna is the oldest person *in* my ralatives" is likely transferring the use of the preposition *fii* from Arabic into the closest preposition equivalent in English.

A second example relates to the use of punctuation (e.g., "My granma is the oldest person in my relatives, she's nice and really cares"). Arabic often uses commas rather than periods to separate sentences with complete thought units. A third instance of possible native language interference is the lack of capital letters, as in the phrases "When i came to her house" and "When im not happy." Arabic does not make a distinction between capital and lowercase letters.

Given that Tasir has relatively well developed reading and writing skills in Arabic—she completed the second grade in Egypt before coming to Arkansas—it is likely that her writing reflects some of the ways texts are structured in Arabic. In addition, because her English academic language skills are not as well developed, she will benefit from instruction that advances her writing and reading in English. Her teachers might consider discussing how text structures differ when reading and writing in English and Arabic. Articles such as Robert Kaplan's "Cultural Thought Patterns Revisited" might be helpful in this regard.[15] This type of direct instruction will help her develop an awareness of how messages are communicated in writing across both languages. In addition, Tasir will benefit from direct teaching of how information is structured in various text types. Specific strategies might include activities that enable her to learn about and produce different organizational patterns such as stories, directions, comparison-contrast, cause and effect, and description, along with the appropriate language structures that support the reading and production of these text types.

MR. GRANT'S PERSUASIVE ARGUMENT WRITING LESSON ON RENEWABLE ENERGY

This lesson is the language arts portion of the thematic unit on renewable energy presented in chapter 5. Tasir's seventh-grade class had to develop a written argument in support of providing local or state funding to private households that switch to renewable energy sources. However, because Mr. Grant feared that the students would think of the final product as yet other written essay on a predetermined topic, he decided to up the ante a little bit and incorporate a verbal component—a mock city hall meeting during which everyone would have to deliver their argument. The group with the most votes would win. This way, he hoped, all the students could work on presentation skills, which have become more important to the school in view of career readiness.

Since the students would be learning about the various types of renewable energy available in the United States, would conduct research on current energy usage and available renewable energy sources in various regions in geography, and would work out budgetary consideration of conversion to renewable energy in mathematics, Mr. Grant felt confident that the students would be able to fully concentrate on the construction of a persuasive argument and the writing process rather than having to spend time locating materials that support the argument.

As he constructed his lesson plan Mr. Grant quickly realized that, in this instance, the CCSS would not only drive his instruction in terms of goals, but they could actually provide a rough blueprint of activities or instructional steps.

Literacy Standards:

CCSS.ELA-LITERACY.W.7.1: Write arguments to support claims with clear reasons and relevant evidence.

CCSS.ELA-LITERACY.W. 7.5: With some guidance and support from peers and adults, develop and strengthen writing as needed by planning, revising, editing, re-writing, or trying a new approach, focusing on how well purpose and audience have been addressed.

CCSS.ELA-LITERACY.SL.7.1: Engage effectively in a range of collaborative discussions (one-on-one, in groups, and teacher-led) with diverse partners on grade 7 topics, texts, and issues, building on others' ideas and expressing their own clearly.

CCSS.ELA-LITERACY.SL.7.3: Delineate a speaker's argument and specific claims, evaluating the soundness of the reasoning and the relevance and sufficiency of the evidence.

CCSS.ELA-LITERACY.SL.7.4: Present claims and findings, emphasizing salient points in a focused, coherent manner with pertinent descriptions, facts, details, and examples; use appropriate eye contact, adequate volume, and clear pronunciation.

OBJECTIVE

With the standards providing Mr. Grant with a clear outline of his lesson, he chose only one objective: create and orally present a written argument in support of a given topic.

LESSON DESCRIPTION

To hook the students into working on persuasion, Mr. Grant projects five choices such as "diet soda OR regular soda?," "basketball OR baseball?," and so on at the beginning of the lesson, instructing each member of a pair to choose one option and explain in three sentences why it is the better choice. Next, he writes "We should have more time for lunch" on the board and asked the class how they would go about constructing an argument to convince the principal of the school.

After a discussion about common features of a convincing argument (i.e., claims and evidence) and how the argument should be presented (i.e., sequence, consideration of the audience), Mr. Grant planned to have the students write a persuasive argument for why the local government of the geographic area they had researched should provide residents with financial incentives to convert to renewable energy sources in their homes.

Following a brainstorm during which the students were encouraged to use elements for constructing the argument from discoveries they made in their science, mathematics, and geography projects, Mr. Grant's lesson plan then transitioned to sequentially teaching the students the steps for writing their arguments:

1. Lead the students sequentially through writing the first draft while circulating to offer guidance:
   a. Write an introductory statement.
   b. Review the summary points of their findings from the GIS research and financial calculations conducted in the other classes; then select three arguments for why the city council should offer financial incentives.[16]
   c. Still consulting the prior projects, draft evidence to back up the chosen arguments.
   d. Write a concluding statement.
2. Lead the students sequentially through revising and editing cycles while circulating to offer guidance:
   a. Students read their paper/argument; partners listen.
   b. Partners make suggestions for improvement of the argument, including introductory and closing statements.
   c. Peer consultations after revisions are made: each student reads a partner's revised draft and focuses on word choice.
   d. Peer consultations after editing: different sets of partners read the draft for language conventions.
   e. Students make final edits.
3. Argument delivery:
   a. Show short video clips of good speeches.[17] Hold class discussion of posture, eye contact, voice projection, and pace.
   b. Students rehearse their speeches with two different partners.
   c. Class conducts a mock city hall meeting. Each group's argument is rated for effectiveness as a whole.

EVALUATION

To evaluate the persuasive argument project, Mr. Grant designed two rubrics that he displayed in the classroom, as was his practice: one to assess the written product and one for the presentation. Because the project had included a substantial amount of peer interaction, however, he also added a peer feedback component to the evaluation in which each student could rate his partner's engagement in providing assistance during the planning and editing phases.

APPLICATION OF THE LANGUAGE ARTS PROTOCOL
to the Writing Lesson

When observing Tasir's interactions in the classroom it is apparent that she should be able to comprehend grade-level instruction. Her high oral language proficiency does indeed help her comprehend most of what is said, aside from some content-specific language and less commonly used idioms and collocations. However, though English learners at the top of level 5 proficiency possess language skills comparable to those of native English speakers, it is important to remember that Tasir's overall proficiency is at the lower end of level 5. Mr. Grant thus needs to take a close look at his goals for this writing project in terms of Tasir's specific needs.

PHASE I: Understanding the Needed Language Skills and Tasir

As he worked on the lesson steps, Mr. Grant thought ahead, comparing the language demands of the lesson to Tasir's language proficiency. He felt reasonably certain that Tasir would not only be able to engage in the lesson when pushed, but would be an active participant because he had designed multiple avenues for students to consult with peers rather than having to work on their own. He knew how important verbal interaction is for her, but was unsure about how demanding writing a persuasive argument would be for Tasir, whose recent writing sample contained a number of syntactic, semantic, and spelling errors.

Although Tasir's English language proficiency assessment data indicates that overall she is at level 5, that is because of her high oral proficiency; her reading and writing scores are still in the high level 4 range. After constructing the comparison in table 9.1, Mr. Grant saw quickly that the gap between grade-level instruction and Tasir's successful completion of this lesson squarely fell in the realm of writing, and language conventions in particular.

When comparing Tasir's specific English language proficiency in writing to the grade-level Common Core State Standards in English language arts, it is clear that she can support her claims in writing with evidence. Her interlanguage, however, as her writing sample shows, includes numerous grammatical and mechanical errors that would be marked as unacceptable in a native English-speaking student's writing. Mr. Grant is not overly concerned about this fact, given that the lesson he constructed provides ample opportunity for Tasir to become aware of her errors through peer editing. He does, however, make a mental note that he should look at how this and future writing lessons can help Tasir develop more solid English grammar and word usage.

Additionally, Mr. Grant recognized a gap between Tasir's reading skills, which show a lack of fluency and difficulty in decoding unfamiliar words, and the fluency expected of a seventh grader. Again, for the purpose of this lesson, this did not cause him much concern because Tasir would have several opportunities to rehearse reading her persuasive argument out loud with a peer before having to perform it before the class.

PHASE II: Targeted Language Arts Instruction for Tasir

Available resources and personnel will obviously affect how the four Ps of language arts scaffolding are provided for Tasir. With professional development to learn about the process of second language acquisition, Mr. Grant could meet Tasir's needs in the regular classroom, partially due to her high oral proficiency, at least in social language. However, since he currently lacks training in teaching English learners, Tasir's specific areas that need scaffolding would best be addressed in a separate English language

TABLE 9.1

Language Demands and EL Proficiency Analysis for Persuasive Writing Lesson

Language Skill	Lesson Steps (designed for all students)	English Proficiency Level Descriptors
Listening	• Follow teacher-guided class discussions. • Follow teacher's instructions. • Listen to partners' verbally expressed opinions and arguments. • Listen to partners' written speeches.	• Comprehend central idea of conversations. • Analyze arguments presented.
Reading	• Consult previously produced work (i.e., geography project, science research). • Read two peer-produced drafts, focusing first on word choice, then on mechanics. • Read multiple versions of own written argument. • Read aloud own text during rehearsal and performance.	• Gather and evaluate information from multiple sources. • Differentiate multiple meanings of words.
Speaking	• Express and support opinions. • Negotiate claims to be included in each group member's speech. • Share observations based on video clips. • Provide suggestions for peer's content revision. • Deliver speech (rehearsals and performance).	• Defend point of view using several sentences, with some rhetorical or grammatical errors present. • Pose relevant questions to negotiate meaning. • Critique peers' arguments. • Occasionally hesitate over academic vocabulary.
Writing	• Go through writing process (draft, revision, editing, production). • Follow through on partners' suggestions for argument improvement.	• Construct and support claim in logical order. • Expand simple and compound sentences. • With support, adapt word choices. • Use transitional words.
Language Conventions	• Grade-level mechanics.	• Occasional errors in word order in complex sentences. • Some predictable spelling and morphological errors present.

development class or by having her work with the ELD teacher before, during, or after the lesson for the seventh-grade class.[18]

STEP 1: SCAFFOLDING LANGUAGE ARTS INSTRUCTION

We know from Tasir's interview in chapter 1 that she struggles when her grade-level teachers present information in pure lecture or textual form and test how well students learned it. Adjustments for the four Ps that are appropriate for Tasir are mainly for pace and perspective.

PITCH. With appropriate adjustments to the pace and perspective of instruction, the readings that support the writing activity (discussed in chapter 4) and the language the teacher uses to review features of persuasive writing and to give directions can be the same as the grade-level discourse and text used with the other students.

PACE. Tasir's developing academic language skills will require a slight adjustment to the pace of instruction so that the teacher can pause between points; restate, paraphrase, and identify key points; and check more frequently for comprehension. Because the pace adjustment is minimal, it should be integrated well into whole-class instruction and probably will also benefit other students.

PORTION. The amount Tasir is expected to write and the amount of reading she is expected to complete to prepare for supporting her opinion should be virtually equal to what is expected of the other students.

PERSPECTIVE/POINT. This is where the most scaffolding for Tasir is needed. With regard to word meaning, she may need certain terms explained that native speakers would know—for instance, students from English-speaking homes might have heard a parent mention the term *thermostat*, but Tasir may have heard only the Arabic word. It is difficult to anticipate which words and phrases an English learner at Tasir's level might not know, so the best strategy is for the teacher to stay attuned to Tasir's comprehension, asking if there are any words that she is unfamiliar with or unsure about. Remember that terms unfamiliar to Tasir may be the same as or different from words that are new to native speakers. Even for level 5 English learners, unfamiliar terms may consist of nonacademic language, such as idioms (let the cat out of the bag), proverbs (you can lead a horse to water . . .), or words that are typically encountered in the early grades but thereafter are not commonly used (curds and whey).

Paying attention to Tasir's errors in speaking and writing can help identify areas to focus on during writing instruction. Knowledge about common developmental patterns for different levels of English proficiency can help teachers anticipate potential areas of difficulty so they can be discussed before students use them in an assignment. For instance, Tasir's writing sample gives Mr. Grant clues to her developmental patterns of English grammatical structures. She sometimes uses the *-s* at the end of present tense verbs when needed (my granma cares, gets me out of trouble), and other times she doesn't (she read to me). Because she alternates between the correct and incorrect forms, this would be a good area to focus on in grammatical accuracy in writing. Her writing also demonstrates that she is still developing accuracy with verbs that use indirect objects (she explains me everything), so focusing on this aspect might also help advance her competence in correct word order. For this lesson, Mr. Grant will make an effort to briefly attend to Tasir's writing before peer editing conferences begin so that she can be better prepared for her classmates' suggestions. While Mr. Grant feels comfortable teaching grammar in ways all students can comprehend, he should still consult with the ELD specialist to find out what types of errors he should help Tasir focus on over the next few months.

STEP 2: USE OF SCAFFOLDING SUPPORTS

Given the small gap between the selected English language arts Common Core State Standards and Tasir's proficiency in writing and speaking, the scaffolding necessary to provide targeted language instruction can be supplemental. The materials for native speakers can be used with or without ancillary materials, but instruction will have to include the scaffolding adjustments noted previously in the pace and perspective sections.

STEP 3: TIME AND SCAFFOLDING PROVIDER

TIME. Ideally, most of the perspective issues would be explained before the lesson, but if that isn't possible, Mr. Grant will need to check frequently with Tasir during each phase of the lesson. He will adjust pace during the lesson. Additional follow-up could include referring Tasir to a short online grammar tutorial, such as those available on the app ShowMe (or Mr. Grant could make a ShowMe tutorial for each area of difficulty his English learners have so they could be used again with other students).

PROVIDER. As stated earlier, if he gets additional training in teaching English learners, Mr. Grant can provide the necessary scaffolding by adjusting the four Ps in the grade-level lesson. In the absence of this expertise, he needs to collaborate with the ELD teacher for pre-teaching, co-teaching, or following-up.

STOP AND REFLECT QUESTIONS

1. Reflect on the ELs in your class. Which students do you think would consider themselves to be "grammatically competent" and which ones would describe themselves as being more "communicatively competent"? Which students would say they are equally balanced between the two? In other words, how do you think your students would categorize their acquisition strengths?
2. How would you rate your knowledge of English grammar? Would you say you are (a) very knowledgeable, (b) somewhat knowledgeable, or (c) you don't remember English grammar rules very well but you get by. If you selected *b* or *c*, what should you do to improve your knowledge of English grammar?

GO AND PRACTICE ACTIVITIES

1. Review a book on English grammar to refresh your knowledge on the rules that govern the English language. Then, in simplified language, explain to your ELs some of the grammatical features of the English language that are described as being most problematic to second language learners in general.
2. Start a portfolio of your ELs' writing samples. Have your students engage in a writing activity each day. It can be a structured activity, where you provide a prompt

and your students write about it, or it can be unstructured, where they are free to write on any topic they choose. Collect the samples at the end of each day and conduct an informal analysis. Highlight all of the errors made using different colors for the different types of errors. At the end of the week, you should have a clear visual representation of the types of errors your ELs are consistently making.

3. Write feedback reports for each student. Select three of the major errors committed and write possible reasons for those errors. Include exercises/activities that would help your ELs to edit their writing by recognizing their own errors. Then give one copy of your report to your English learner and place another in the student's portfolio. The feedback forms demonstrate progress over time as you document the reduction in errors made each week.

4. Research the various aspects of reading and writing found in the cultures of your English learners. A bilingual aide and the ELs in the class should participate in this activity. Allow the bilingual aide to provide input on the native language. If no aide is available, find a community volunteer or a native speaker of the language to verify whether the information found in your search is indeed correct. (Allow similar language groups to work together.) Along with your students, create a Venn diagram identifying the similarities and differences between English and each EL's native language. Be sure to keep a copy for your reference. If possible, allow your English learners to share their Venn diagrams with ELs in other classes.

CHAPTER 10

Teaching Edgar to Analyze a Text-Based Argument

Language and Literacy in High School

On the table were a lidded glass quart jar, half a quart of milk, and a plastic cylinder filled with pH strips. Edgar approached the objects and immediately began pouring. "Hold on there, Edgar," said Mr. Otto. "I can see you are excited to get started, but we need to follow the correct procedures." Edgar set the milk down and turned toward the front of the room. A girl who sat in the first row began handing out copies of a data table with three columns, one for listing the day, one for recording the pH, and one for noting the appearance of the jar of pasteurized milk in a 37°C incubator. Mr. Otto called Edgar back to help set up while he stated the directions for the weeklong experiment.

Every day Edgar entered his observations, carefully noticing the changes. The activity objective was to help students understand ecosystems and their functions, and Edgar was working steadily toward this end. Now that he had developed a sense of the changes over time, Edgar had to show his comprehension. Today the front-row girl handed out another paper, but this time it wasn't a data table. It was a quiz, with questions such as, "What might happen to an ecosystem if all the decomposers were to die?" and "Explain how the flow of energy contributes to and overlaps with the steps of the carbon cycle." Edgar's biology class was implementing the Common Core State Standards for disciplinary literacy with a science writing assessment, and he had no idea how to respond. After Edgar handed his teacher a blank page, Mr. Otto decided to contact Ms. Myers for help.

You might have expected to find Edgar in his language arts class like our other English learners in chapters 7 through 9. But because the gap is so vast between Edgar's intermediate (level 3) proficiency and the language demands of tenth-grade language arts instruction, the classroom application presented in this chapter details Edgar's experiences in a separate ELD class, showing in detail what type of language is used. We also show how his ELD teacher supports his use of academic language in other subjects and classes.

GRADE-LEVEL EXPECTATIONS FOR LANGUAGE AND LITERACY IN TENTH GRADE

Teachers at Highpoint High School are implementing the new and more rigorous English language arts Common Core State Standards that all students in all grades, including Edgar's tenth-grade class, are expected to meet. The following sections summarize the language demands established by these expectations and explain their accessibility for Edgar.

Reading

Analysis of complex, grade-level narrative and informational texts is the focus of most of the reading standards. Tenth graders are expected to cite evidence; analyze and summarize the central theme, character interaction, and plot development; comprehend figurative and connotative meanings and the impact of word choice on tone; and analyze text structure and order, development of ideas, rhetoric, and argumentation. The language standards impacting reading include comprehension of unknown words by using context, parts of speech, and reference materials; interpretation of figures of speech; and analysis of nuances in word meaning.

The following passage gives a sense of grade-level text for tenth grade:[1]

> When two people speak the same first language, they occasionally misunderstand each other. Imagine the difficulties that interpreters have when they must first understand what the speaker of one language has said and then translate the message into another language. Translators are challenged when the speaker makes a reference to an event or story character that is not known to listeners from another country. A speaker may refer to someone as a "Cinderella," meaning that a person was once poor and is now wealthy, but if the listeners do not know the story, the meaning is lost.

Writing

In writing, tenth graders are required to make claims and counterclaims; supply evidence; write cohesively; use formal style and objective tone; introduce, develop, and conclude an argument using facts and details; use transitions and precise language; use dialogue, pacing, description, reflection, and multiple plot lines; and use appropriate style for the task. The language standards pertaining to writing include the use of parallel structure and various types of phrases (noun, verb, adjective, adverbial, participial, prepositional, and absolute) and clauses (independent, dependent, noun, relative, and adverbial) as well as accurate use of academic and discipline-specific terms. They are also expected to use semicolons and colons and spell correctly.

The following paragraph provides a sense of the expectations for satisfactory writing at the high school level. It is an excerpt from a tenth-grade writing sample graded a 4 on a 6-point scale:[2]

> The fame, the fortune, the glitz and the glamour, is what some people try to achieve by becoming famous. Being famous is a life altering experience that takes you from being a nobody to being a somebody. Fame comes in many different ways, from being a politician to an athlete, but still they enjoy the rewards that it brings. Being famous would affect someone's life in many different ways.

Speaking, Listening, and Language

Students in tenth grade read in preparation for discussions; sustain conversations; respond thoughtfully; present information clearly, concisely, and logically, using substance and style that is appropriate to the audience; adapt their speech to the context; and use formal style.

LEVEL 3 ENGLISH LEARNERS' LANGUAGE AND LITERACY IN TENTH GRADE

To understand the gap between the grade-level expectations and what a typical English learner who was assessed at level 3 can understand and express, it is helpful to examine the descriptors for this proficiency level in detail. The following English Language Proficiency (ELP) standards, established by the Council of Chief State School Officers, represent the forms and functions English learners in tenth grade know and can perform in English by the end of level 3 of English proficiency, Edgar's current level.[3] They were developed to show English learners' effective language use during their progress toward independent participation in grade-level curriculum, instruction, and assessment.

Teachers can refer to the ELP standards to better understand where the gap is between their students' English proficiency and the CCSS language arts and literacy standards that their classes are expected to meet by year's end. Comparing them to the CCSS standards can highlight where extra support and time may be required in instruction and assessment.

Language Forms

By the end of level 3, the English learner will be able to demonstrate the knowledge, skill, or ability described in the standard, using frequently occurring words and phrases and an increasing number of idiomatic expressions.

Language Functions

The following language function descriptors begin with a CCSS grade-level standard, followed by its adaptation for English learners at level 3 of English proficiency (the *italicized* descriptor after the colon).

A level 3 English learner in tenth grade can:

- determine the meaning of words and phrases in oral presentations and literary and informational text: *determine the meaning of general academic and subject-specific words and phrases and frequently occurring expressions in texts about familiar topics, experiences, or events, using context, some visual aids, reference materials, and a basic knowledge of morphology (e.g., affixes, roots, and base words).*
- extract evidence from grade-appropriate oral presentations and literary and informational texts through close listening or reading: *determine the central idea or theme in oral presentations and written texts, and explain how it is developed by specific details in the texts.*
- speak and write about grade-appropriate complex literary and informational texts and topics: *compose short oral or written reports on informational topics or events, developing the topic with a few details, using simple and some compound or complex sentences and a few general academic and subject-specific words or phrases.*
- adapt language choices to purpose, task, and audience when speaking or writing: *adapt word choices and style according to purpose, task, and audience, with developing ease, using some general academic and subject-specific words and expressions in speech and written text.*
- construct a grade-appropriate oral or written claim and support it with reasoning and evidence: *construct a claim about familiar topics: introduce the topic, provide sufficient reasons or facts to support the claim, and provide a concluding sentence, using a variety of sentences and some general academic and subject-specific words.*
- participate in grade-appropriate oral and written exchanges of information, ideas, and analyses, responding to peer, audience, or reader comments and questions: *participate in conversations, discussions, and written exchanges on familiar topics, texts, and issues: build on the ideas of others and express his or her own views, ask and answer relevant questions, add relevant information and evidence, and restate some of the key ideas expressed.*
- research and/or obtain, evaluate, and communicate grade-appropriate oral and written information in a clear and effective response to a defined task and purpose: *carry out short research projects to answer a question; gather information from multiple provided print and digital sources and paraphrase key information in a short written or oral report, using modeled sentences and simple sentences, with labeled illustration, diagrams, or graphic organizers; and provide a list of sources.*
- analyze and critique the arguments of others orally and in writing: *explain the reasons an author or speaker gives to support a claim, and cite textual evidence to support the analysis, using mostly simple and a few compound sentences and using some academic and subject-specific words and phrases.*

- use grade-appropriate standard English forms to communicate in speech and writing: *use a limited variety of phrases (e.g., noun, verb, adjectival, adverbial, and prepositional) and clauses (independent, dependent, relative, and adverbial), and produce and expand simple compound and a few complex sentences.*
- create clear and coherent grade-appropriate speech and text: *narrate a sequence of events or present ideas and information, using transitional words and phrases to show logical relationships among events and ideas.*

The description for language form shows that level 3 English learners generally use frequently occurring words and phrases and idiomatic expressions. Comparing the CCSS English language arts standards for tenth grade with Edgar's assessed level of English proficiency (level 3), as described by the ELP language forms and functions above, indicates a number of outcomes that Edgar may not reach by year's end. For example, a tenth grader is expected to explain or draw inferences from a grade-level text in English, but Edgar's knowledge and use of frequent words, phrases, and idiomatic expressions in English do not yet equip him to comprehend complex sentences or verb tenses. The ELP language functions give reasonable suggestions on addressing a CCSS standard given the level of English proficiency. They do not, however, provide specifics on how to teach lessons addressing those standards for English learners. Of course, as Edgar's English language proficiency develops, he will be able to comprehend and express concepts with more complex language.

CCSS grade-level descriptors that Edgar can meet include comprehension of unknown words through using context, parts of speech, and reference materials, interpretation of figures of speech, and analysis of nuances in word meaning, as long as appropriate scaffolding is provided.

Although there are some CCSS English language arts standards that Edgar can achieve without modification, he is faced with more standards that require a much higher level of English proficiency. In the Classroom Application section, we present guidelines for teaching English language arts to Edgar based on formal and classroom assessment of his oral proficiency and literacy skills in English.

RESEARCH ON TEACHING LANGUAGE AND LITERACY TO ENGLISH LEARNERS IN HIGH SCHOOL

Supporting English learners' literacy development at the high school level is multifaceted. Effective reading requires proficiency in three interrelated sets of factors pertaining to language, literacy, and world knowledge.[4] Linguistic factors relate to knowledge of textual elements such as word, sentence, and text structures. Literacy factors pertain to cognitive and metacognitive awareness and use of reading strategies such as setting a purpose for reading, monitoring one's understanding, solving reading comprehension difficulties during reading, and monitoring comprehension. Knowledge factors consist of the background information that readers already possess and may use to fill in gaps in the explicit linguistic elements in a text.

Oral Proficiency in English

As noted in previous chapters, oral proficiency in English is necessary for reading comprehension and writing proficiency. The degree of oral proficiency necessary for most English learners to participate in class is not sufficient for successful reading in a second language, however. Indeed, significant numbers of students have a great deal of proficiency in conversational English and yet read very slowly and with poor comprehension. In other words, good oral language proficiency skills are a necessary but not sufficient condition for effective reading and understanding of academic subjects, which require proficiency in academic English. Even students with advanced conversational English skills need time and support to develop proficient academic English skills, which usually takes from four to seven years. EL students with no prior schooling or support in the native language may take seven to ten years to catch up to their peers.[5]

Language arts and literacy teachers in high school often face the challenge of working with English learners who have adequate oral language proficiency but below-grade literacy skills. When English learners, like Edgar, experience difficulty in reading and text understanding, it is common for teachers to focus on vocabulary knowledge as a major source of difficulty. However, language arts and literacy teachers also know that while vocabulary knowledge is crucial to reading, writing, and content learning, effective reading comprehension requires much more. Research indicates that almost any kind of vocabulary instruction can improve students' performance on vocabulary tests. Unfortunately, many commonly used methods of vocabulary instruction do not reliably increase students' reading comprehension.[6] English learners, even those with high levels of oral proficiency in English, may be less sensitive to certain types of information supplied by context, particularly details supplied by morphological (word structure) and syntactic (word sequence) components of language. In fact, for struggling EL and non-EL readers and writers in upper elementary, middle, and high school classrooms, morphological and syntactic aspects of language have been shown to play more important roles in reading development than previously assumed.

Because reading comprehension requires more than knowing word meanings, we encourage language arts and literacy teachers to incorporate in their teaching a healthy balance of formal and informal instruction by focusing on (a) what readers need to know about language and text features to apply reading and learning strategies effectively and (b) what good readers do when they engage in text reading and understanding.

For example, teaching students how certain aspects of language such as morphology and syntax work might include information about important prefixes, suffixes, and root words. It is helpful for developing language learners, readers, and writers to know, for instance, that inflectional morphemes such as the plural suffix *-s*; or the past tense *-ed* do not change the meaning of the words, but they convey information about agreement, tense, and plurality. On the other hand, derivational morphemes change word meanings and parts of speech, as in the words *read-reader*; *magic-magician*; *teach-teacher*;

clever-cleverly. Teachers can help students like Edgar develop morphological knowledge and skills by incorporating instruction that focuses on prefixes, suffixes, and root words while emphasizing that words are related in meaningful ways (e.g., *create, creation, creativity*, etc.). This type of instructed second language acquisition, or focus on form, helps students decode morphologically complex words, understand word meanings, and comprehend what they read. It can also help English learners develop grammatical competence in all four skills—listening, speaking, reading, and writing—as well as further their acquisition of new forms in English and avoid fossilization or stabilization of errors. Pointing out that the added *s* in, for example, *she likes* is required can help English learners notice that feature and develop competence in using it correctly over time.

In addition to teaching EL students about important morphological and syntactic aspects of language, language arts and literacy teachers should help students develop strategic or metacognitive knowledge about reading. Examples of this type of knowledge might include strategies for unlocking the meanings of unknown words, using what they already know about a topic to make sense of what they read, restating the meaning of a text or passage using one's own words, and evaluating what one reads in a critical way. To help students develop this type of knowledge, it is best for teachers to first explain the strategic processes involved in reading, model these strategies using different types of texts, and provide students opportunities to practice these strategies, first with teacher guidance and then on their own using self-selected texts.

First Language Influences on English Language Literacy

Students like Edgar possess a wealth of knowledge about their native languages. Edgar's language arts and literacy teachers should take advantage of the similarities and differences between Spanish and English when designing instruction to support his language and literacy development. There are well-established similarities and differences between first and second language reading. We suggest that teachers consider integrating in their teaching explicit instruction in how languages are different and similar in terms of sound structure, word and sentence formation, vocabulary, and text structure. Differences and similarities across languages can then be reinforced by engaging Edgar and his peers in reading sample texts that address similar topics in Spanish and English, and in comparing the texts to see how they differ in their expression of ideas in writing and their use of vocabulary, grammar, and text structure. These activities will help Edgar expand his knowledge of how both languages work, and ultimately use what he knows about his own language to advance his listening, speaking, reading, and writing skills in English.

Students need to know that writing is used as a means of communication to express ideas, thoughts, and feelings across all human languages. Writers in all languages use a variety of genres (e.g., essays, poems, stories), formats (e.g., narrative, descriptive, explanatory texts), and styles (e.g., formal, casual). Students should know that all languages have conventions, guidelines and procedures for writing, and that, developmentally, the process of learning to write in any language takes greater time and effort than learning to speak it.

When learning to write in a second language, students should know that different languages apply different conventions, guidelines, and procedures in their writing systems. These conventions vary a great deal depending on the linguistic distance between any two languages. For instance, while all human languages have subjects, verbs, and objects, some languages, such as English, German, and French, have a subject-verb-object (SVO) structure, while others languages, such as Pashto and Turkish, require a subject-object-verb (SOV) construction. German is one of the languages that use the SVO structure in main clauses, but subordinate clauses follow the SOV structure. Yet other languages, such as Arabic and Hebrew, use a verb-subject-object (VSO) structure. In addition, some of these languages differ in terms of script and direction. For instance, Arabic and Hebrew have twenty-eight letters and are read from right to left; English and French have twenty-six letters and are read from left to right. It is also important to note that there are significant differences in spelling systems. English spelling, for instance, is said to be more irregular than spelling in languages such as Spanish, which has a more regular orthography. It is estimated that about four hundred words in English have irregular spellings, and these are among the most frequently used words in the language.[7] Finally, different languages use different rhetorical structures and devices to organize writing and convey meaning.

◆ CLASSROOM APPLICATION ◆

To assess Edgar's reading skills in English, Ms. Myers asked him to read aloud for her.

"I don't like read." "Yeah, Edgar, I know," Ms. Myers said, laughing a bit as she let out a shallow sigh. "Let's go ahead and try this story. Edgar, please do your best for me." Ms. Myers reached under the table and pulled up a plastic-wrapped hardcover book, already open to the first page. She set it in front of Edgar, holding her palm in the crease until Edgar gripped the sides. Now that it was in Edgar's hands, Ms. Myers put her cupped hand to her ear, raising her eyebrows. Edgar half-smiled and rolled his eyes, unapproving, yet obliging Ms. Myers, and began:

"Um . . . William . . . um . . . we are going out. Um . . . We will be . . . um, at the movies . . . uh . . . and . . . we go out to dinner." Edgar read word by word, flatly. There was no rise and fall in tone—just monotone expression, virtually meaningless.

"Uh . . . We will not be out late. Please be good for the baby sister. Miss Lane may will be coming over, says Mom. Okay, Mom, say William. He was not ha . . . happy. He did not like, not like it, when Mom and Dad went out. They left h-him at home. William did not like having a babysit . . . sitter." One syllable, one syllable, one syllable, two. One syllable, one syllable, two syllable, two. Edgar read like a typewriter. A typewriter with Spanish accents on the vowels.

"Miss Lane made him eat all his dinner. She did not let him play outside. She was afrai William wo get hurt. Miss Lane was no fun. She never play . . . play any games with William. Miss Lane walk-ed in the door, Hello, William, how are you? say Miss Lane. OK, (I don't know how to say that) say William. He walk he walk-ed back to his room. He decide to read for (I don't know that). He like to read books."

Edgar read the way he spoke, with final consonants dissolving like his confidence. Many times he had been told to pronounce all the letters at the end of words, so he made sure to pronounce *walked* not as *walkt* or *walk*, but *walk-ed*. When he came across words he didn't know, he just said so. He was trying to read a story many grade levels below his own, and he was trying his best.

"That's good, Edgar," said Ms. Myers. "That's enough for now. Thank you for reading for me." "Uh-huh," replied Edgar, as he shut the book and pushed it toward the edge of the table.

ANALYZING EDGAR'S CLASSROOM LANGUAGE SAMPLES

This language sample makes clear that Edgar is reading far below tenth-grade level, struggling with a third-grade story. He clearly needs targeted instruction in learning to read English. And because so much of the new content in his academic classes is transmitted through reading, he also needs to make as quick a transition to reading to learn as possible. Ms. Myers's ELD class is exactly what he needs.

Mainstream teachers in upper elementary, middle, and high school classrooms should be mindful of all students, including EL students, who appear to struggle when reading disciplinary content materials. It is evident that while Edgar seems to be doing fairly well and to enjoy being in Ms. Myers's ELD class, he is clearly not doing as well in his subject-area classes like mathematics, science, and social studies. The intriguing thing is that he finds these classes "boring," most likely because he does not feel he is getting the same level of attention and help from his teachers or fellow students. Edgar has relatively good conversational skills in English, which are helpful when communicating with his teachers and peers. However, he doesn't have the requisite academic language skills (e.g., depth and breadth of academic vocabulary, understanding of the structure of words, sentences, and textual materials) to read and understand academic materials. As we indicated in previous sections of this book, the learning demands for reading, writing, and comprehending texts in grades 4 through 12 are far greater than in the earlier grades, in part due to text complexity, conceptual density, and arduous language demands. EL students such as Edgar may have difficulties with one or more of these issues, which contribute in different and yet complementary ways to their ability to read and write.

Ms. Myers regularly requires her English learners to write, giving them both structured and open assignments. For a free-writing assignment about his little brother's birthday present, Edgar wrote these lines:

The TriCycle is good for childrens Like 3 or 2 year because the tricycle has wheel and the childrens don't fold wen The are playing.

The brevity of Edgar's composition shows a number of areas that he is struggling with. First, he was able to write only one sentence during the ten-minute writing activity. He has difficulties with basic language conventions in English such as capitalization, plural forms (childrens, 3 or 2 year, wheel), and spelling of vowel sounds that he hears and pronounces according to his native language sound system, causing the confusion between the spelling of *fall* and *fold*. Because his variety of Spanish often eliminates final consonant sounds, he is confused about when a consonant is pronounced in English word endings. It can't be overemphasized how much Edgar needs targeted English language instruction, which, given the gap between his current level of English proficiency and the expectations for tenth-grade English language arts instruction, must take place in a separate instructional environment with a qualified ELD teacher.

Because we are not comparing this separate ELD instruction to a grade-level (tenth-grade) English language arts lesson, we are not applying phase I of the Language Arts Protocol as we did in chapters 7 through 9, where we needed that analysis to determine appropriate adjustments (phase II). Instead, we describe the lesson as it takes place in an ELD classroom.

MS. MYERS'S TEXT MESSAGING LESSON

As described in the first section of this chapter and as demonstrated through Edgar's reading and writing samples, it is clear that there are a number of grade-level English language arts standards that Edgar cannot currently meet. For example, CCSS.ELA-LITERACY.L.9-10.6 (Acquire and use accurately general academic and domain-specific words and phrases, sufficient for reading, writing, speaking, and listening at the college and career readiness level) is a standard that Edgar can work toward, but as a level 3 English learner he does not yet have the English proficiency to attain. On the other hand, many ELA standards are broad enough for Edgar to meet with targeted language instruction in an ELD classroom. This lesson reaches toward the ELA knowledge and skills that Edgar needs to develop to be college and career ready, but it is targeted to Edgar's skills at this point in time.

The lesson described here is one lesson in a unit framed around the topic "Does all communication serve a positive purpose?"[8] It is targeted to level 3 students and is designed to address a number of grade-level English language arts Common Core State Standards for reading informational text as well as listening and speaking. Specifically, the lesson concentrates on reading with the goal of identifying a main idea and supporting details.

The lesson description provides transcripts of teacher and student speech to give insights into how this lesson is different from grade-level language arts instruction. We then discuss these specifics using our four Ps of language arts scaffolding for English learners.

Literacy Standards:

CCSS.ELA-LITERACY.RI.9-10.2: Determine a central idea of a text and how it is conveyed through particular details; provide a summary of the text distinct from personal opinions or judgments.

CCSS.ELA-LITERACY.SL.9-10.1: Initiate and participate effectively in a range of collaborative discussions (one-on-one, in groups, and teacher led) with diverse partners on grades 9–10 topics, texts, and issues, building on others' ideas and expressing their own clearly.

CCSS.ELA-LITERACY.SL.9-10.1.D: Respond thoughtfully to diverse perspectives, summarize points of agreement and disagreement, and, when warranted, qualify or justify their own views and understanding and make new connections in light of the evidence and reasoning presented.

CCSS.ELA-LITERACY.L.9-10.4: Determine or clarify the meaning of unknown and multiple-meaning words and phrases based on grades 9–10 reading and content, choosing flexibly from a range of strategies.

OBJECTIVES

Ms. Myers's objectives for this lesson are for students to support their opinion about a topic in discussion (if they use text messaging and whether it is good or harmful for teens) and then to analyze a text for its main idea and the details that support it.

LESSON DESCRIPTION

Ms. Myers holds up her smartphone and says, "Raise your hand [raises her hand] if you like to text [mimes texting on her phone] with your friends [points to the class]." After students raise their hands, she asks two complex questions, chunking each sentence segment and pausing to gauge comprehension and engagement. She clearly states her first question:

Is texting different [pauses, looks at class]

from how we communicate [pauses]

when we talk? [pauses]

How?

"I talk like text," Edgar answers as he smiles at the girl sitting beside him. "Why you so DDG [drop dead gorgeous]?"

"Okay, Edgar," says Ms. Myers, "we get what you mean. Some people text more than they talk. Maybe texting has influenced the way we talk now. Texting's influence could be big, or it could be a drop in the bucket. *A drop in the bucket* is an idiom that means a small influence. It comes from adding water to a bucket, or pail. We can add a cup [she mimes holding a cup and tilting it upside down], or we can add a drop [she mimes pinching an eye dropper pointed downward]. A drop is a small amount." She writes *drop in the bucket* on the Idiom of the Day wall chart.

Ms. Myers follows up with another chunked question:

Is texting different [pause]

from how we communicate [pause]

when we write at school? [pause]

How?

A student replies, "Is different. For write at school, we use word. For texting, we say thing like LOL." Everyone nods and smiles knowingly.

"Yes, that's right," says Ms. Myers. "When we write [pauses and scans the class for comprehension], we use full words [holds hands out at waist level, about two feet apart]. Full words like *laughing out loud*. When we write, we don't use [shakes head] abbreviations like *LOL*." She then writes *abbreviations* on the board, saying the word slowly, syllable by syllable, and asks the students to repeat each syllable, then the entire word, in chorus.

"An abbreviation is a short way of saying something. What examples of abbreviations can you think of?" Students offer more examples, yelling out terms like BFF (best friend forever), F2F (face to face), and JK (just kidding), as the teacher writes the abbreviations and their full forms on the board. Ms. Myers goes on, "When we write, we use correct grammar. When we text, we break a lot of grammar rules. The topic of our lesson today is why some people think text messaging is a bad form of communication. Let's read this article [points to article in textbook]." The students follow silently as she expressively reads the article the first time, paragraph by paragraph.

Do you like to send text messages? Text messaging through cell phones is popular among teens, but it can be controversial among adults. People who think it's harmful have put texting on trial.

Ms. Myers pauses after each point: "Text messaging through cell phones [pause] is popular among teens [pause] but it can be controversial [pause] among adults." After reading the short paragraph, she tells students to pair up and state in their own words what the paragraph means. She also asks them to identify any words or phrases that they don't understand. Once they have discussed the paragraph, she asks for a volunteer to paraphrase the paragraph. She then asks if anyone needs a definition for any words or clarification of any information in the paragraph. The students ask what *put on trial* means, and Ms. Myers explains that it means to examine the evidence to determine whether something is *right/good* or *wrong/bad*, like in a courtroom. Another question is the meaning of the word *among*, to which Ms. Myers not only offers *between* or *with* but also mentions that these words are synonyms.

Once everyone states that they understand the paragraph, Ms. Myers moves on, reading the following text with appropriate pauses:

> The first argument against text messaging is that the constant use of abbreviations takes away from a student's ability to write clear and well-organized papers. Supporters of texting say that language happens on a continuum, from very casual to very formal, and that it's unlikely that teens will confuse the two.

As they work together on paraphrasing the paragraph, some students ask what *takes away from* means. Does it mean steal or subtract? Ms. Myers happily notices that the students make a connection to mathematics with their second guess. She responds that another way to say *takes away from* is *detracts*, and it means to weaken or lessen something. This word is a cognate of *detractar* in Spanish, which helps some students gather its meaning. When students ask what a *continuum* is, Ms. Myers draws a horizontal line on the whiteboard and writes "very casual" on one end and "very formal" on the other.

Following two more paragraphs that repeat the process, Ms. Myers explains that now each student will complete the daily table [holds up the blank table her class uses each day to identify main ideas and supporting details] for this article. She reminds them that they write each main idea in the left column [points to left column] and each of the main idea's supporting details in the right column [point to right column].

Once all students have completed the table, Ms. Myers uses a student selector app on her iPad to identify individuals to answer questions. Her first question is "What is an argument the article presents against text messaging?" The selected student refers to the table he completed to respond, and Ms. Myers summarizes the reply with bullet points on the whiteboard. She continues the process, then changes the question to, "How do people who support text messaging respond to these arguments?"

TABLE 10.1

Sample Daily Table

Main Idea	Supporting Details

Now Ms. Myers asks the students to take turns in their groups, expressing their personal opinion by completing the following sentence frame:

"I think text messaging is/is not harmful for teens because_____."

When the students are done writing, she asks them to stand up, pick up their completed sentence frame handout, and line up according to their opinion on text messaging. One side of the room has a label that says "very harmful"; the opposite side's label says "not harmful at all." After they are situated, she asks each student to state his or her opinion as she moves from one side of the issue to the other.

EVALUATION

Ms. Myers conducts formative assessment through a journal entry, "My opinion on text messaging and teens." Summative assessment is conducted through a unit test.

APPLYING THE LANGUAGE ARTS PROTOCOL
to the Writing Lesson

PHASE I: Understanding the Needed Language Skills and Edgar

Since this is a self-contained ELD class in which all students are at Edgar's proficiency level (level 3), Ms. Myers does not need to conduct steps 1 and 2 of phase I. Instead, her instructional planning starts with phase II.

PHASE II: Targeted Language Arts Instruction for Edgar

As you read through the following description of the four Ps, scaffolding use, and time considerations that constitute phase II of the Language Arts Protocol, you may want to occasionally move back to the preceding detailed lesson description, which shows what these features look like when put into action.

STEP 1: SCAFFOLDING LANGUAGE ARTS INSTRUCTION

As an ELD specialist, Ms. Myers has extensive experience in identifying specific challenges the English language poses for second language learners and how to scaffold her instruction so that her students can move toward attainment of the grade-level English language arts standards and simultaneously move up in language proficiency.

PITCH. A number of elements in this lesson reflect research and theory on second language acquisition and literacy development. Ms. Myers's word and phrase choices are geared toward a level 3 English learner. She paraphrases and defines idiomatic expressions (*drop in the bucket*) and phrasal verbs (*take away from*) and uses sentence structure that level 3 English learners comprehend. She is mindful of "processability" when setting expectations for Edgar's comprehension and production of grammatical structures.[9] She has in-depth knowledge of Edgar's proficiency in listening, speaking, reading, and writing through continuous assessment, using regularly collected samples of his spoken and written work as well as performance assessment and paper and pencil tests of his listening and reading skills. When speaking, Ms. Myers chunks long sentences, adding nonverbal support when introducing terms or phrases she believes are unfamiliar to the students. She also selected a reading passage that is just slightly above what students at this level can read independently in terms of grammatical complexity, vocabulary, and infrequent or unusual structure and form. The text uses present tense sentences, either in simple present (*parents also complain*) or present continuous form (*when kids get bored, they start sending messages*).

PACE. Ms. Myers's pace is markedly slower than what a grade-level language arts teacher would use. She breaks up long sentences, even in oral presentation and discussion, and pauses between clauses and phrases, checking for comprehension through attentiveness to students' expressions as well as frequent questions directed at her English learners' level of proficiency. In addition, her frequent elaboration of unfamiliar terms to further clarify meaning, as described under pitch, slows the pace of instruction and the amount of content she can address. Her associated nonverbal support, as well as her frequent transcription of new terms and definitions on the whiteboard, also slow the pace of instruction.

PORTION. The topic of the lesson and the required reading are restricted to a manageable amount for a level 3 English learner. Although there is likely new terminology and phrasing for Edgar, there is ample time for Ms. Myers to discuss, expand, and explain it because the content is limited. The amount of writing is also kept to a reasonable task for the allotted time.

PERSPECTIVE/POINT. There are a number of perspective aspects in the lesson for English learners. The meaning of terms and phrasing is frequently expressed, with definitions, cognates, paraphrasing, and nonverbal support used. On the following day, Ms. Myers follows up this lesson with a focus on form, looking at the difference in when we use simple present and present continuous tenses and analyzing how they are formed in affirmative and negative statements as well as questions. This follow-up lesson for ELs is an example of language arts instruction that has an entirely different point than it would if designed for native speakers.

STEP 2: USE OF SCAFFOLDING

Because Edgar's English proficiency level is well below grade-level language arts instruction, his targeted language instruction is an alternative to what is being taught to the native speakers. It occurs entirely in the ELD classroom.

TIME. This lesson is in a self-contained, dedicated ELD class that is held during Edgar's language arts period.

PROVIDER. As the specialist teaching this ELD class, Ms. Myers is clearly the provider of the lesson. However, she also coordinates with Edgar's academic subject teachers to provide support for the language demands of those courses.

STOP AND REFLECT QUESTIONS

1. What resources do you have at your school for ELD instruction? Talk with your colleagues about their support of English learners and any resources they have identified.
2. Can you recall a time when an English learner in your class demonstrated visible frustration from an inability to pronounce a word or read a sentence correctly? How was his/her frustration displayed? As the teacher, what did you do?

GO AND PRACTICE ACTIVITIES

1. Research the specific differences between narrative and expository (informational) text. Create a chart comparing the two. Simplify the chart and share it with your ELs. Discuss which aspects of each they find to be easy or difficult.
2. Work with your ELD specialist and your speech-language pathologist to identify any morphological or syntactic difficulties your English learners may be experiencing.
3. Instruct your English learners to find a book written in their native language. Assign them to work with their parents to identify the nouns, verbs, and articles in the book and then highlight them on a poster, using different colors. Have them create a poster display of sample sentences selected from their book with the highlighted words to share with the class. Allow the students to discuss the differences between their sentence structures. Finally, have them compare those structures to English.
4. Identify the various writing systems of the languages spoken in your class. Collect writing samples from your ELs and determine which syntactical structures from your students' writing systems are being transferred into their writing in English.

A Call for Collaboration

We've spent all the previous chapters navigating the gap together. We looked at it from the top, the bottom, and everywhere in between. We assessed its depth in kindergarten, and we worked our way right on over to high school. Grade-level expectations keep rising, and English learners keep striving to catch up. After everything we've experienced with the gap, we know, thankfully, that teachers can help close it. If English learners receive the highest quality and quantity of accessible communication and targeted language instruction, their language development and academic subject achievement will increase.

The reality is that most English learners—who have varying life and school experiences and different levels of English proficiency—are placed in mainstream classrooms for at least part of the day. This has implications not only for their teachers, but also for the entire school. This means that all educators have the responsibility, and the privilege, of supporting English learners' achievement. We can all share their struggles, help shoulder their burdens, rejoice in their successes, and broaden and brighten our outlook through experiencing the newness of our own language and culture through their eyes.

In the introduction, we noted that our goal is not to explain how to teach language arts or academic subjects. Rather, we aim to help already practicing educators or preservice teachers teach their subjects by concentrating on what is unique about reaching different types of English learners in the mainstream classroom. Subsequent chapters offered practical guidance focused on what academic subject as well as language arts and literacy teachers can do to make curriculum, instruction, and assessment accessible for English learners. In this conclusion, we illustrate two key elements to successful teaching of English learners in mainstream classrooms—professional learning and collaboration—and call on individual teachers, as well as school-based teams, to engage in both.

ONE PLUS MODEL OF PROFESSIONAL LEARNING AND COLLABORATION

Being informed about English learners and how to support their achievement is critical for all educators. But one size doesn't fit all for professional learning. Different types of educators have different knowledge, skills, and needs, so why should they all complete the same courses or in-service components about teaching English learners? During our work with school districts we have witnessed counterproductive results when professional learning about ELs is delivered as an add-on rather than embedded within the specific subjects and grade levels of future or practicing teachers. So over the years we developed a framework for professional learning and collaboration—the One Plus Model. We described its theoretical and practical details in our previous book, *Preparing Every Teacher to Reach English Learners: A Practical Guide for Teacher Educators*. It is a good companion to this book because it explains how to integrate a focus on English learners into professional learning about most any academic subject or discipline.

EL-Focused Professional Learning

We believe that all teachers need targeted knowledge and skills to reach ELs, and that each professional contributes to EL achievement and English language development in a unique and important way. Each type of educator has a different role in supporting English learners' success and has different background knowledge and skills and, therefore, different needs for professional learning. Our work over the past two decades has been aimed at identifying which second language acquisition and teaching research, theory, and instructional practices teachers of English learners in mainstream classrooms need to know and be able use. We take into account the existing pedagogical content knowledge and skills of academic subject and language arts teachers, build on them, and add a laser focus on what is different about teaching those subjects to English learners.

Given the many demands on teachers' time, we believe there is a point of diminishing returns in identifying the knowledge and skills for teaching English learners that every teacher must acquire, which should generally be less extensive than the knowledge and skills required of ELD specialists. Of course, the proportion of English learners to native speakers in these teachers' classrooms also affects the instructional practices they use and the amount of professional learning required to implement them. Although some may feel that more is always better, we have found that relevance and usefulness of the content of professional learning are better criteria for selection than sheer quantity.

From our work with teachers in different states we have concluded that not only the type but also the extent of knowledge and skills are different for different educators, with a further distinction for academic subject and language arts/literacy teachers. Recognizing the differences in purpose of and approach to teaching language arts and academic subjects, our One Plus Model of professional learning establishes basic knowledge regarding English learners that is beneficial for all types of educators. This is followed by additional knowledge and skills for adapting curriculum, instruction, and assessment that all teachers of English learners can apply in preK–12 classrooms, then yet more in-depth knowledge and skills required to teach language arts and literacy to English learners.

Figure C.1 illustrates this stratified approach to the content of professional learning. At the top layer of the pyramids, we indicate that all educators need to know

FIGURE C.1
One Plus Model of Professional Learning

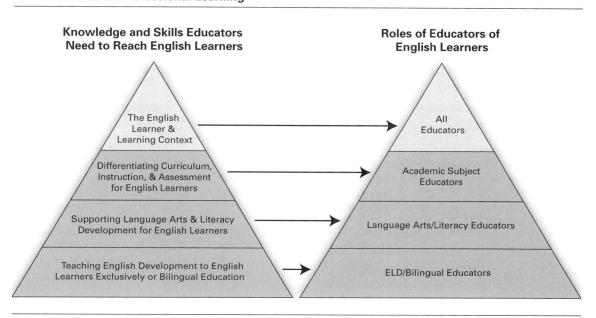

basic information about English learners and the context in which they learn. This entails a general understanding of the factors affecting second language acquisition, especially those over which educators have some control, such as the comprehensibility of classroom communication. Other factors, such as age and native language of the learner, are important to be aware of, especially in how they affect language development, regardless of whether they are outside the teacher's sphere of influence. The learning context spans issues such as the program model and family and community support and their roles in EL language development and academic achievement. Teachers, principals, counselors, and so on need a foundational degree of understanding of these important topics.

In addition to these foundational topics, all teachers need specific information about differentiating curriculum, instruction, and assessment for English learners. Those who teach primarily academic subjects benefit from understanding how to engage English learners and support their achievement in those subjects, represented by the second layer from the top of the two pyramids. While academic subject teachers certainly support language and literacy in their content areas, that is not the main purpose of their instruction. For language arts and literacy teachers it is, and therefore the linguistic nature of their subject requires more expertise in teaching language.

Language arts and literacy teachers also benefit from knowing how to support the academic subject learning of ELs. Primarily, however, these teachers need deeper understanding of the second language acquisition process, the influence of the first language on the acquisition of English, and best practices for second language and literacy development, represented by the third layer from the top of the pyramids.

The base layers of the pyramids depict the specialized knowledge and skills required of ELD and bilingual education teachers. These teachers are experts who co-teach and serve as resources for classroom teachers of English learners. Accordingly, their depth and breadth of knowledge and skills regarding teaching and assessing English learners is greater than what other types of teachers need.

This book is broadly organized by the One Plus Model of professional learning, offering information on key concepts and instructions about best practices for meeting English learners where they are, within the context of the mainstream classroom. While the limits on book length prevent the inclusion of the entire professional learning curriculum, we have organized the main sections of the book by the top three layers of the pyramids. In the introductory chapter, we offered a brief discussion of key points relative to the English learner and the learning context. In part I, we presented highlights of research and theory as well as practical guidance for differentiating curriculum, instruction, and assessment for academic subjects, and in part II, we provided essential information for reaching English learners in the curriculum, instruction, and assessment of language arts and literacy.

Schoolwide Collaboration for English Learner Success

We have outlined our approach to raising the achievement of English learners in the mainstream classroom, showing how educators can share expertise and combine efforts to improve classroom communication and language instruction for English learners. In describing and applying both the Academic Subjects Protocol and the Language Arts Protocol, we offered many suggestions for planning and delivering curriculum, instruction, and assessment that are linked to the sharing of expertise among mainstream content-area teachers, language arts teachers, and ELD specialists. Indeed, the One Plus Model is constructed on the very premise that all school-based educators have important contributions to make in assuring that the English learner population in our preK–12 schools receive the attention they deserve and require to reach their highest potential. Each educator in the school building carries out essential duties consistent with his or her areas of expertise and experience. Therefore, we submit that they do not all need to have the same knowledge and skills to work effectively with these students. It is the implementation of everyone's duties in a *coherent, collaborative manner* that leads to the academic achievement of English learners in the mainstream classroom.[1]

Educators often refer to effective schools as "communities of learners." Rooted in that description is the belief that these communities experience deep interpersonal connections that encourage teachers, administrators, noninstructional personnel, volunteers, and parents to address and openly communicate the needs of all students, including English learners. Creating such a culture of commitment and interconnectedness through communication promotes success for English learners.

Educator Roles

Schools are multidimensional centers of activity that run best when there is cross-disciplinary consultation, collaboration, and teamwork. Teachers are undoubtedly the most visible educators working with students. In a typical week, most English learners, depending on their age and grade level, spend a significant portion of their school time in mainstream classrooms with instructional personnel, including content-area teachers (e.g., science, mathematics, or social studies), language, and/or literacy teachers. ELD specialists assume various amounts of direct instructional time with English learners, depending on the school's program model for English language development. Occasionally, these students also interact with various other noninstructional school personnel such as school psychologists, language/speech pathologists, counselors, and school administrators.

Mainstream English learners in elementary school spend the majority of the day with the same teacher who teaches most of the academic subjects, including language arts/literacy. Like the mainstream language arts/literacy teacher, the ELD specialist always focuses on English language development, but both the depth of involvement and the amount of time they interact with ELs vary greatly. Some have their own classrooms where they teach self-contained ELD content, as in Gero's and Edith's cases, to kick-start the second language acquisition process. Others go from classroom to classroom where they teach ELs in small groups for fifteen to thirty minutes, while the regular teacher continues instruction with the rest of the class.[2]

In secondary schools, where the students have a different teacher for each subject, ELD teachers may conduct self-contained ELD classes that EL students attend in addition to their regular language arts/literacy class, or they may provide targeted language instruction in place of the mainstream class that is designed to catch students up to grade-level instruction. This was the case with Edgar, whose English language proficiency was not compatible with grade-level language arts instruction.[3] Therefore, English learners at the secondary level typically spend approximately one class period per day with ELD teachers.

Noninstructional personnel have mostly intermittent contact with ELs that does not add up to a lot of time throughout a school year. Nonetheless, they perform essential functions *in support of classroom teachers*, who depend on these professionals' knowledge of the intersection of second language acquisition issues and their specialized expertise. For example, school psychologists follow up on requests from teachers to test for giftedness or assist in determining and carrying out interventions for ELs who fail to meet state or district benchmarks for reading instruction, while school counselors or administrators help families of newly arrived immigrants to navigate the American school system.[4]

Because of their deep knowledge of second language acquisition, ELD specialists are best equipped to assist all instructional and noninstructional personnel in meeting their respective responsibilities of educating English learners.[5] By collaborating with each other and with ELD specialists through cycles of examining student work, and creating and implementing instructional supports focused on students' language and content needs, teachers can find effective ways of helping all students reach these learning goals while still maintaining their individual teaching styles and flexibility.

In the following sections we highlight the type of knowledge educators need to gain, depending on their roles, as well as suggestions for how this learning can take place in a collaborative fashion.

Knowledge and Skills Needed to Reach English Learners

Figure C.2 provides an overview of the knowledge that the different school professionals highlighted in this book need to build in order to meet the unique needs of English learners. Most of the topics were addressed briefly in the introduction and chapters 1 and 6. This framework summarizes the "stackable" knowledge and skills each type of educator needs to effectively teach English learners. All educators, both instructional and noninstructional personnel, start out needing the same knowledge and skills.

The depth and breadth of needed knowledge then increases at each subsequent level. While all classroom teachers need to be able to recognize the academic language demands of their curriculum and implement appropriate best practices for English learners, language arts/literacy teachers of ELs need more in-depth knowledge in second language acquisition and applied linguistics than academic subject teachers.

Job-Embedded Professional Learning

One of the main tenets of the One Plus Model is that all educators do not need the same knowledge and skill set as ELD specialists. They do, however, need to enhance

FIGURE C.2

One Plus Model—Content by Educator Type

All Educators		Academic Subject Teachers		Language Arts/Literacy Teachers
The English learner and the learning context • EL demographics • EL legal issues • EL policy issues, including assessment accommodations • EL family issues • EL cultural and acculturation issues • EL proficiency levels • EL program options, including instructional models	**+** **+** **+**	**Differentiation of curriculum, instruction, and assessment** • Academic language demands • Content-specific research and best practices for ELs • Curricular adaptations • Instructional (and assessment) modifications by English proficiency level	**+** **+** **+**	**Support of language arts/ literacy development** • Academic language/literacy development • Interlanguage analysis • Applied linguistics (common phonological, morphological, semantic/lexical, and syntactic development patterns) • First language/second language contrasts between EL first languages and English • Contrastive rhetoric • Error correction in second language acquisition • Commonalities and differences in first language/second language reading and writing

their knowledge and skills regarding the unique needs of English learners. The same principle holds true for noninstructional personnel. For example, school psychologists, who are already versed in child development as a result of their professional training and experience, need to become aware of how second language acquisition affects an EL's academic development. The knowledge base they require is different from that of a mental health counselor or a principal because the role they fulfill in educating the child is different.

Millions of dollars have been spent on professional learning for teachers across content areas and grade levels, often without the expected results. As a consequence, funding agencies and educational researchers have been investigating what practices lead to systematic improvement of student achievement. There is ample evidence that one-size-fits all quality professional development does not exist.[6] However, after studying professional learning opportunities around the world, Linda Darling-Hammond and her colleagues concluded that professional development is most successful when it takes place in the school context; is intensive, ongoing, and directly connected to classroom practice; and invites collaboration among various education professionals.[7] Several of these findings, namely the importance of personalized, job-embedded, and technology-enabled instruction, are also represented in the key elements of quality professional education identified by the Bill and Melinda Gates Foundation reform efforts.[8] The research that underpins their recommendations has demonstrated a relationship between sustained and intensive professional development and student achievement gains. It also found that professional learning that is collaborative benefits the entire school, and that effective professional development focuses on specific academic content. Researchers also determined that approximately fifty hours of professional training in a specific area is the minimum amount necessary to improve students' learning. Professional learning should further school goals and build working relationships among teachers. The positive effects of this type of sustained, job-embedded, collaborative professional development are supported by research.[9]

Working Together to Support English Learners' Achievement

Few schools districts have an EL programming framework that provides substantive support for ELD experts—mainstream classroom collaboration that includes co-taught or co-planned content classes.[10] Nonetheless, some schools without this support have found ways to implement co-teaching principles where ELD and mainstream teachers work closely together on planning, teaching, or assessment of student learning. In many cases these teams have adapted models previously developed by exceptional education specialists and mainstream teachers. More common than co-teaching, however, is the situation where the various instructional personnel work quite independently of one another. Our Academic Subjects Protocol and Language Arts Protocol both encourage ELD specialist assistance in planning and implementing curriculum, instruction, and assessment, reflecting our assumptions that models that provide ELD services are valuable. However, the protocols also allow for real, but less than ideal, circumstances, such as when there are too few ELs to warrant a school-based ELD specialist, and classroom teachers rely on a different provider of support. Nonetheless, if schools want to provide the necessary support for English learners to reach their full academic potential, continued communication and collaboration between mainstream teachers and the ELD specialist is most beneficial.

While the implementation of a truly collaborative schoolwide model may at the outset have challenges, it has tangible benefits for school administrators, teachers, and students. We believe that all schools should be able to find ways in which some level of ELD specialist–mainstream teacher collaboration can occur. To that end, we have designed a three-level joint effort model (see figure C.3) that schools can adapt. The three levels range from a coordination of efforts where the teacher of ELs and the ELD specialist coordinate lesson planning, with the ELD specialist acting as a resource while still pursuing her own curriculum, to slightly more cooperative efforts in which the ELD specialist adjusts her own instruction to assist the mainstream teacher through pre- or reteaching of difficult concepts, to two types of collaborative efforts where co-teaching takes place. Schools and individual teachers can adapt the model to their specific contexts.

Research shows that the collaboration between ELD and mainstream teachers is a complex process that is highly dependent on mutual understanding and willingness to take ownership of the model. On one hand, mainstream classroom teachers have to understand that the ELD specialist's expertise is not limited to methodology or strategies for teaching a second language, but extends into curriculum content. On the other hand, the ELD specialist has to be willing to take ownership of the subject area and to take on content instruction to support the mainstream teacher in teaching the academic language of the content.[11] Figure C.3 shows that the *coordinated effort level* of our One Plus Model requires the fewest scheduling changes. In settings where the EL goes to the ELD specialist for part of the day, her two teachers can communicate in writing, simply coordinating their lessons. Similarly, if the teacher who provides ELD push-in services starts to co-teach with the mainstream teacher, no schedule change is needed because the specialist is already in the classroom for the fifteen to thirty minutes they would otherwise spend at the back of the room in small-group EL instruction.[12] Time commitment on the part of both teachers for the coordinated effort is relatively low because both can accomplish the planning of tasks at a time that is convenient for them.

Moving from coordinated to cooperative efforts and then to collaborative efforts calls for an increasing amount of commitment to work together as a team. This cannot be accomplished without the school principal's commitment to facilitating this journey. While individual mainstream teachers and ELD specialists can enter into coordinated-effort relationships on their own, a principal's suggestion for forming such partnerships sends the message that the administration encourages teachers to share expertise and pay close attention to ELs' academic achievement. The schoolwide adoption of a teacher collaboration model requires tangible administrative support and resources. Mainstream teachers and ELD specialists need to be afforded opportunities to meet outside of their "spare" time or during faculty meetings and/or professional

FIGURE C.3

One Plus Model—Continuum of Systemic Instructional Support for ELs

	Commitment to Working Together			
	Lower ⟶			Higher
	Coordinated Efforts	**Cooperative Efforts**	**Collaborative Efforts**	
Who and What	• Mainstream teacher shares info on upcoming lesson concepts. • ELD teacher assists with language objectives and suggests scaffolding for ELs in class. • ELD teacher continues teaching own curriculum in push-in or separate ELD class.	• Mainstream teacher shares info on upcoming lesson concepts. • ELD teacher assists with language objectives and suggests scaffolding for ELs in class. • ELD teacher adjusts push-in lessons or own lesson to pre-teach and/or reteach parts of mainstream lesson.	• ELD teacher in classroom assists ELs in a supportive role part-time or full-time.	• ELD teacher in classroom co-teaches with content teacher part-time or full-time.
Means and Frequency of Communication	• Lesson plans or inquiry notes in box or via e-mail.	• Weekly/monthly meetings for planning. • Notes in box when needed.	• Weekly meetings for planning. • Daily debriefing.	

development time, and noninstructional personnel should be encouraged to attend planning sessions or debriefings with the teams on a regular basis.

Approaching Professional Learning in Your School

As stated previously, research has shown that collaborative approaches to professional learning improve school performance and student achievement beyond what teachers can accomplish on their own.[13] In a recent study aimed at examining what research and practice reveal about engaged, school-based teacher learning teams, the National Commission on Teaching and America's Future showed that teachers who collaborate in learning teams hold themselves to a higher standard, improve their practice, and accelerate student achievement.[14] Studies reviewed in this report further showed that "when teachers are given the time and tools to collaborate, they become life-long learners, their instructional practice improves, and they are ultimately able to increase student achievement far beyond what any of them could accomplish alone."

Our view is that job-embedded professional learning is key to advancing instructional practices and enhancing English learners' language, literacy, and content achievement. We advocate a broad-based approach to professional development that is framed around local school district specific needs; that integrates research-based language, literacy, and content instructional practices for EL students; and that is focused on increasing these students' achievement in language, literacy, mathematics, science, and other academic subjects.

Starting up this type of professional learning naturally depends on a number of factors, such as the school's English learner population, available programming and specialized personnel, the model adopted for in-service professional development, and the individual commitment of school personnel to collaborate. Rather than waiting for a district- or principal-led initiative that may never come, we encourage you to take the first steps. Look around for existing relationships and common interests; approach your closest colleagues and inquire whether they would be willing to start an informal study group or undertake some research on how you can better serve your English learners. As soon as your group shows success in moving English learners forward, others will likely want to go on the journey with you!

SUGGESTIONS FOR TEACHER-INITIATED TEAMWORK AND COLLABORATION

Educators reap great benefits when they regularly collaborate with colleagues in their own school—or beyond their district—to brainstorm new ideas or exchange best practices. Building relationships with other teachers, collaborating, and sharing best practices are critical for enhancing instruction and improving student achievement outcomes. Teacher consultation and collaboration contribute significantly to the improvement of school climate, teacher retention, career satisfaction, and student achievement, according to findings published in the *Collaborating for Student Success* report.[15]

The reality is that even though schools are multidimensional centers of activity, they may not always provide the structures and conditions under which teachers feel prepared to engage in meaningful interaction and professional stimulation. One obstacle to starting systematic collaboration is the lack of time available for the concentrated efforts that productive consultation, collaboration, and teamwork require. When teachers do have time to consult with colleagues, it is likely to be during professional development sessions, but these are often highly structured and too short to permit meaningful interaction. However, individual mainstream teachers of EL students who want to at least approach others to work collaboratively need not feel alone in a school that lacks the appropriate structures.

For these teachers, we offer the following simple suggestions:

- Reach out. Teachers are very busy and typically hesitate to ask for or offer assistance without being invited to do so because they do not want to give the impression that they are not good teachers or that they think the other teacher is not doing a good job. If you are not sure what ELD specialists do when they work with English learners or how they determine the students' needs, ask them! Content-area teachers should not wait for expert colleagues (e.g., ELD teacher, reading specialist, speech-language pathologist, school psychologist, librarian) to come knocking on the door. Alternatively, ELD specialists, especially at the secondary level, are rarely subject-matter experts and may be uncertain about teaching dense, content-specific text in their ELD classes. The goal of all teachers is the academic achievement of the students, and at times a little encouragement from colleagues is all that's needed to start collaborating.

- Build rapport first. Before reaching out to colleagues to ask for specific assistance, though, show interest in their work and expertise. A social studies teacher may want to initiate a conversation with the ELD specialist right before or immediately following a faculty meeting simply by asking how many children at which proficiency level they teach. By and large, all they need to do after that is nurture the relationship and move to the next step by making simple, yet specific requests. For example, the social studies teacher could ask his ELD colleague for some tips in chunking reading assignments for an English learner at the intermediate proficiency level.

- Clarify the purpose of your call for assistance. Mainstream teachers should not assume that the colleagues to whom they are reaching out automatically know what kind of help is wanted. For instance, assume that you are teaching a science unit on water cycles and discover that your English learner has difficulty answering questions about the text relating specifically to key concepts of evaporation, condensation, and precipitation. In such a case, you may want to share a copy of the water cycle text with the student's ELD specialist or language arts teacher and discuss how he or she might assist in helping him advance his academic vocabulary, particularly as it relates to science learning. Understanding the content teacher's needs will help a language arts teacher or ELD specialist provide focused advice.

- Make it easy for colleagues to provide assistance to you and your students. Because educators are busy all day, they may not respond to requests for assistance if the only option is meeting face to face. We suggest that mainstream teachers ask for assistance that the expert colleague can fulfill by placing tips, articles, notes, curricula, and so on in the teacher's mailbox. Other requests for assistance, at least until a more systematic model of collaboration has been established, can be as simple as an invitation to meet once in a while and informally discuss how particular students are doing in each other's classes, and what can be done to support these students across the disciplines. Of course, snacks and other treats help, too!

- Reassure colleagues that their time and energy are well spent. When teachers reach out to expert colleagues for assistance, they should give a compelling reason to respond to the call for collaboration and teamwork. The key is to offer value to colleagues by helping them see the benefits of working together to meet the language, literacy, and content needs of EL students in all classrooms.

- Share the free, open source, multimedia resources that we have curated for mainstream teachers of English learners, available at http://www.englishlearnerachievement.com and http://tapestry.usf.edu. Both sites have a multitude of professional learning materials and classroom resources for teachers of English learners.

All in all, the time you spend collaborating to help your English learners will be repaid in triplicate by their resulting progress. As we will see in the following stories, our English learners have progressed since we last left them.

END-OF-YEAR EVENTS FOR GERO, EDITH, TASIR, AND EDGAR

Nearly nine months have passed since we first met Gero, Edith, Tasir, and Edgar, and their lives have changed in many ways. They live in different parts of the country and their families come from different places, but they have one thing in common. They have teachers who care about them and are trying to help them succeed.

✦ Gero—Pine Woods Elementary School

"Bienvenus, Mr. and Mrs. Jantiy! Come have a seat next to Mrs. Confidante. She will interpret for me." Gero's parents moved in unison toward Ms. Levin. "Thank you, Ms. Levin. I understand English, but my wife is still learning." They huddled on the miniature chairs as Ms. Levin handed them a stack of papers. "I want you to see what Gero has accomplished this year," she said, pausing to allow the interpreter to speak. "This is his writing from last August." Ms. Levin pointed to the first page. "Alligator!" exclaimed Mrs. Jantiy. "I remember when he told us he could say alligator in three languages!" Ms. Levin gently held each page, as if she were a white-gloved archivist, and explained how each piece showed Gero's progress. "And look at what he's writing now!" Ms. Levin boasted. She went on to show them Gero's reading assessments and other measures of his achievement. Mrs. Jantiy, dabbing the corner of her eye with a pressed linen handkerchief, whispered, "I thought that Gero would be lost and would fall behind. I was so . . . I was so afraid to come here tonight." Mrs. Jantiy took a deep breath, reached out her hand, and said, "Ms. Levin, thank you for teaching our son." Speaking directly to Gero's mother, Ms. Levin replied, "Merci pour votre fils. Il est un cadeau pour notre classe."[16]

✦ Edith—Pine Woods Elementary School

As she reflected on the events of the past school year, Ms. Oliver thought back to early spring, when she first felt Edith was ready to reply to a question requiring a full sentence. Her class was discussing career and college readiness, so she asked Edith what career she would like. Everyone leaned in to hear Edith state softly and slowly, "I want to be a teacher. I want to teach at this school." Ms. Oliver looked up to the left, took a short breath, and acknowledged Edith with a nod before going on to the next student. It wouldn't be until later, when the room was empty and private, that she could experience the magnitude of that moment. She kept a journal in the middle drawer of her desk for such occasions. It was a place she could deposit the intangible rewards of teaching.

She pulled the bottom of the ribbon holding her place from the last entry and placed her pen on the remaining empty space. Then she lifted her hand and turned to a new page.

✦ Tasir—Freedom Middle School

"You know, Ms. Marlin, sometimes I feel like I can't pass the state test because my other teachers don't help me understand. But I mostly wonder whether it's just me. Maybe I'm not very smart. Maybe I *don't* try hard enough. I don't know why I'm having so much trouble passing." Ms. Marlin stopped erasing the whiteboard and walked over to Tasir. "Learning a second language isn't easy. If it were, everyone would be bilingual, at least. Also, it's not a quick process. It takes time." Tasir slumped in her chair. "I've had a lot of time, four years, and I'm still behind." "Look here, Tasir," Ms. Marlin said. "Let me show you something about learning second languages."

Ms. Marlin took out a diagram showing a steep slope rising from left to right across the page. "See, this is the grade you entered school in Arkansas, the third grade." Tasir put her finger on the x axis. "You were a true beginner, and as you learned English, you were expected to use your new language in more and more complex ways. You had a moving target, and you are getting caught up now." Ms. Marlin traced her finger up the slope to the seventh grade, and pointed out the gap between that point and the horizontal line representing advanced English learners. "You still have a little gap, and now that our school is writing learning goals for English language development, you will start to see exactly what you need to accomplish to pass the test." Tasir peered at Ms. Marlin's new planner with sample scales. "So, what does *complex sentence* mean, Ms. Marlin?" Tasir and Ms. Marlin sat side by side, looking over Tasir's current English language proficiency assessment descriptors and those of level 6. Seeing where she was headed and the breakdown of how she would get there made passing the state test begin to seem possible. "Can I have a copy of level 6?" Tasir asked. Realizing her copy quota had long been exceeded, Ms. Marlin replied, "C'mon, Tasir, let's walk to the office and I'll buy a booklet for you."

✦ Edgar—Highpoint High School

"Hey, what you listen to?" Edgar asked as he walked into the classroom. The unmistakable *búh-buh-duhm-buhm, búh-buh-duhm-buhm* beat of reggaeton rattled the speakers connected to Mr. Otto's computer. "I just got into reggaeton," Mr. Otto replied. "Remember the students who performed at the cultural festival last month? Well, now I'm really hooked. It makes grading during my planning period a lot more fun."

"Ms. Myers, she teach us with reggaeton. We writing our own song and reading the words of a lotta reggaeton singer." Mr. Otto set aside his red pen and looked squarely at Edgar. "Do you think you could teach me about reggaeton? Like what the music is about, who the coolest artists are?" he asked. "Yeah, I can teach you," Edgar replied as he sat down and began scrolling through his playlist.

Ms. Myers had been working reggaeton into her reading and writing lessons since the day of the school festival. From the very first lesson, she had seen how her students related to the songs' themes. For someone who refused to write during the first weeks of school, Edgar was now writing daily, making up new lyrics and discussing the meaning of his favorite songs.

Above the whiteboard, prominently displayed, was Edgar's latest composition:

I Write/Yo Escribo
I write because
I want to say
Who I am
Yo soy orgulloso
I am bilingual
I am Edgar.

YOUR TURN TO ACT

Perhaps just as important as what sets English learners apart from other students is what holds true for English learners and native speakers alike. English learners can be just as lovable or incorrigible as any other student. Sometimes they try their best, sometimes they don't. They make good choices and irreparable mistakes. But there's something special about their connection with teachers who go above and beyond for them, who take the time to learn about how they learn, and try to better understand and address their needs. You can be that teacher.

We have stressed that all English learners, no matter who they are or where they attend school, deserve educators who are competent in meeting their needs. In our view, only when those who work directly with English learners think and act in interdisciplinary ways can their broad and varied goals and needs be addressed effectively. Educator collaboration guides support for English learners, but most importantly, it advances professional learning and educator best practices, which in turn improves student achievement. In other words, learning to effectively teach these students is no longer preparation for the job. It *is* the job.

We believe that close interdisciplinary collaboration is critical to advancing academic achievement and access to college and careers for all students, and EL students in particular. Our collective experiences over the past two decades indicate that working across the disciplines may not be easy, but it has tremendous benefits for teachers and their students. Interdisciplinary collaboration and teamwork require extraordinary commitment, intense determination, and a forward-looking vision, all of which are key characteristics that define effective teaching of all students, not just English learn-ers. This is consistent with the recommendation by teacher effectiveness and student achievement experts that learning organizations should promote long-term and con-tinuous professional learning that takes into account new teacher roles, and that creates new structures for advancing student learning and engagement.[17]

Now that we have presented the principles and practices of our One Plus Model and the research and theory behind it, we can affirm that whatever good comes from this book is due to collaboration. We talked through every issue together as a group, or sometimes one to one as time and place allowed, and then we wrote, read, and tried out each other's ideas with teachers in regular, imperfect schools. And so, it is fitting that a book about the importance of communication for, between, and of English learners was only made possible through communication between educators who want to help im-prove English learners' education.

Each of this book's authors has experienced being lost in an unknown language and culture. With the right circumstances, and with the type of support we detailed in this book, each of us found our way. Wishing the same for every English learner, we urge you to act. You have read this book. You understand your role in supporting Eng-lish learners' needs, and you know what your colleagues can do to support ELs as well. Now it is your turn. We believe you now have the knowledge to *take action* to advance the academic achievement of the English learners in your school or district. We urge you to do all you can within your own classroom and to reach out to your colleagues and administrators to work together for the success of all English learners at your school. *Yon sel dwèt pa manje kalalou.*[18]

STOP AND REFLECT QUESTIONS

1. Why do the authors consider collaboration and professional development as key el-ements to the successful teaching of English learners?

2. Given the respective skills of personnel at your school, how can they help assure the academic success of English learners?

3. How do you define the term *community of learners*? How can you assure that such a community exists within your school? What are the first steps in designing or cre-ating such a community?

4. What framework or model has been designed and implemented in your district to support the educational needs of all ELs in the district?

5. What is the role of all principals in assuring that English learners receive a quality education?

6. The authors of this book chose to end this chapter with the Haitian proverb, *Yon sèl dwèt pa manje kalalou.* What does the proverb mean and why was this used to summarize the chapter and the essence of the book?

GO AND PRACTICE ACTIVITIES

1. Schedule a time to meet with the ELD specialist at your school to find out what he/she does when working with English learners. Prepare a list of questions you wish to ask before your meeting. Be sure to include topics such as what research-based strategies are appropriate to use at varying levels of English proficiency in the mainstream classroom.

2. Assist in the creation of a quality professional development activity at your school. Be sure to invite the many professionals at your school to provide input, suggestions, and ideas in the spirit of true collaboration.

3. Visit the http://www.tapestry.usf.edu Web site, designed for teachers, noninstructional personnel, and teacher preparation faculty. Once you have perused the site and acknowledge its usefulness firsthand, invite others at your school to visit it as well.

4. Organize a Tapestry club! Invite educators at your school or in your education program to meet at a regularly scheduled time to discuss the videos viewed on the Web site. The club can decide the format by which the videos will be discussed. Be sure to include new ideas developed from viewing the videos.

The Academic Subjects Protocol

Making Curriculum, Instruction, and Assessment
Accessible for English Learners

The flowchart on the following page provides a visual summary of decision points for planning and providing instructional adaptations for English learners. We suggest you keep it in your planner and refer to it when developing or adapting lessons that are suitable for your EL students. A full explanation of each phase and step is provided in chapter 1.

ACADEMIC SUBJECTS PROTOCOL

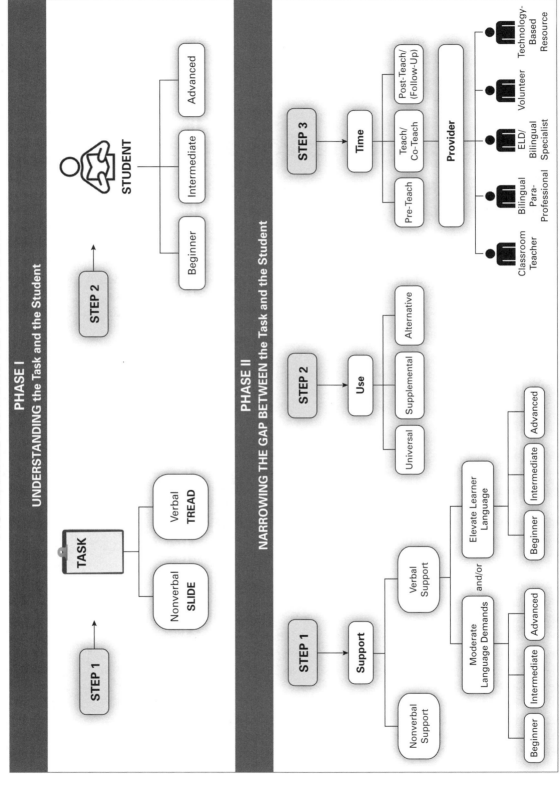

PHASE I
UNDERSTANDING the Task and the Student

STEP 1

TASK

Nonverbal SLIDE

Verbal TREAD

STEP 2

STUDENT

Beginner · Intermediate · Advanced

PHASE II
NARROWING THE GAP BETWEEN the Task and the Student

STEP 1 → Support

Nonverbal Support

Verbal Support

Moderate Language Demands and/or Elevate Learner Language

Beginner · Intermediate · Advanced

Beginner · Intermediate · Advanced

STEP 2 → Use

Universal · Supplemental · Alternative

STEP 3 → Time

Pre-Teach · Teach/Co-Teach · Post-Teach/(Follow-Up)

Provider

Classroom Teacher · Bilingual Para-Professional · ELD/Bilingual Specialist · Volunteer · Technology-Based Resource

The Language Arts Protocol

Scaffolding Instruction to Support English Learners'
Language and Literacy Skills

The flowchart on the following page provides a visual summary of decision points for planning and providing targeted instruction for English learners. We suggest you keep it in your planner and refer to it when developing or adapting lessons that are suitable for your EL students. A full explanation of each phase and step is provided in chapter 6.

LANGUAGE ARTS PROTOCOL

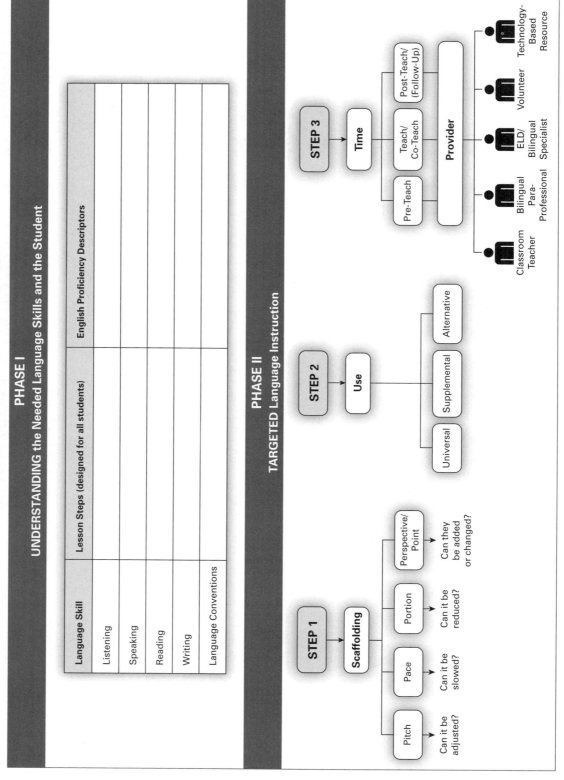

PHASE I
UNDERSTANDING the Needed Language Skills and the Student

Language Skill	Lesson Steps (designed for all students)	English Proficiency Descriptors
Listening		
Speaking		
Reading		
Writing		
Language Conventions		

PHASE II
TARGETED Language Instruction

STEP 1 → Scaffolding

- Pitch — Can it be adjusted?
- Pace — Can it be slowed?
- Portion — Can it be reduced?
- Perspective/Point — Can they be added or changed?

STEP 2 → Use

- Universal
- Supplemental
- Alternative

STEP 3 → Time

- Pre-Teach
- Teach/Co-Teach
- Post-Teach/(Follow-Up)

Provider

- Classroom Teacher
- Bilingual Para-Professional
- ELD/Bilingual Specialist
- Volunteer
- Technology-Based Resource

Resources

The English Learner Achievement and ESOL Tapestry Web Sites

We maintain two Web sites that complement the content of this book. Districts that use this book for professional learning and university-based teacher preparation programs that use it as a course textbook can access on-line multimedia, print, and other current information that corresponds to the content of each chapter. These sites offer plentiful readings, videos, and other resources for augmenting various teacher preparation courses, offering a full course on teaching English learners, or providing a complete in-service component.

THE ENGLISH LEARNER ACHIEVEMENT WEB SITE

This Web site (http://www.englishlearnerachievement.com) follows the organization of the book, with resources provided for each of the chapters herein. It also contains English learner topic summaries from the One Plus Model and materials we created for classroom and professional learning, as well as links to multiple resources, including professional organization position papers and other materials, multimedia resources, and print media references and linked content. In addition, this site includes a blog where readers can ask us their questions about teaching English learners.

ESOL TAPESTRY WEB SITE

This Web site (http://tapestry.usf.edu) includes three sections: a video lecture series, an annotated list of articles on topics regarding English learners, and a journal focused on preK–12 English learners.

Expert Video Series

The expert video series currently consists of fourteen one-hour video tutorials, each presented by a prominent expert through lecture or interview, or as a workshop. The featured experts include Jodi Crandall, Peter Roos, Sandra Fradd, Deborah Short, Walt

Wolfram, Joyce Nutta, Neil Anderson and Vicky Zygouris-Coe, Carine Strebel and Bruce Perry, Jamal Abedi and Florin Mihai, Julia Esparza Brown and Linda Rosa-Lugo, Dana Ferris and Keith Folse, Catherine Snow, Eugene Garcia, and Jim Cummins. The topics include teacher preparation, legal issues, best practices in content-area instruction, first and second language reading, error correction in writing, young dual-language learners, and the implications of the Common Core State Standards for the education of English learners in the United States.

ESOL Resources

As a supplement to the video modules, the ESOL Tapestry Web site also contains a large, routinely updated compilation of Web-based and print-based articles and other documents relating to the education of English learners. The resources, divided into online and print-based references, are organized by subject area (art, music, physical education, disciplinary literacy, counseling, early childhood education, language arts, literacy development, literature, mathematics, methods and curriculum, psychological foundations, reading, research and theory, science, social foundations, social studies, exceptional education, teacher professional learning, testing, and writing) and are all focused on the specific needs and issues of English learners from each discipline's perspective.

The Tapestry Journal: An International Multidisciplinary Journal on English Language Learner Education

The Tapestry Journal is an online free, open-access biannual journal. It accepts articles, commentaries, and book reviews with the goal of integrating research and best practices into a variety of subjects relating to English learners' academic achievement and English language development. Topics in the archive range from case studies concerning ELs' social, emotional, and language growth within school to practical methods for teachers to incorporate explicit linguistic and cultural instruction in mainstream classrooms. The journal invites manuscript submissions in the following three categories: research and theory, effective field practices, and commentaries. Additionally, a supplementary blog functions as an informal forum for discussing issues, controversies, and viewpoints relating to the education of ELs and second language acquisition. We invite you to add to this professional journal by submitting accounts of your school's collaborative initiative to help English learners succeed or by sharing your thoughts as you change your professional practice with a special focus on the English learner.[1]

Notes

Introduction

1. Figures are for the 2010–2011 school year. Susan Aud, Sidney Wilkinson-Flicker, Paul Krista-povich, Amy Rathbun, Xiaolei Wang, and Jijun Zhang, *The Condition of Education 2013* (NCES 2013-037), U.S. Department of Education, National Center for Education Statistics (Washington, DC: U.S. Government Printing Office, 2013), retrieved February 21, 2014, http://eric.ed.gov /?id=ED542714; Claude Goldenberg, "Teaching English Language Learners: What the Research Does—and Does Not—Say," *American Educator*, Summer 2008, 11–23, 42–43.
2. Claude Goldenberg, "Teaching English Language Learners."
3. Wendy Grigg, Patricia Donahue, and Gloria Dion, *The Nation's Report Card: 12th-Grade Reading and Mathematics 2005* (NCES 2007-468), U.S. Department of Education, National Center for Educa-tion Statistics (Washington, DC: U.S. Government Printing Office, 2005).
4. U.S. Congress, "No Child Left Behind Act of 2001," § 6319: 2008; U.S. Congress, "Higher Edu-cation Opportunity Act," Public Law 110-315, 110th Congress (2008). Our queries on the Na-tional Education Achievement Program's Data Explorer have shown that this achievement gap has not changed significantly in reading and mathematics for students in grades 4, 8, and 12 since the program started (National Center for Education Statistics, *NAEP Data Explorer,* Institute of Educa-tion Sciences, http://nces.ed.gov/nationsreportcard/naepdata/).
5. Joyce W. Nutta, Kouider Mokhtari, and Carine Strebel, *Preparing Every Teacher to Reach English Learners: A Practical Guide for Teacher Educators* (Cambridge: Harvard Education Press, 2012).
6. There are many different program models to support English learners' language development and academic achievement. Most of those models include an English language development (some-times referred to as ESL or ESOL) or bilingual specialist who works with the classroom teacher to help English learners, either in the mainstream class during instruction or in a separate classroom composed of English learners only.
7. Mary Ellen Good, Sophia Masewicz, and Linda Vogel, "Latino English Language Learners: Bridg-ing Achievement and Cultural Gaps Between Schools and Families," *Journal of Latinos and Educa-tion* 9, no. 4 (2010): 321–339; Suzanne Panferov, "Increasing ELL Parental Involvement in Our Schools: Learning from the Parents," *Theory into Practice* 49, no. 2 (2010): 106–112.
8. Gero is a bilingual French/Haitian Kreyòl speaker, but because of his dominance in Haitian Kreyòl, we use it as the primary language of discussion when referring to Gero's native language.
9. Those who build a new life in a different culture go through four stages of cultural adjustments: Honeymoon, Hostility, Integration/Acceptance, and Home stage. Gregory J. Trifonovitch, "Cul-ture Learning/Culture Teaching," *Educational Perspectives* 16, no. 4 (1977): 18–22.
10. Jim Cummins, "The Role of Primary Language Development in Promoting Educational Success for Language Minority Students," in *Schooling and Language Minority Students: A Theoretical Frame-work,* ed. Charles F. Leyba (Los Angeles: California State University, Evaluation, Dissemination and Assessment Center, 1981), 3–49; Jim Cummins, *Bilingual Education and Special Education: Issues in Assessment and Pedagogy* (San Diego: College Hill, 1984).

11. Wayne Thomas and Virginia Collier, *School Effectiveness for Language Minority Students* (Washington, DC: National Clearinghouse for Bilingual Education, 1997).

12. Patsy M. Lightbown and Nina Spada, *How Languages Are Learned* (Oxford: Oxford University Press, 2013); Rod Ellis, *Understanding Second Language Acquisition* (Oxford: Oxford University Press, 2008); John Schumann, *The Pidginization Process: A Model for Second Language Acquisition* (Rowley, MA: Newbury House Publishers, 1978).

13. Robert C. Gardner and Wallace E. Lambert, *Attitudes and Motivation in Second Language Learning* (Rowley, MA: Newbury House, 1972).

14. Lightbown and Spada, *How Languages Are Learned*.

15. Consistent with recent trends in U.S. Department of Education terminology and in published scholarship, we use the term *English learner* (abbreviated as EL) rather than the older term *English language learner* (ELL) to refer to the students who are the focus of the book. Other terms that have been used to describe this population include *English as a Second Language (ESL) students* and *English for Speakers of Other Languages (ESOL) students.* Another commonly used term, *culturally and linguistically diverse (CLD) students,* broadly describes students whose language or culture differs from the dominant language or culture, but this does not necessarily mean that they are not yet fully proficient in English. Similarly, a subset of these students is termed "language minority" students—those for whom a language other than English is the first or heritage language—but this group may include individuals who are balanced bilinguals or who have been exited from the EL category because they have attained full proficiency in English. English learners are a subset of language minority students since their heritage or first language is not English and they are not yet fully proficient in English. Mistakenly, Hispanic or Latino students are sometimes conflated with English learners. However, although the majority of English learners in the United States are Latinos, a Latino student may not be an English learner, and an English learner may not be Latino. Our operating definition of EL is based on descriptors found in federal legislation and includes the following characteristics: a student who communicates in a language other than English exclusively or in addition to English and who lacks adequate English proficiency for successful written and spoken communication in academic and/or social settings. It is important to note that English learners' language proficiency can range from non-English-speaking newcomers to long-term English learners (those who are classified as English learners for generally seven years or more), to so-called Generation 1.5 learners—postsecondary students described as being "caught between two generations and cultures," fully literate in neither their first nor their second language. Elizabeth D. Oudenhoven, *Caught in the Middle: Generation 1.5 Latino Students and English Language Learning in a Community College* (doctoral dissertation AAT3212980, Loyola University, 2006).

16. Michael A. K. Halliday, "The Notion of 'Context' in Language Education," in *Text and Context in Functional Linguistics*, ed. Mohsen Ghadessy (Amsterdam: John Benjamins, 1999), 1–24.

Chapter 1

1. James Carey, *Communication as Culture: Essays on Media and Society* (New York: Routledge, 2008); John Dewey, *Experience and Nature*, vol. 1 (New York: Dover Publications, 1958).

2. Carey, *Communication as Culture.*

3. Michael A. K. Halliday, "The Notion of 'Context' in Language Education," in *Text and Context in Functional Linguistics*, ed. Mohsen Ghadessy (Amsterdam: John Benjamins, 1999), 1–24.

4. Educators lack a complete understanding of what the Common Core demands are, how they impact learning, and how they can be assessed in ways that will help teachers track student attainment of these skills and competencies. In pursuit of a full, research-based definition of the language demands of standards, curriculum, instruction, and assessment of academic subjects, researchers such as Sato and colleagues (Edynn Sato, Stanley Rabinowitz, Carole Gallagher, and Chun-Wei Huang, *Accommodations for English Language Learner Students: The Effect of Linguistic Modification of Math Test Item Sets* [NCEE 2009-4079], U.S. Department of Education, Institute of Education Sciences, National Center for Education Evaluation and Regional Assistance [Washington, DC: U.S. Government Printing Office, 2010]) have developed criteria to enable measurement of academic language demands in receptive, or listening and reading, and productive, or speaking and writing, skill areas. Issues such as length, repetition, detail, abstraction, visual aspects, familiarity,

complexity, sophistication, text structure, and style of discourse can be considered when examining the language demands placed on students in academic subjects.

5. With the integrated language and academic subjects approach that the Common Core State Standards require, language arts teachers will increasingly use texts from academic subjects as a focus for skill development in listening, speaking, reading, and writing. This, in turn, will raise students' achievement in academic subjects, whose instruction and assessment depend largely on language.

6. Douglas Fisher and Nancy Frey, "Releasing Responsibility," *Educational Leadership*, November 2008, 32–37.

7. Rod Ellis, *The Study of Second Language Acquisition*, 2nd ed. (Oxford: Oxford University Press, 2008).

8. We use the term *nonverbal communication* to mean any way of communicating other than primarily through language. We use the term *verbal communication* to mean primarily language-based (both oral and written language) communication.

9. Stephen D. Krashen, *The Input Hypothesis: Issues and Implications* (New York: Longman, 1985).

10. Merrill Swain, "Communicative Competence: Some Roles of Comprehensible Input and Comprehensible Output in Its Development," in *Input in Second Language Acquisition*, eds. Susan M. Gass and C. G. Madden (Rowley, MA: Newbury House, 1985), 165–179.

11. An audience evaluating output at a later time could also be a group of listeners, as with a speech or broadcast.

12. Michael H. Long, "The Role of Linguistic Environment in Second Language Acquisition," in *The New Handbook of Second Language Acquisition*, eds. William C. Ritchie and Taj K. Bhatia (San Diego: Academic Press, 1996).

13. We speak mainly about the school environment, as that is what the classroom teacher has influence over, but for ELs in the U.S. mainland, input, interaction, and output have an impact on their acquisition of English outside of school. Availability of English media at home, including technology such as television, computers, and the Internet, as well as participation in community and extracurricular activities, such as fellowship at places of worship or playing on local sports teams, provide opportunities for exposure to English to which those who study English only at school (such as students of English as a foreign language in China) lack access. In addition, trips to the store, driving along the streets and highways, and many other places outside the home provide exposure to spoken and written English and opportunities to interact with native and more proficient speakers.

14. Our approach to providing accessible curriculum, instruction, and assessment for English learners is based on a theoretical perspective of second language acquisition referred to as an interactionist model (Ellis, *The Study of Second Language Acquisition*), which studies input, interaction, and output in school and other learning environments. We view the interactionist model as complementary to other theoretical perspectives, many of which are more focused on social aspects of second language acquisition. Theoretical underpinnings are critical for informed practice, and we have grounded the contents of this book in a model that we have experience putting into practice with educators who are not ELD specialists. In addition, it places the emphasis in second language development on factors over which the classroom teacher and other educators have some control, such as the quality of input, interaction, and output. Other factors, such as social distance between the first and second languages, are important to be aware of but do not bear the same significance to the daily decision making of a classroom teacher. Although this book is written primarily from a second language acquisition disciplinary standpoint, we also present insights from other disciplines, including research and theory on first language and literacy learning issues, where they shed light on specific second language learning processes and outcomes.

15. Michael H. Long, *Problems in SLA*, Second Language Acquisition Research Series (Mahwah, NJ: Lawrence Erlbaum Associates, 2006).

16. Jim Cummins, "The Role of Primary Language Development in Promoting Educational Access for Language Minority Students," in *Schooling and Language Minority Students: A Theoretical Framework*, ed. California State Department of Education (Los Angeles: Office of Bilingual Bicultural Education, Evaluation, Dissemination, and Assessment Center, California State University, 1984).

17. For more discussion on this discrepancy, we recommend research on Systemic Functional Linguistics or on corpus-based linguistics.

18. Thomas W. Stewart and Nathan Vaillette, eds., *Language Files: Materials for an Introduction to Language and Linguistics*, 8th ed. (Columbus: The Ohio State University Press, 2001).

19. Although nonverbal communication can imply body language, our use of this term is broader and includes any means of communication using something other than or in addition to listening, speaking, reading, or writing to deliberately convey a message. One of the definitions of *verbal* implies oral expression (as in a verbal, or spoken, contract), but our use of the term is based on the definition that encompasses both spoken (oral) and written (print) language.

20. We believe that the communication environment in the early grades is more conducive to comprehensibility of instruction and English language development for ELs than that in the upper grades. We are not suggesting that tenth-grade classrooms should resemble kindergarten classrooms. Instead, we are comparing a highly contextualized classroom to one with very limited context. Moving from highly contextualized to less contextualized instruction allows native English speakers to develop academic proficiency in and through the use of English over a twelve-year span. However, a second language learner placed, for example, in a tenth-grade classroom with little to no contextual support never had access to this progression from a highly contextualized environment to low or limited context. This poses unique challenges for English learners entering U.S. schools beyond the primary grades.

21. James Asher, *Learning Another Language Through Actions: The Complete Teachers' Guidebook* (Los Gatos, CA: Sky Oaks Publications, 1977).

22. Jim Cummins, *Bilingual Education and Special Education: Issues in Assessment and Pedagogy* (San Diego: College Hill, 1984).

23. Diane August and Timothy Shanahan, *Developing Literacy in Second-Language Learners: Report of the National Literacy Panel on Language-Minority Children and Youth* (Mahwah, NJ: Lawrence Erlbaum Associates, 2006).

24. TESOL also has published standards for ELs' language use in specific academic subjects, available at http://www.tesol.org/advance-the-field/standards/prek-12-english-language-proficiency-standards. These are very useful for ELD teachers following a content-based instruction approach, and they can be a helpful resource for academic subject teachers of English learners.

25. Another common categorization of English learners' proficiency levels comes from a second language teaching method called the Natural Approach. See Stephen D. Krashen and Tracy D. Terrell, *The Natural Approach: Language Acquisition in the Classroom* (Oxford: Pergamon,1983). It uses four levels: preproduction, early production, speech emergence, and intermediate fluency. We have found that mainstream teachers of English learners are able to individualize instruction following these four general stages or levels. Because we have observed that in the mainstream environment the first two stages tend to blend together fairly rapidly and the means of supporting communication at this level are very similar, we have adapted its classification of proficiency levels for our approach to differentiating academic subject instruction for English learners. We combined preproduction and early production into beginning level, called speech emergence the intermediate level, and termed intermediate fluency the advanced level for clarity and simplicity of expression. From our research with academic subject teachers of English learners in mainstream classes, dividing the process of second language acquisition into these three levels for differentiating curriculum, instruction, and assessment balances feasibility of implementation with effective instruction for English learners.

26. In a research synthesis study, Genesee, Lindholm-Leary, Saunders, and Christian reported on the relationship between first language literacy, background knowledge, and conceptual knowledge: Fred Genesee, Kathryn Lindholm-Leary, William M. Saunders, and Donna Christian, "English Language Learners in U.S. Schools: An Overview of Research Findings," *Journal of Education for Students Placed at Risk* 10, no. 4 (2005): 363–385. They found that first language oral proficiency and reading comprehension skills, in combination with ELs' general knowledge about the topic of study, enabled ELs to successfully transfer academic skills and conceptual knowledge from their first language to English.

27. August and Shanahan, *Developing Literacy in Second-Language Learners*.

28. In a study conducted by García-Vázquez, Vázquez, López, and Ward, Spanish-speaking English learners' standardized achievement test scores for tests administered in English were significantly related to Spanish language proficiency in reading and writing: Enedina García-Vázquez, Luis A.

Vázquez, Isabel C. López, and Wendy Ward, "Language Proficiency and Academic Success: Relationships Between Proficiency in Two Languages and Achievement Among Mexican American Students," *Bilingual Research Journal* 21, no. 4 (1997): 395–408. Moreover, writing proficiency in Spanish was significantly related to their mathematics achievement test, which was administered in English.

29. Stephen D. Krashen, *The Power of Reading: Insights from Research* (Portsmouth, NH: Heinemann, 2009).

30. Robert T. Jiménez, Georgia E. García, and P. David Pearson, "The Reading Strategies of Bilingual Latina/o Students Who Are Successful English Readers: Opportunities and Obstacles," *Reading and Research Quarterly* 31 (1996): 90–112.

31. While the verbs encompassed by SLIDE and TREAD are quite clearly linked to more or less verbal student or teacher actions, there is a third group teachers should keep in mind when analyzing established lessons or designing their own. The language load of this third group of verbs depends to a large extend on the context. For example, when students are directed to "find" something, it could be a place in a text where something specific happens (i.e., demanding language use), or it could involve finding a visual clue in a picture or around the classroom (i.e., nonverbal). Similarly, the verbs *provide* and *give* could mean an opinion or proof (i.e., language use) or literally to hand something to a person. The important point to keep in mind is not the literal meaning of the verb but *what it is asking the teacher or students to do*.

32. Cummins refers to this nonverbal communication as *context-embedded instruction*; Krashen uses the term *extra-linguistic cues*.

33. See http://dailyinfographic.com or http://www.easel.ly or http://pinterest.com/officialascd/education-infographics/ for information on infographics.

34. Many topics' complexity can be represented through diagrams, graphic organizers, and interactive media with associated verbal explanations slightly above the current English proficiency of the EL, promoting not only comprehension of the subject but also English language development.

35. Other examples of verbal support are provided in the lessons presented in chapters 2–5.

36. It is important to note that reading materials developed for English learners at beginning, intermediate, and advanced levels of English proficiency are not the same as graded readers for native speakers of English.

37. If our goal is to help English learners learn the academic content, such as history, while they are learning the language, the language used to present the content must be comprehensible. Reading passages that unpack embedded phrases and clauses (simplify text) and that expand details and build in redundancies that help define terms that less-proficient ELs may not know (elaborated text) can help promote comprehension. In a mainstream classroom environment, where there may be only one or just a few English learners, providing unpacked (rephrased or elaborated) texts to supplement more complex texts is more feasible than expecting the classroom teacher to individually unpack each grade-level text with ELs of varying proficiency levels during whole-class instruction. Of course, unpacking complex texts for native speakers likely will be close enough to advanced ELs' level of proficiency to benefit their comprehension as well.

38. Jamal Abedi, Carol Lord, and Joseph R. Plummer, National Center for Research on Evaluation, Standards, and Student Testing, Center for the Study of Evaluation, *Final Report of Language Background as a Variable in NAEP Mathematics Performance* (Los Angeles: Graduate School of Education & Information Studies, University of California, 1997).

39. Margaret Heritage, *Formative Assessment in Practice: A Process of Inquiry and Action* (Cambridge, MA: Harvard Education Press, 2013).

Chapter 2

1. The National Council for the Social Studies defines social studies on its Web site as "the integrated study of the social sciences and humanities to promote civic competence" (http://www.socialstudies.org/about). Social studies, the council further specifies, "covers disciplines such as anthropology, archaeology, economics, geography, history, law, philosophy, political science, psychology, religion, and sociology, as well as appropriate content from the humanities, mathematics, and natural sciences."

2. Thomas Misco and Martha E. Castaneda, "Now, What Should I Do for English Language Learners? Reconceptualizing Social Studies Curriculum Design for ELLs," *Educational Horizons* 87, no. 3 (2009): 182–189.

3. Isabel L. Beck and Margaret G. McKeown, "Outcomes of History Instruction: Paste-Up Accounts," in *Cognitive and Instructional Processes in History and the Social Sciences,* eds. Mario Carretero and James F. Voss (Mahwah, NJ: Lawrence Erlbaum Associates, 1994), 237–256; Margaret G. McKeown and Isabel L. Beck, "Making Sense of Accounts of History: Why Young Students Don't and How They Might," in *Teaching and Learning in History,* eds. Gaea Leinhardt, Isabel L. Beck, and Catherine Stainton (Mahwah, NJ: Lawrence Erlbaum Associates, 1994), 1–26.

4. Macmillan McGraw-Hill, *TimeLinks: Third Grade, Communities* (Columbus: Macmillan McGraw Hill, 2007).

5. Manfred Pienemann, ed., *Crosslinguistic Aspects of Processability Theory* (Amsterdam: John Benjamins, 2005).

6. Jim Cummins, "The Role of Primary Language Development in Promoting Educational Success for Language Minority Students," in *Schooling and Language Minority Students: A Theoretical Framework,* ed. Charles F. Leyba (Los Angeles: California State University, Evaluation, Dissemination and Assessment Center, 1981): 3-49; Jim Cummins, "Empowering Minority Students: A Framework for Intervention," *Harvard Educational Review* 56, no. 1 (1986): 18–37.

7. Even children and families from Western countries that made up the early waves of immigrants and whose values contributed to the formation of those in the United States hold different values and refer to different frames of reference. For example, a Swiss middle school student would likely view democracy differently from American children, as Switzerland is a direct democracy as opposed to the American representative democracy. The greater the socioeconomic, cultural, and political differences between American norms and those of other countries, the more teachers need to consider background building prior to lessons.

8. Carlos J. Ovando, Mary Carol Combs, and Virginia P. Collier, *Bilingual and ESL Classrooms*, 4th ed. (New York: McGraw-Hill, 2006).

9. Evelyn Marino Weisman and Laurie E. Hansen, "Strategies for Teaching Social Studies to English-Language Learners at the Elementary Level," *The Social Studies* 98, no. 5 (2007): 180–184.

10. The Tennessee Department of Education's 2009 Tennessee Vocabulary Project is available at http://www.tn.gov/education/ci/doc/VOCABULARY.pdf.

11. Robert J. Marzano, *Building Background Knowledge for Academic Achievement* (Alexandria, VA: Association for Supervision and Curriculum Development, 2004).

12. To be precise, the hierarchy of this example is actually individual food items that are grouped under the generic terms *vegetables*, *fruit*, or *meat* before they get grouped under *food*, which in turn is part of the actual social studies concept that is to be taught—"basic needs."'

13. The types of services offered to assist English learners in mainstream classrooms depend on factors such as the number of ELs in a given school or district and the availability of appropriately trained personnel. Therefore, services vary greatly throughout the United States. *Push-in* and *pull-out* services are widely used in schools with only a handful of ELs per class. In the push-in model, an ELD specialist or bilingual paraprofessional moves from class to class to provide small-group instruction for ELs (typically twenty to thirty minutes per day during any content-area instructional time), whereas in the pull-out model, the ELs leave their mainstream classroom to join an ELD specialist in her classroom for a specific period of time each day, preferably during English language arts time.

    Another commonly used instructional model is the Specially Designed Academic Instruction in English (SDAIE), also referred to as sheltered instruction. SDAIE/sheltered instruction falls under the umbrella of content-based language instruction. While the focus of instruction for ELs is content, the model has a strong emphasis on language development for listening, speaking, reading and writing. The most widely used model of SDAIE is the Sheltered Instruction Observation Protocol (SIOP). See Jane M. Echevarría, Mary Ellen Vogt, and Deborah Short, *Making Content Comprehensible for English Language Learners: The SIOP Model* (Boston: Allyn & Bacon, 2000). ELs attend sheltered classes for all core subjects (becoming mainstreamed in some academic subjects as they develop English proficiency until they are fully integrated in mixed classrooms), but they typically go to music, art, physical education, electives, and lunch with their grade-level peers.

14. Several ideas for this unit were taken from Erika Crowder's blog: http://sprinklestokindergarten.blogspot.com/2012/02/american-symbols.html.

15. In the absence of Common Core State Standards for social studies, we selected a Georgia kindergarten social studies/history standard that fits the overarching unit. Various states have similarly worded standards for this topic and grade level. Each center and day would of course have different individual content and literacy/language objectives, which we omitted for space reasons.

16. The best way to start with the protocol is to <u>underline</u> the verbs that indicate *what the teacher and student(s) are doing* during the activity. The verbs and verb phrases are already underlined in the lesson description for illustration purposes.

17. One symbol is explored each day. The lesson starts with the American flag. The tasks are always the same.

18. For example, see http://www.superteacherworksheets.com/patriotic-symbols/flag-fitb_FLAGS.pdf. Modifications for the students' grade and preparation levels should be made.

19. This can be done in PowerPoint, through an interactive whiteboard presentation, or by using a whiteboard app to be viewed on tablets; for example, ShowMe for the iPad (http://www.showme.com) or Lensoo for Android devices (http://www.lensoo.com).

20. The writing spaces will be used during independent daily journaling time. A sample of such a work sheet can be seen at Mrs. Williamson's blogspot: http://mrswilliamsonskinders.blogspot.com/search/label/presidents.

21. The symbol from another country is preferably from a nation that is represented in the student body. For example, printable foreign flags can be found at http://www.education.com/worksheets/kindergarten/national-symbols/?page=2.

22. All teachers should learn about the surface and deep cultural elements of their English learners' origins.

23. According to Herrell and Jordan, read-aloud strategies are especially useful to English learners because the mixture of gestures, change in intonation patterns, questioning, and so forth reduces anxiety and allows the students to focus on the verbal and nonverbal elements of the activity. Adrienne L. Herrell and Michael Jordan, *Fifty Strategies for Teaching English Language Learners*, 4th ed. (Upper Saddle River, NJ: Merrill, 2012).

24. We assume here that Gero had not yet joined Ms. Levin's class when she originally introduced the Venn diagram.

Chapter 3

1. National Science Teachers Association, *Scope, Sequence, and Coordination of Secondary School Science* (Washington, DC: National Science Teachers Association, 1991).

2. Zhihui Fang and Mary Schleppegrell, *Reading in Secondary Content Areas: A Language-Based Pedagogy* (Ann Arbor: Michigan University, 2010).

3. Ibid.

4. Ibid.; Suzanne Eggins, *An Introduction to Systemic Functional Linguistics*, 2nd ed. (London: Pinter, 2004).

5. Okhee Lee and Sandra H. Fradd, "Science for All, Including Students from Non-English Language Backgrounds," *Educational Researcher* 27, no. 4 (1998): 12–21.

6. Ibid.

7. Trish Stoddart, America Pinal, Marcia Latzke, and Dana Canaday, "Integrating Inquiry Science and Language Development for English Language Learners," *Journal of Research in Science Teaching* 39, no. 8 (2002): 664–687.

8. Joyce Nutta, Nazan Bautista, and Malcolm Butler, *Teaching Science to English Language Learners* (New York: Routledge, 2011).

9. Additional cognate examples among English, Spanish, and Haitian Kreyòl, respectively, are accident—accidente—aksidan; addition—adición—adisyon.

10. They also learn about the centrality of verbs and discover how sentences in English grow from the position of the verbs to construct the remainder of the sentence.

11. Lee and Fradd, "Science for All."

12. Cory A. Buxton, "Creating Contextually Authentic Science in 'Low-Performing' Urban Elementary Schools," *Journal of Research in Science Teaching* 43, no. 7 (2006): 695–721; Okhee Lee and Aurolyn Luykx, "Science Education and Student Diversity: Race/Ethnicity, Language, Culture, and

Socioeconomic Status," in *Handbook of Research in Science Education*, 2nd ed., eds. Sandra K. Abell and Norman G. Ledereman (Mahwah, NJ: Lawrence Erlbaum Associates, 2007), 171–198.

13. Eleanor L. Babco and Nathan E. Bell, *Professional Women and Minorities: A Total Human Resources Compendium* (Washington, DC: Commission on Professionals in Science and Technology, 2008); Alberto J. Rodriguez, *Turning Despondency into Hope: Charting New Paths to Improve Students' Achievement and Participation in Science Education* (Greensboro, NC: Southeast Eisenhower Consortium, 2004).

14. Emily Gallmeyer's original lesson plan on the earth's rotation from 2007 can be found on her Web site under the portfolio section, curriculum, C5: http://users.manchester.edu/student/ekgallmeyer/ProfWebpage/default.htm. The lesson teaches students to use critical thinking and problem-solving strategies. We slightly changed the lesson objective, standards, and evaluation.

15. As an inquiry approach, the 5E Learning Cycle Model is attributed to the category of constructivist learning. The 5Es represent a sequence of five steps: Engaging or exciting (the learner), Exploring or investigating (the topic), Explaining (students report what they have learned), Extending (allowing the students to use their new knowledge by making connections to other related concepts and the world around them), and Evaluating (the understanding—by both teachers and students). The 5E Learning Cycle Model was first developed by a team of the Biological Science Curriculum Study: Rodger W. Bybee et al., *Science and Technology Education for the Elementary Years: Frameworks for Curriculum and Instruction* (Washington, DC: National Center for Improving Instruction), 1989.

16. In the absence of Common Core State Standards in science, we used Florida's fourth-grade science standard.

17. The best way to start with the protocol is to underline the verbs that indicate what the teacher and students are doing during the activity. The verbs and verb phrases are already underlined in the lesson description for illustration purposes.

Chapter 4

1. Robert Geier et al., "Standardized Test Outcomes for Students Engaged in Inquiry-Based Curricula in the Context of Urban Reform," *Journal of Research in Science Teaching* 45, no. 5 (2008): 922–939; Mehmet Gültekin, "The Effect of Problem Based Learning on Learning Outcomes in the 5th Grade Social Studies Course in Primary Education," *Educational Sciences: Theory and Practice* 5, no. 2 (2005): 548–556.

2. Stephanie Bell, "Project-Based Learning for the 21st Century: Skills for the Future," *The Clearing House* 83 (2010): 39–43.

3. Phyllis C. Blumenfeld et al., "Motivating Project-Based Learning: Sustaining the Doing, Supporting the Learning," *Educational Psychologist* 26 (1991): 369–398; Cindy E. Hmelo-Silver, "Problem-Based Learning: What and How Do Students Learn?" *Educational Psychology Review* 16 (2004): 235–266.

4. Bell, "Project-Based Learning for the 21st Century"; Linda Torps and Sara Sage, *Problems as Possibilities: Problem-Based Learning for K–12 Education* (Alexandria, VA: ASCD, 2002).

5. Many English learners underestimate their abilities because they feel lost for much of the day while engaging in tasks that require academic language skills. Therefore, we suggest that teachers compile a list of resources appropriate for the ELs' English proficiency level from which the students can choose. When unsure whether an alternative Web site, text, or personal contact is appropriate for English learners, teachers should consult with an ELD specialist.

6. J. Emmett Gardner, Cheryl A. Wissick, Windy Schweder, and Loralee Smith Canter, "Enhancing Interdisciplinary Instruction in General and Special Education: Thematic Units and Technology," *Remedial and Special Education* 24, no. 3 (2003); Betty Shoemaker, "Integrative Education: A Curriculum for the Twenty-First Century," *Oregon School Study Council* 33, no. 2 (1989).

7. We acknowledge that the term *technology* encompasses a whole array of tools that may or may not be computer based. For the purpose of this discussion, however, we limit ourselves to multimedia and computer technologies.

8. Teresa S. Foulger and Margarita Jimenez-Silva, "Enhancing the Writing Development of English Language Learners: Teacher Perceptions of Common Technology in Project-Based Learning," *Journal of Research in Childhood Education* 22, no. 2 (2007): 115.

9. Although many of these tools are also beneficial for focused language and literacy development (e.g., language conventions, organization of text, fundamental reading skills), we list these tools here with a focus on academic content instruction. For explanations and examples of specific considerations in using technology for language acquisition, the reader may want to refer to Mary Ellen Butler-Pascoe and Karin M. Wiburg, *Technology and Teaching English Language Learners* (Boston: Pearson, 2003) or Denise E. Murray, "Technologies for Second Language Literacy," *Annual Review of Applied Linguistics* 25 (2005).

10. Arkansas Department of Education, http://www.arkansased.org/public/userfiles/Learning_Services /Curriculum%20and%20Instruction/Frameworks/Social%20Studies/soc_studies_k_8_051308.pdf.

11. The best way to start with the protocol is to underline the verbs that indicate *what the teacher and student(s) are doing* during the activity. The verbs and verb phrases are already underlined in the lesson description for illustration purposes.

12. The investigation portion of this unit takes place in the media center/computer lab so that each student can complete the WebQuest and no more than two students have to share a computer while searching for/constructing GIS maps with the information needed for the presentation.

    Several government sites offer mapping tools free of charge. See, for example, the National Atlas (http://www.nationalatlas.gov/mapmaker) or the National Map by the United States Geographic Survey (http://nationalmap.gov/viewer.html).

13. Available at http://www.nrel.gov/gis/mapsearch.html.

14. The teacher may need to provide verbal and/or nonverbal support to the groups. Also, some students may need more assistance with computer literacy to select and interpret maps, whereas others may encounter some technological difficulties in creating the map.

Chapter 5

1. Walter Kintsch, "Understanding Word Problems: Linguistic Factors in Problem Solving," in *Language and Artificial Intelligence*, ed. Makoto Nagao (Amsterdam: Elsevier, 1987), 197–208.

2. Jingzi Huang and Bruce Normandia, "Comprehending and Solving Word Problems in Mathematics: Beyond Key Words," in *Reading in Secondary Content Areas: A Language-Based Pedagogy,* eds. Zhihui Fang and Mary J. Schleppegrell (Ann Arbor, MI: Michigan Teacher Training, 2008), 64–83.

3. Christine A. Coombe, Keith S. Folse, and Nancy J. Hubley, *A Practical Guide to Assessing English Language Learners* (Ann Arbor: University of Michigan Press, 2007).

4. To illustrate the nature of vocabulary in mathematics, we extracted an example of specialized vocabulary used in algebra from the Tennessee Vocabulary Project, available at http://www.tn.gov /education/ci/doc/VOCABULARY.pdf.

5. JoAnn Crandall, ed., *ESL Through Content-Area Instruction: Mathematics, Science, Social Studies. Language in Education: Theory and Practice*, no. 69 (West Nyack, NY: Prentice Hall, 1987).

6. Lily W. Fillmore and Catherine E. Snow, *What Teachers Need to Know About Language* (Washington, DC: U.S. Department of Education, Office of Education Research and Improvement, Education Resources Information Center, 2000).

7. The best way to start with the protocol is to underline the verbs that indicate *what the teacher and student(s) are doing* during the activity. The verbs and verb phrases are already underlined in the lesson description for illustration purposes.

8. Note that *give* at the start of this sentence is a "TREAD" word because Mr. Leibniz will "give" the news verbally.

9. See note 13 in chapter 2 for an explanation of "sheltered instruction," or SDAIE.

Chapter 6

1. By verbal symbols we mean language; by nonverbal symbols we mean graphic images and diagrams, real objects and models, hands-on experiences, gestures and expressions, and so on.

2. WIDA provides Performance Definitions and Can Do Descriptors for five levels: Level 1, Entering, through Level 5, Bridging. At Level 6, Reaching, the EL is presumed to have mastered all criteria of the lower levels.

3. Marshall McLuhan was a Canadian scholar on communication theory. James Carey, *Communication as Culture: Essays on Media and Society* (New York: Routledge, 2008).

4. We believe that the still undefined status of the language demands of schooling is a testament to this general lack of language awareness. In communicating about various school subjects, educators typically pay no mind to the structure, form, and function of *spoken* discourse, nor do they necessarily sense how these linguistic aspects affect the listeners' comprehension of intended meaning. Likewise, when teachers design tasks that require students to communicate to and with others about academic subjects, they often fail to identify how these activities require a certain facility with language. Although there is a sounder record of attentiveness to the structure, form, and function of language used in written texts rather than in oral communication, much of it has been limited to literary analysis or language study, or it has been oversimplified into formulas of informational text complexity that are not substantiated by strong research and theory.

5. Count nouns can be stated in plural form (most commonly by adding an *s*), and can therefore be counted. Noncount nouns cannot be stated in plural form, so they cannot be counted. If noncount nouns can't be counted, then they also can't be preceded by the indefinite article *a*, which indicates there is one of them.

6. Keith S. Folse, *Keys to Teaching Grammar to English Language Learners: A Practical Handbook* (Ann Arbor: University of Michigan Press, 2009).

7. M. A. K. Halliday, *Language as Social Semiotic: The Social Interpretation of Language and Meaning* (London: Arnold,1978).

8. With the implementation of the Common Core State Standards, English language arts teachers will become well acquainted not only with the four strands of reading, writing, listening and speaking, and language, but also with the individual standards at each of the grade levels they teach. In the area of reading, the CCSS expect all students to build knowledge, gain insights, explore possibilities, and broaden their perspective through reading relevant and diverse selections from classic and contemporary literature as well as challenging informational texts in a range of subjects. Certain critical types of reading materials, including classic myths and stories from around the world, foundational U.S. documents, seminal works of American literature, and the writings of Shakespeare, are required. In writing, the standards aim to develop students' ability to write logical arguments based on substantive claims, sound reasoning, and relevant evidence. The writing standards provide annotated samples of student writing in order to help establish adequate performance levels in writing arguments, informational or explanatory texts, and narratives. The speaking and listening standards emphasize gaining, evaluating, and presenting increasingly complex information, ideas, and evidence through listening and speaking as well as through media. These standards emphasize academic discussion in one-on-one, small-group, and whole-class settings. They aim to develop necessary skills for formal presentations as well as the more informal discussion that takes place as students collaborate to answer questions, build understanding, and solve problems. The language standards emphasize language accuracy and vocabulary development. Vocabulary and language conventions are treated in their own strand not because skills in these areas should be handled in isolation but because their use extends across reading, writing, speaking, and listening.

9. We use the term *second language learning* to encompass both foreign language learning, which takes place in environments where the language studied is not the language spoken in the country or region of the school, and second language learning, which takes place in environments where the language studied is the language spoken in the country or region of the school.

10. Rod Ellis, *The Study of Second Language Acquisition*, 2nd ed. (Oxford: Oxford University Press, 2008). These are not either/or propositions, as an instructed environment could incorporate naturalistic features, such as requiring French 1 students to converse one-on-one with native speakers, and naturalistic environments may include instructed second language acquisition, such as living in a second language community while taking an online grammar course to help understand the mechanics of the language.

11. See http://online.stanford.edu/course/classroom-conversations-fall-2013 for a great resource on supporting constructive classroom conversations.

12. What Stephen Krashen calls i + 1, or comprehensible input, focuses on understanding input. Stephen D. Krashen, *The Input Hypothesis: Issues and Implications* (New York: Longman, 1985).

13. The term *communicative competence* was extended to language pedagogy by Michael Canale. For more information see Michael Canale, "From Communicative Competence to Language Pedagogy," in *Language and Communication*, eds. Jack Richards and Richard Schmidt (London: Longman, 1983).

14. Ellis, *The Study of Second Language Acquisition*, 28–31; 764–765.

15. Ibid, 6.

16. Manfred Pienemann, "An Introduction to Processability Theory," in *Cross-Linguistic Aspects of Processability Theory*, ed. Manfred Pienemann (Amsterdam: John Benjamins, 2005), 1–60.

17. The Defense Language Institute categorizes languages by their similarity to English for purposes of establishing the number of weeks required of full-time, intensive study to develop basic skills in social language comprehension and use. Association of the United States Army, "DLI's Language Guidelines," http://www.ausa.org/publications/ausanews/specialreports/2010/8/Pages/DLI'slanguageguidelines.aspx.

18. Larry Selinker, *Rediscovering Interlanguage* (New York: Longman, 1992); Susan M. Gass and Alison Mackey, "Input, Interaction, and Output: An Overview," *AILA Review* 19, (2006): 3–17.

19. Ibid.

20. Ellis, *The Study of Second Language Acquisition,* 846–847.

21. This tends to be more possible in a separate or sheltered classroom since native speakers often do not need the same type of instruction in the forms and structures of English as do English learners such as Edgar.

22. *Literacy* remains a dynamic concept, evolving and changing over time, reflecting different societies' forms of and needs for expression. Literacy activist Paulo Freire defined literacy as "discursive forms and cultural competencies that construct and make available the various relations and experiences that exist between learners and the world." Paulo Freire and Donaldo Macedo, *Literacy: Reading the Word and the World* (New York: Routledge–Taylor & Francis, 2013), 7. Even more technically, María Torres-Guzmán defines literacy as an "asset of cultural practices that includes the encoding and decoding of print and that is used to convey a message that has specific shared meaning for a group of individuals in a particular context." Bertha Pérez and María E. Torres-Guzmán. *Learning in Two Worlds: An Integrated Spanish/English Biliteracy Approach,* 3rd ed. (New York: Allyn and Bacon, 2002), 4. Similar to the culture-bound definitions we presented in previous chapters for communication and language, these definitions of literacy situate culture at its core. Similarly, our perspective on literacy is meaning and culture centered, encompassing the ability to perceive meaning from and express meaning in the *social semiotic system* of text.

23. An excellent synthesis of this research is summarized in Diane L. August and Timothy Shanahan, eds., *Developing Literacy in a Second Language: Report of the National Literacy Panel* (Mahwah, NJ: Lawrence Erlbaum Associates, 2006).

24. Nonie K. Lesaux, Keiko Koda, Linda S. Siegel, and Timothy Shanahan, "Development of Literacy of Language Minority Learners," in *Developing Literacy in a Second Language: Report of the National Literacy Panel*, eds. Diane. L. August and Timothy Shanahan (Mahwah, NJ: Lawrence Erlbaum Associates, 2006), 75–122.

25. Nonie K. Lesaux, Amy C. Crosson, Michael J. Kieffer, and Margaret Pierce, "Uneven Profiles: Language Minority Learners' Word Reading, Vocabulary, and Reading Comprehension Skills," *Journal of Applied Developmental Psychology* 31, no. 6 (2010): 475–483.

26. Catherine E. Snow, "Cross-Cutting Themes and Future Research Directions," in *Developing Literacy in a Second Language: Report of the National Literacy Panel*, eds. Diane. L. August and Timothy Shanahan (Mahwah, NJ: Lawrence Erlbaum Associates, 2006), 631–651.

27. Proctor, Carol, August, and Snow tested a second language reading comprehension model incorporating decoding and oral language measures on a sample of 135 Spanish- and English-speaking fourth graders and reported a high correlation of .73 between students' vocabulary knowledge and reading comprehension outcomes. C. Patrick Proctor, Diane August, María S. Carlo, and Catherine E. Snow, "The Intriguing Role of Spanish Language Vocabulary Knowledge in Predicting English Reading Comprehension," *Journal of Educational Psychology* 98, no. 1 (2006): 159–169. In another study, van Gelderen et al. administered tests of English vocabulary knowledge and reading comprehension to 397 Dutch students in grades 8 through 10 and found a strong correlation of .63. Amos van Gelderen, Rob Schooner, Kees de Glopper, Jon Hulstijn, Annegien Simis, Patrick Snellings, and Marie Stevenson, "Linguistic Knowledge, Processing Speed, and Metacognitive Knowledge in First-and Second-Language Reading Comprehension: A Componential Analysis," *Journal of Educational Psychology* 96, no. 1 (2004): 19–30.

28. Catherine E. Snow, M. Susan Burns, and Peg Griffin, *Preventing Reading Difficulties in Young Children* (Washington, DC: National Academy Press, 1998), 74.

29. See Kate Cain, *Reading Development and Difficulties* (West Sussex, UK: British Psychological Society and Blackwell, Ltd., 2010) for an extensive discussion of this research and its application for practice.

30. One study that relates directly to the impact of text structure is Jill Fitzgerald and Alan Teasley, "Effects of Instruction in Narrative Structure on Children's Writing," *Journal of Educational Psychology* 78, no. 6 (1986): 424–432. For an extensive discussion of how awareness of text structure relates to children's and adult readers' reading and writing performance, see Walter Kintsch, *Comprehension: A Paradigm for Cognition* (Cambridge: Cambridge University Press, 1998).

31. See http://www.wida.us/assessment/access/ for information on the WIDA ACCESS for ELLs English proficiency assessment and http://www.elpa21.org/ for ELPA 21. You may wonder why it is necessary to use a test designed to measure English learners' listening, speaking, reading, and writing when all children are given standardized reading tests. Tests for English learners are sensitive to the stages they go through in developing proficiency in all four skill areas. In addition to language complexity, cultural content can also affect assessment of English learners' knowledge of academic subjects. Culture-free testing does not exist. This is a result of the strong connection between culture and cultural content, on the one hand, and language, on the other, as our earlier discussion of communication, culture, and language described. In well-written tests, English learners can understand the cultural content of test questions through context. Depending on an English learner's cultural heritage, what may be a common cultural occurrence in many places in the United States may be completely unfamiliar to the EL. Consider this sentence:

    Tommy had cereal after he got up.

    If ELs are not familiar with cereal, they might not understand the meaning of the sentence, and the word *had* would not provide the specificity necessary to infer the general meaning. However, if the wording provides more background through specificity of terms, it becomes clear that *cereal* refers to food:

    Tommy ate cereal for breakfast.

    More specific word choices, such as *ate* rather than *had*, and specifying *breakfast* to provide additional context (*after he got up* may not be understood as rising in the morning), provide information that makes the content more comprehensible to the EL.

32. The most recent update of the TESOL standards is from 2006: http://www.tesol.org/advance-the-field/standards/prek-12-english-language-proficiency-standards. WIDA stands for World-Class Instructional Design and Assessment. The latest set of standards was released in 2012. See http://www.wida.us/assessment/access/background.aspx.

33. We chose to present the WIDA English Language Development Standards for several reasons. First of all, the consortium is composed of thirty-one U.S. states, meaning that a majority of teachers will use them for their yearly testing of English learners to satisfy the requirements of the Elementary and Secondary Education Act. Furthermore, the latest set of standards was released in 2012, whereas the latest TESOL language proficiency standards date back to 2006, and the TESOL standards were based on the language proficiency levels developed by WIDA.

34. Pienemann, "An Introduction to Processability Theory."

35. William M. Saunders, Barbara R. Foorman, and Coleen D. Carlson, "Is a Separate Block of Time for Oral English Language Development in Programs for English Learners Needed?" *Elementary School Journal* 107 (November 2006): 181–198.

36. Jim Cummins, *Bilingual Education and Special Education: Issues in Assessment and Pedagogy* (San Diego: College Hill, 1984).

37. William Saunders, Claude Goldenberg, and David Marcelletti, "English Language Development: Guidelines for Instruction," *American Educator* (Summer 2013): 13–25.

38. A reading development class may or may not be the best place for an English learner whose reading is below grade level. It might be more advantageous to invest more time in the instructed second language acquisition that occurs in an ELD class, which integrates the four skills of listening, speaking, reading, and writing at the student's level of proficiency and which has been shown to

expedite second language development. Wherever language arts and literacy instruction takes place, it should be targeted as closely as possible to the English learner.

39. The Can Do Descriptors can be downloaded from: http://www.wida.us/standards/CAN_DOs/

40. WIDA sells some very handy Can Do Name Charts that can simplify the process of reusing charts. See the above Web site for more information.

41. We wanted to help mainstream classroom teachers understand how ELD teachers provide this quality of targeted language instruction for their English learners. To determine what might help, we designed an empirical exploration of what qualified ELD teachers actually do differently when they use language arts and literacy teaching techniques that are common to both the first language (L1) and second language (L2) instructional environments. To isolate what is different about targeted language instruction, we recorded videos of ELD teachers using a dozen different language arts techniques that are commonly applied in mainstream elementary and secondary classrooms. The classes that participated in these videos were composed exclusively of English learners in grades K–2, 3–5, 6–8, and 9–12, and their teachers were certified and experienced in teaching ELD.

After the videos were produced, we showed them over a year's time to more than a hundred mainstream language arts teachers and asked them to take notes regarding what was different in the execution of those teaching techniques and strategies with the English learners. In other words, we asked them to note what the teacher and students did that was different from if a language arts teacher had been using the same strategy or technique with a class composed solely of native speakers of English. From teachers' observations and subsequent reflections, we identified qualities of scaffolding that made sense to mainstream language arts and literacy teachers. We held subsequent professional development sessions with the teachers, sharing these qualities of scaffolding for English learners, which we termed pitch, pace, portion, and perspective/point (the 4 Ps of language arts scaffolding for English learners).

42. Teachers who work in bilingual education and dual-language classrooms regularly use students' home language for instruction. They do so purposefully to build upon and make use of students' home language to support language development as well as academic subject learning in English. We believe it is helpful for language arts and literacy teachers to use what are referred to as "translanguaging" or "translingual practices" to enable students to communicate and access academic subjects, using a mix of their first language and English. Translanguaging and translingual strategies are especially helpful when working with EL students such as Gero, Edith, or Edgar, who are at beginning or intermediate language proficiency levels. Researchers and practitioners agree that teachers who share the same home language as their students can and should use the home language as a valuable resource to communicate with their students and support their language learning, literacy development, and academic subject learning. They should also allow students to mix languages as well as code-switch from their first language to their second language, and from everyday informal uses of the second language to more formal or academic uses to reduce language barriers to communication. Being bilingual is an asset, and knowledge from one language can transfer to the other.

Ms. Levin, Gero's teacher, doesn't speak Haitian Kreyòl or French. Ms. Oliver, Edith's teacher, doesn't speak Spanish. Nonetheless, they can support Gero's and Edith's language and literacy development through various strategies. For instance, in her fourth-grade language arts classroom, Ms. Oliver can build upon Edith's first language, Spanish, as a resource for literacy development and academic subject learning. In the beginning of a lesson, Ms. Oliver can use multilingual word walls to introduce new vocabulary in Spanish and English, pointing out distinctions between true cognates, such as *national* and *nacional*, and false cognates, such as *embarrassed* and *embarazada* (pregnant). When reading to or with beginning EL students like Gero, Ms. Levin can use multilingual versions of selected classics such as Eric Carle's *The Very Hungry Caterpillar* or Bill Martin's *Brown Bear, Brown Bear, What Do you See?* which are available in French (and choose from a smaller collection of bilingual books that are available in Haitian Kreyòl). For intermediate English learners like Edgar, in the middle or end of a lesson, Ms. Myers can enable him to engage in discussions and meaningfully participate in instruction even if with "imperfect" language. In fact, she regularly encourages Edgar to take notes about what he's reading and discuss what he is learning in both languages. When EL students engage in activities such as these, they have a unique opportunity to simultaneously develop not only the conceptual and academic understandings, but also the language resources to express them.

43. Another example is using a grammatical focus rather than a semantic one for a cloze procedure, which means omitting specific parts of speech, rather than every nth word, to check an English learner's grammatical competence.

44. Roland Tharp and Ronald Gallimore, *Rousing Minds to Life: Teaching, Learning, and Schooling in Social Context* (New York: Cambridge University Press, 1988).

45. This can also be accomplished through technology, using grammar mini-lessons available at free resources such as the app Show Me.

46. Emily C. Bouck, Sara Flanagan, Bridget Miller, and Laura Bassette, "Technology in Action: Rethinking Everyday Technology as Assistive Technology to Meet Students' IEP Goals," *Journal of Special Education Technology* 27, no. 4 (2012): 47–57.

Chapter 7

1. Gero is a bilingual French/Haitian Kreyòl speaker, but because of his dominance in Haitian Kreyòl, we will use Haitian Kreyòl as the primary language of discussion when referring to Gero's native language.

2. Bader Reading and Language Assessment Inventory, http://staging.indyreads.org/wp-content/uploads/2012/09/BaderAssessment.pdf.

3. See http://www.elpa21.org/.

4. Diane August and Timothy Shanahan, eds., *Developing Literacy in Second-Language Learners: Report of the National Literacy Panel on Language-Minority Children and Youth* (Mahwah, NJ: Lawrence Erlbaum Associates, 2006).

5. Ibid.

6. Catherine Snow, "Cross-Cutting Themes and Future Research Directions," in August and Shanahan, *Developing Literacy in Second-Language Learners*, 641–642.

7. Nonie K. Lesaux and Esther Geva, "Development of Literacy in Language-Minority Students," in August and Shanahan, *Developing Literacy in Second-Language Learners,* 27–60.

8. National Institute of Child Health and Human Development, *Report of the National Reading Panel, Teaching Children to Read: An Evidence-Based Assessment of the Scientific Research Literature on Reading and Its Implications for Reading Instruction, NIH 00-4769* (Washington, DC: U.S. Department of Health and Human Services, 2000).

9. Ibid., 639.

10. David L. Share, "Phonological Recoding and Self-Teaching: Sine Qua Non of Reading Acquisition," *Cognition* 55 (1995): 151–218, cited in Catherine Snow, "Cross-Cutting Themes and Future Research Directions," 646–647.

11. Catherine Snow, "Cross-Cutting Themes and Future Research Directions," 646.

12. Diane August, Margarita Calderón, and María Carlo, *Transfer of Skills from Spanish to English: A Study of Young Learners: Report For Practitioners, Parents, and Policy Makers* (Washington, DC: Center for Applied Linguistics, 2002), 647.

13. Nonie K. Lesaux, Amy C. Crosson, Michael J. Kieffer, and Margaret Pierce, "Uneven Profiles: Language Minority Learners' Word Reading, Vocabulary, and Reading Comprehension Skills," *Journal of Applied Developmental Psychology* 31, no. 6 (2010): 475–483.

14. August and Shanahan, *Developing Literacy in Second-Language Learners*.

15. For more information on commonalities and contrasts between Spanish, Haitian Kreyòl, and English, please see the following sites:

> Spanish—http://esl.fis.edu/grammar/langdiff/spanish.htm
> http://www.angelfire.com/fl/espanglishtips/
> Haitian Kreyòl—http://www.confidentvoice.com/blog/
> american-english-pronunciation-problems-for-speakers-of-haitian-creole/

16. Michael DeGraff, "Haitian Creole," in *Comparative Creole Syntax: Parallel Outlines of 18 Creole Grammars*, Westminster Creolistics Series 7, eds. John A. Holm and Peter L. Patrick (London: Battlebridge Publications, 2007).

17. William Grabe, "Notes Toward a Theory of Second Language Writing," in *On Second Language Writing,* eds. Tony J. Silva and Paul K. Matsuda (Mahwah, NJ: Lawrence Erlbaum Associates, 2006).

18. Common Core State Standards Initiative, http://www.corestandards.org/ELA-Literacy/W/K.

19. For this and the LAP examples in chapters 8–10, we developed a composite of a variety of English proficiency standards, indicators, and English language development curriculum elements to describe Gero's, Edith's, Edgar's and Tasir's proficiency in listening, reading, speaking, writing, and language conventions. We believe this composite, compiled from a number of regional consortia, national organizations, and state initiatives, blends the best definitions of what English learners at different levels of proficiency can do. We call this composite the English proficiency descriptors. The full list of our five-level composite descriptors for the K–12 grade bands can be accessed at http://englishlearnerachievement.com. Additionally, we encourage readers to consult the various organizations from which we derived the descriptors (e.g., TESOL, WIDA, ELPA21) as well as their own state English proficiency standards.

Ms. Levin keeps a table with Gero's English proficiency level descriptors filled in for all of the five skills and then writes the steps of any lesson she is planning in the second column.

Chapter 8

1. Bader Reading and Language Assessment Inventory, http://staging.indyreads.org/wp-content/uploads/2012/09/BaderAssessment.pdf.

2. Florida Department of Education, *2012 FCAT Writing. Grade 4 Expository Calibration Scoring Guide* (Tallahassee, FL: Florida Department of Education, 2011). Available at http://www.palmbeachschools.org/ec/Writing/documents/G42012ExpositoryCalibrationGuide.pdf.

3. See http://www.elpa21.org/.

4. J. S. Chall and V. A. Jacobs, "Writing and Reading in the Elementary Grades: Developmental Trends Among Low-SES children," *Language Arts,* 60, no. 5 (1983): 617–626.

5. Pauline Gibbons, *Scaffolding Language, Scaffolding Learning: Teaching Second Language Learners in the Mainstream Classroom* (Portsmouth, NH: Heinemann, 2002).

6. Donald Meichenbaum and Andrew Biemiller, *Nurturing Independent Learners: Helping Students Take Charge of Their Learning* (Cambridge: Brookline Books, 1998).

7. Nonie K. Lesaux, Amy C. Crosson, Michael J. Kieffer, and Margaret Pierce, "Uneven Profiles: Language Minority Learners' Word Reading, Vocabulary, and Reading Comprehension Skills," *Journal of Applied Developmental Psychology* 31, no. 6 (2010): 475–483.

8. Mienke Droop and Ludo T. Verhoeven, "Language Proficiency and Reading Ability in First- and Second-Language Learners," *Reading Research Quarterly* 38 (2003): 78–103.

9. Elizabeth Bernhardt, *Understanding Advanced Second-Language Reading* (New York: Routledge, 2011).

10. Levi McNeil, "Extending the Compensatory Model of Second Language Reading," *System* 40 (2011): 64–76.

11. Bernhardt, *Understanding Advanced Second Language Reading.* Bernhardt's model is influenced by and dependent on the concept of compensatory information processing first developed by Keith Stanovic, a prominent first language literacy researcher.

12. Keiko Koda and Annett M. Zehler, eds., *Learning to Read Across Languages: Cross-Linguistic Relationships in First- and Second-Language Literacy Development* (New York: Routledge, 2008).

13. See http://www.conaliteg.gob.mx/index.php/directorio for more information on this free program.

14. This list will be displayed for the remainder of the school year and additional prefixes and suffixes will be added as they are discovered.

15. For space reasons, only one lesson with three prefixes is shown here, but Ms. Oliver also plans to conduct similar lessons with suffixes.

Chapter 9

1. Bader Reading and Language Assessment Inventory, http://staging.indyreads.org/wp-content/uploads/2012/09/BaderAssessment.pdf.

2. Florida Department of Education, *2012 FCAT Writing. Grade 4 Expository Calibration Scoring Guide,* (Tallahassee, FL: Florida Department of Education, 2011). Available at http://www.palmbeachschools.org/ec/Writing/documents/G42012ExpositoryCalibrationGuide.pdf.

3. See http://www.elpa21.org/.

4. See Common Core State Standards for English Language Arts at http://www.corestandards.org/ELA-Literacy.

5. Jacquelyn Schachter, "An Error in Error Analysis," *Language Learning* 24, no. 2 (1974): 205–214; Joy M. Reid, *Writing Myths: Applying Second Language Research to Classroom Teaching* (Ann Arbor: University of Michigan, 2008).

6. Robert B. Kaplan, "Cultural Thought Patterns in Inter Cultural Education," *Language Learning* 16, no. 1–2 (1966): 1–20.

7. Min Wang, Keiko Koda, and Charles A. Perfetti, "Alphabetic and Nonalphabetic L1 Effects in English Word Identification: A Comparison of Korean and Chinese English L2 Learners," *Cognition* 87, no. 2 (2003): 129–149.

8. Megumi Hamada and Keiko Koda, "Similarity and Difference in Learning L2 Word-Form," *System* 39, no. 4 (2011): 500–509.

9. Minh Nguyen-Hoan and Marcus Taft, "The Impact of a Subordinate L1 on L2 Auditory Processing in Adult Bilinguals," *Bilingualism: Language and Cognition* 13, no. 2 (2010): 217–230; Wang, Koda, and Perfetti, "Alphabetic and Nonalphabetic L1 Effects."

10. Alison Holm and Barbara Dodd, "The Effect of First Written Language on the Acquisition of English Literacy," *Cognition* 59, no. 2 (1996): 119–147.

11. Dana R. Ferris, *Treatment of Error in Second Language Student Writing* (Ann Arbor: University of Michigan, 2011); Keith S. Folse, *Vocabulary Myths: Applying Second Language Research to Classroom Teaching* (Ann Arbor: University of Michigan, 2004).

12. Hamada and Koda, "Similarity and Difference in Learning L2 Word-Form."

13. Ibid.

14. See http://tapestry.usf.edu/responding_to_errors/ for more information.

15. Robert B. Kaplan, "Cultural Thought Patterns Revisited," in *Writing Across Languages Analysis of L2 Text*, eds. Ulla Connor and Robert B. Kaplan (Reading, MA: Addison-Wesley, 1987), 9–21.

16. Encourage individuals not to all pick the same arguments so that as a whole, the group will be able to present a well-rounded argument.

17. For example, choose a few minutes of both "Persuasive Speech (Stop Eating Fast Food)," available at http://www.youtube.com/watch?v=bVJ8GlqbxkU, and "Speech 110-Summer 2011 (Persuasive Speech-Say No to Fast Food)," available at http://www.youtube.com/watch?v=XvkH-SXyH_E.

18. See the One Plus Model of professional learning presented in the conclusion for our discussion of what we suggest minimal preparation would encompass.

Chapter 10

1. Bader Reading and Language Assessment Inventory, http://staging.indyreads.org/wp-content/uploads/2012/09/BaderAssessment.pdf.

2. Florida Department of Education, *2012 FCAT Writing: Grade 8 Expository Calibration Scoring Guide* (Tallahassee, FL: Florida Department of Education, 2011), http://www.palmbeachschools.org/ec/Writing/documents/G42012ExpositoryCalibrationGuide.pdf.

3. See http://www.elpa21.org.

4. Elizabeth Bernhardt, *Reading Development in a Second Language: Theoretical, Empirical, and Classroom Perspectives* (Norwood, NJ: Ablex, 1991).

5. Wayne Thomas and Virginia Collier, *School Effectiveness for Language Minority Students* (Washington, DC: National Clearinghouse for Bilingual Education, 1997).

6. William Nagy and Dianna Townsend, "Words as Tools: Learning Academic Vocabulary as Language Acquisition," *Reading Research Quarterly* 47, no. 1 (2012): 91–108.

7. David Crystal, *The English Language: A Guided Tour of the Language* (London: Cambridge University Press, 2002).

8. The lesson is gleaned from the tenth-grade Pearson's textbook series *Language Central*: Jim Cummins, Lily Wong Fillmore, Jill Kerper Mora, and Georgia Earnest García, *Language Central: English Language Development (ELD), Grade 10* (New York: Pearson Education, 2013). A commercial

product was used because it highlights best how integrated English language instruction teaches all four language skills one by one, while allowing a focus on form.

9. Manfred Pienemann, ed., *Crosslinguistic Aspects of Processability Theory* (Amsterdam: John Benjamins, 2005).

Conclusion

1. For research on the positive correlation between student academic achievement and levels of collaboration in schools, at both the elementary and secondary levels, you may wish to consult Steve Gruenert, "Correlations of Collaborative School Cultures with Student Achievement," *National Association of Secondary School Principals Bulletin* 89, no. 43 (2005): 43–55; or Yvonne L. Goddard, Roger D. Goddard, and Megan Tschannen-Moran, "A Theoretical and Empirical Investigation of Teacher Collaboration for School Improvement and Student Achievement in Public Elementary Schools," *Teachers College Record* 109, no. 4 (2007): 877–896.

2. Some schools may not have an in-house ELD teacher and depend on bilingual aides who work alongside English learners for a majority of the day. For descriptions of the most frequently used ELD and bilingual program models that use ELD specialists, see Cheryl A. Roberts, "Bilingual Education Program Models: A Framework for Understanding," *Bilingual Research Journal* 19, no. 3–4 (1995): 369–378, or Jeanne Rennie, "ESL and Bilingual Program Models," Center for Applied Linguistics, Sept. 1993, http://www.cal.org/resources/digest/rennie01.html.

3. Please see the discussion of language learning in academic settings in chapter 1 for more detail.

4. More teachers and school counselors need to become aware of the fact that English learners can be gifted and can thrive in a gifted class, even though they still have to acquire academic English, and teachers need to learn how to better identify such students. As it stands, English learners are vastly underrepresented in gifted classes, but make up a disproportionate number of the students diagnosed with a disability, following a similar pattern to their culturally diverse native English-speaking peers.

5. Since the 1980s foreign and second language educators, ELD teachers included, have used a language teaching approach called content-based instruction with success. Rather than teaching language through dialogues, exercises, and discussions on the structure and form of language to develop general fluency and accuracy, with content-based instruction the focus shifts to teaching a foreign or second language through using it to teach academic subjects. Many schools with high percentages of English learners use a content-based approach to teaching English. With content-based language instruction, ELD teachers, in tandem with academic subject teachers, support their students' English language development, especially as it relates to the subjects they are studying. In the past, ELD instruction focused primarily on teaching language for language's sake, but more current approaches focus on teaching language through the content. This involves using "sheltered content" materials that are designed with a degree of verbal complexity appropriate for the ELs' level of English proficiency and that focus on the vocabulary and grammar inherent in the text or discourse. Alternatively, ELD teachers can provide the necessary unpacking and support that English learners require to access materials that are above their English proficiency levels. In addition, they use language arts exercises such as listening, speaking, reading, and writing activities that are appropriate for the level of English proficiency and relevant to the subject matter. For example, an ELD teacher may teach a proficiency-level-appropriate language lesson focusing on the properties of an atom, but the main focus of the lesson would be to learn specific vocabulary and grammar used in science texts describing the topic and give English learners practice in writing scientific descriptive sentences on the topic at their level of English proficiency. This approach complements what the mainstream science teacher would do with a class of native speakers and one or more English learners. When both teachers collaborate to plan their lessons and coordinate their efforts, the ELs benefit most. In addition, where there are enough English learners enrolled in specific academic subject classes, such as biology or U.S. history, sheltered instruction can bridge the language and academic subject instruction divide. Many ELD teachers use a sheltered approach to teaching language through academic content called the Sheltered Instruction Observation Protocol (SIOP), developed by Echevarria, Vogt, and Short: Jane M. Echevarría, Mary Ellen Vogt, and Deborah

Short, *Making Content Comprehensible for English Language Learners: The SIOP Model* (Boston: Allyn & Bacon, 2000). These teachers also use the Teachers of English to Speakers of Other Languages (TESOL) PreK–12 English Language Proficiency Standards for identifying social and academic language use for communicating in language arts, mathematics, science, and social studies: http://www.tesol.org/advance-the-field/standards/prek-12-english-language-proficiency-standards.

6. Linda Darling-Hammond and Nikole Richardson, "Teacher Learning: What Matters?" *Educational Leadership* 6, no. 5 (2009): 4–-53.

7. Linda Darling-Hammond, Ruth Chung Wei, Alethea Andree, Nikole Richardson, and Stelio Orphanos, *Professional Learning in the Learning Profession: A Status Report on Teacher Development in the U.S. and Abroad* (Oxford, OH: National Staff Development Council, 2009). http://learningforward.org/docs/pdf/nsdcstudy2009.pdf.

8. Amy Hodges Slamp, "iPD: Rethinking Professional Development in Districts" (presentation at the TeachLive summer conference, Bill & Melinda Gates Foundation, College Ready Work Team, Orlando, FL, May 24, 2013).

9. Linda Darling-Hammond et al., *Professional Learning in the Learning Profession.*

10. Multilingual Department and Minneapolis Public Schools, "2011–2012 ELL Programming Framework," http://ell.mpls.k12.mn.us/uploads/programming_framework.pdf.

11. Sophie Arkoudis, "Negotiating the Rough Ground between ESL and Mainstream Teachers," *International Journal of Bilingual Education and Bilingualism* 9, no. 4 (2006): 415–433; Chris M. Davison, "Key Assumptions about Effective Collaboration between ESL and Content-Area Teachers," *International Journal of Bilingual Education and Bilingualism* 9, no. 4 (2006): 454–475.

12. For a description of ELD specialists and mainstream teachers co-teaching, see Maria Dove and Andrea Honigsfeld, "ESL Coteaching and Collaboration: Opportunities to Develop Teacher Leadership and Enhance Student Learning," *TESOL Journal* 1, no. 1 (2010).

13. Ibid.; Linda Darling-Hammond et al., *Professional Learning in the Learning Profession.*

14. National Commission on Teaching and America's Future, *Team Up for 21st Century Teaching and Learning: What Research and Practice Reveal About Professional Learning* (Washington, DC: NCTAF, 2010).

15. A. Richardson Love, "Collaborating for Student Success: Perspectives from the MetLife Survey of the American Teacher," *National Civic Review* 99, no. 2 (2010): 10–14.

16. French for "Thank you for your son. He is a gift to our class."

17. Linda Darling-Hammond, *Teacher Quality and Student Achievement: A Review of State Policy Evidence* (Seattle: Center for the Study of Teaching Policy, University of Washington, 1999); Daniel Weisberg, Susan Sexton, Jennifer Mulhern, and David Keeling, *The Widget Effect: Our National Failure to Acknowledge and Act on Differences in Teacher Effectiveness* (Brooklyn, NY: The New Teacher Project, 2009), http://www.tntp.org.

18. Haitian Kreyòl, meaning "one cannot eat okra with one finger," which in turn implies that people must work together to accomplish tasks.

Appendix C

1. Submission guidelines can be accessed at http://journals.fcla.edu/tapestry/about/submissions #onlineSubmissions. For inquiries, manuscript submissions, and blog entries, please e-mail tapestryjournal@gmail.com.

Acknowledgments

Our biggest debt of gratitude is owed to Caroline Chauncey, our awesome editor. The most accurate descriptor of Caroline's role in the composition of this book is coauthor. She was simultaneously critical and encouraging, gently but constantly pushing us to give a little more, do a little better, until we transformed our lecture and workshop slides, notes, activities, and handouts into a freestanding book. She made us think about the education of English learners in universal terms, gave us stellar suggestions, provided us with direction and guidance when we felt lost, and advocated for our work at every turn. Caroline is so good at what she does, that anything she is involved in is always far better for it.

We are very thankful for all the many dedicated and talented professionals at Harvard Education Press who are a key part of this book's success. Sarah Weaver skillfully led us through the copyediting process, Christina De Young energetically guided marketing, Rose Ann Miller creatively oversaw publicity, and Sumita Mukherji expertly managed the production phase.

We would also like to express our gratitude to the many other people who helped make this book a reality, far too many to name here. We thank all those who provided support, talked things over, read drafts of our manuscript, offered comments, and assisted in the editing, proofreading, and design for this book. We thank the anonymous reviewers for their constructive comments and questions that forced us to think about the vision for this book from different angles. We also would like to note the vital role of Raqs Baladi in uniting us and moving the book forward.

We are thankful to doctoral research assistants and colleagues who contributed significantly to the book. Melanie Gonzalez and Alison Youngblood helped us identify recent research and gave up weekend and holiday time to work on formatting. Donita Grissom searched through books and online material to identify academic text we could use for examples and suggested lesson plans that fit well with our four English learners and chosen content areas. Ting "Poppy" Yan checked references and endnotes with precision. Colleague Michele Regalla provided great feedback on drafts (although we're not supposed to disclose this lest others learn about her covert editing skills and start asking her for similar favors). Annette Norwood's keen eye caught typos and other needed corrections. We would like to thank our many teacher preparation colleagues who have wholeheartedly embraced the Academic Subjects and Language Arts Protocols and incorporated the approach into how they require their candidates to adapt lessons for English learners. District and state leaders in Florida, in particular Minnie Cardona, ESOL and world languages coordinator in Seminole County Public Schools, and Chane Eplin, bureau chief at the Florida Department of Education's Bureau of Student Achievement Through Language Acquisition, graciously took time out of their busy schedules to talk to us when we had pressing questions.

Our deep appreciation also goes to Julie Snyder and LaSonya Moore, who provide English learners the support they need to achieve in school and in life and who helped us collect real-life assessment data and language samples. We also greatly benefited from the artistic vision of Wendy Williams, who was able to interpret our drawings and turn them into clear and concise graphics. We are deeply indebted to Simone Basilio, who jumped in at a moment's notice late one Friday evening to help us out with a handful of graphics and stuck with us throughout the weekend.

Most important, we would like to thank the real students who were the basis for the stories of our four English learners. Witnessing their struggles and accomplishments inspired us to tell the story of learning and teaching second languages from their perspectives. We hope they inspire our readers as much as they inspired us.

About the Authors

JOYCE W. NUTTA began her fascination with second languages before elementary school, listening to French- and Spanish-speaking tourists at her parents' ten-unit motel in west central Florida. In the ninth grade, she and her parents moved to a small town in the Dolomites of Italy, where she was enrolled in an Italian-speaking high school even though she knew nothing of the language or culture. She spent two years in the ninth grade and, although her social language developed by the end of her second year, she was unable to pass the rigorous essay exams of academic subjects and language arts in Italian and returned to Florida to continue high school. After volunteering to help immigrant students learn English in her academic classes, she began her profession as a teacher of English as a second language and eventually a teacher educator. She earned teaching certification followed by a master's degree in applied linguistics, and a PhD in second language acquisition/instructional technology. Her research interests include the integration of English learner issues into teacher education curricula, the use of technology to teach second languages, and technology-enhanced instruction in teacher education. She is a coeditor of *The Tapestry Journal: An International Multidisciplinary Journal on English Language Learner Education*. She is a coauthor of *Preparing Every Teacher to Reach English Learners: A Practical Guide for Teacher Educators* (Harvard Education Press) and offers professional development based on its content as well as the content of this book. Her presentations are highly interactive and hands-on applications of research-based approaches to teaching English learners. She currently is a professor of English for Speakers of Other Languages (ESOL) and the ESOL Endorsement and TESOL PhD Track Coordinator of the College of Education at the University of Central Florida.

CARINE STREBEL grew up surrounded by multiple languages. She spent her first five years in Biel/Bienne, a town on the language boundary between the French- and German-speaking parts of Switzerland, near the Jura Mountains. She learned French formally when the family lived in Paris for three years, a course of study that continued when they returned to Switzerland, and then learned English starting in the eighth grade. She credits her parents for inspiring her passion to learn about different cultures and languages as well as her desire to become a language teacher from a young age. After moving to the United States to complete her undergraduate studies, Strebel became a French teacher and pursued graduate studies in francophone literature, but then decided to deepen her understanding of second-language acquisition through formal studies in that field because she wanted to help immigrant children become successful in American schools. Her PhD is in instructional technology with a focus in ESOL. She is a coauthor of *Preparing Every Teacher to Reach English Learners: A Practical Guide for Teacher Educators* and also a coeditor of *The Tapestry Journal: An International Multidisciplinary Journal on English Language Learner Education*. Her research focuses on the infusion of English learner competencies throughout teacher education programs in content-based language instruction. She is the ESOL coordinator at Stetson University, where she also teaches courses in instruction for diverse learners and works with faculty and staff to provide appropriate support for the university's international students.

KOUIDER MOKHTARI grew up in Morocco, a multilingual country, where he learned to read in two languages: Arabic and French. Outside of school, he spoke Moroccan Arabic, which is a colloquial version of Modern Standard Arabic that is rarely written or used in any formal communication. His fascination with the nature of language and its role in learning to read and write intensified in the first year of high school, when he started learning English. After completing teacher certification, he taught English as a foreign language in high school in Rabat and Casablanca, Morocco. He earned a master's degree in applied linguistics and an interdisciplinary doctorate from Ohio University. His research focuses on the acquisition of language and literacy by first and second language learners, with particular emphasis on children, adolescents, and adults who can read but have difficulties with reading comprehension. Mokhtari is a coauthor of *Preparing Every Teacher to Reach English Learners: A Practical Guide for Teacher Educators* (Harvard Education Press) and a coeditor of *The Tapestry Journal: An International Multidisciplinary Journal on English Language Learner Education*, which is dedicated to the advancement of research and instruction for English learners. He currently serves as the Anderson-Vukelja-Wright Endowed Professor of Education within the School of Education at the University of Texas at Tyler, where he engages in research, teaching, and service initiatives aimed at enhancing teacher practice and increasing student literacy achievement outcomes.

FLORIN M. MIHAI grew up in Iasi, Romania. In second grade, he started learning English and became fascinated by it. After earning a BA in English and Romanian from Alexandru Ioan Cuza University in Iasi, he taught English as a foreign language at a private language school in his hometown for several years. Because he wanted to further his education and pursue a postgraduate degree, he enrolled in the Multilingual and Multicultural Education program at Florida State University, where he earned a master's and a PhD. His research interests include language and content-area assessment for English learners, grammar instruction, pre- and in-service teacher education, and curriculum development in global contexts. He is the author of *Assessing English Language Learners in the Content Areas: A Research-into-Practice Guide for Educators* (University of Michigan Press, 2010) and a coauthor of *Language and Literacy Development: An Interdisciplinary Focus on English Learners with Communication Disorders* (Plural Publishing). Mihai is a coeditor of *The Tapestry Journal: An International Multidisciplinary Journal on English Language Learner Education*. Currently, he is an associate professor in the Teaching English to Speakers of Other Languages (TESOL) program at the University of Central Florida.

When **EDWIDGE CREVECOEUR-BRYANT** immigrated to the United States from Haiti with her family, she had no idea what awaited her. Upon arriving in New York, in the winter, she did not expect to see "white things" fall from the sky that caused her toes to feel numb nor to be driven to school on a noisy bus with children laughing and talking instead of walking! More startlingly, she did not expect to paint all day, every day, while the other students did work that she had previously done in Haiti. She could not understand the language but knew she could do the work if the teacher just gave her a chance. At the tender age of seven, during one of those "painting in the back of the classroom" moments, she decided that she would become a teacher to help students who could not speak English. Taught English by her father, she became that teacher! Edwidge C. Bryant was the first student in the United States to earn a bachelor of science degree in bilingual education with an emphasis in Haitian Kreyòl and English from City College of the City University of New York. She continued her education at Teachers College Columbia University, where she earned a master's degree in educational administration and a doctorate in applied linguistics with an emphasis in bilingual education. She has coauthored five bilingual English-Haitian Kreyòl dictionaries, including the latest, *Word by Word*, published by Prentice Hall. Crevecoeur-Bryant serves as codirector of five literacy centers in Petit Goave, Haiti. She also serves as the educational director of the TELL (Technology and English Learning in Leogane) Project in Haiti. She enjoys a national and international reputation for presenting her work on Haitian education, language, and technology. Crevecoeur-Bryant has devoted her career to improving the lives of second language learners in the United States and Haiti through directly teaching ESOL students as well as undergraduate and graduate students at various institutions of higher education. She currently serves as the ESOL coordinator in the College of Education at Jacksonville University, Jacksonville, Florida.

Index